The Photographic Fix

Social History, Popular Culture, and Politics in Germany
Kathleen Canning, Series Editor

Recent Titles

The Photographic Fix: Memory, Ideology, and the First World War in the Weimar Republic
Justin Court

Icon Dresden: Baroque City, Air War Symbol, Political Token
Susanne Vees-Gulani

Socialist Subjectivities: Queering East Germany under Honecker
Scott Harrison, Jeff Hayton, and Katharine White, Editors

Interrogating Integration: Sport, Celebrity, and Scandal in the Making of New Germany
Kate Zambon

German Empires and Decolonial Fantasies, 1492–1942
Patricia Anne Simpson

Women in German Expressionism: Gender, Sexuality, Activism
Anke Finger and Julie Shoults, Editors

Queer Livability: German Sexual Sciences and Life Writing
Ina Linge

Moderate Modernity: The Newspaper Tempo *and the Transformation of Weimar Democracy*
Jochen Hung

African Students in East Germany, 1949–1975
Sara Pugach

The Arts of Democratization: Styling Political Sensibilities in Postwar West Germany
Jennifer M. Kapczynski and Caroline A. Kita, Editors

Decolonizing German and European History at the Museum
Katrin Sieg

Spaces of Honor: Making German Civil Society, 1700–1914
Heikki Lempa

Bankruptcy and Debt Collection in Liberal Capitalism: Switzerland, 1800–1900
Mischa Suter

Marking Modern Movement: Dance and Gender in the Visual Imagery of the Weimar Republic
Susan Funkenstein

Anti-Heimat Cinema: The Jewish Invention of the German Landscape
Ofer Ashkenazi

Dispossession: Plundering German Jewry, 1933–1953
Christoph Kreutzmüller and Jonathan R. Zatlin, Editors

Sex between Body and Mind: Psychoanalysis and Sexology in the German-speaking World, 1890s–1930s
Katie Sutton

Imperial Fictions: German Literature Before and Beyond the Nation-State
Todd Kontje

For a complete list of titles, please see www.press.umich.edu

The Photographic Fix
Memory, Ideology, and the First World War in the Weimar Republic

JUSTIN COURT

University of Michigan Press *Ann Arbor*

Published in the United States of America by the
University of Michigan Press
First published February 2026

A CIP catalog record for this book is available from the British Library.

Library of Congress Control Number: 2025025142
LC record available at https://lccn.loc.gov/2025025142

ISBN 978-0-472-07749-6 (hardcover : alk. paper)
ISBN 978-0-472-05749-8 (paper : alk. paper)
ISBN 978-0-472-90507-2 (open access ebook)

DOI: https://doi.org/10.3998/mpub.12915585

The University of Michigan Press's broader open access publishing program is made possible thanks to additional funding from the University of Michigan Office of the Provost and the generous support of contributing libraries.

Cover photograph: "Vali dressed up as a prisoner," from *Jako Sitzmann, Photo Album, 1914–1918.* Courtesy of the Department of Special Collections, Memorial Library, University of Wisconsin–Madison.

The authorized representative in the EU for product safety and compliance is Easy Access System Europe, Mustamäe tee 50, 10621 Tallinn, Estonia, gpsr.requests@easproject.com

To the memory of Jost Hermand (1930–2021)

Contents

Digital materials related to this title can be found on the Fulcrum platform via the following citable URL: https://doi.org/10.3998/mpub.12915585

Illustrations

Photographs from Walter Bloem, *Deutschland: Ein Buch der Größe und der Hoffnung in Bildern, 1914–1924*

Photographs from the Reichsarchiv and George Soldan

Photographs from Franz Schauwecker, *So war der Krieg!*

Photographs from Franz Schauwecker, *So ist der Friede*

Introduction
Photography and the Afterlives of Memory

German-language picture books of the 1920s promised to reveal to their viewers the First World War through an experiential encounter with photographs. Belief in photography's ability to accurately convey the "reality" of war was widespread and relied on an assertion of the medium's technical impartiality. As Franz Schauwecker, editor of one such volume, *So war der Krieg!* (This is what the war was like; 1927), asserts:

> Framed between forward advance and sacrifice, these images show the true face of war, undistorted, without whitewashing; they reveal the grim tragedy of modern war in the irrefutable, hard, and honest objectivity of the photograph. Here, the war, with its material, people, and landscape, has soberly and wordlessly inscribed itself into the undeceivable light-sensitive layer of the photographic plate.[1]

The claim for photography's inherent truth-telling ability, however, is inconsistent with the volume's actual composition. In *So war der Krieg!* Schauwecker, a war volunteer himself and a prominent nationalist author in postwar Germany, plays freely with the apparently obvious "truth" contained in the frames of photographs. He weaves the visual content of disparately sourced photographs into a polemic that sees new political action taking root in the war experience. The frontline soldier, who willingly said "yes" to a fate of death and destruction, has become the standard bearer of a new German nationalism for the postwar era.[2] Schauwecker's ideological views

1. Schauwecker, *So war der Krieg!*, 3. All translations mine unless otherwise noted.
2. Schauwecker, *So war der Krieg!*, 5.

are not contained in the inherent properties of the selected photographs but are ascribed to the images through the surrounding apparatus of the book: textual accompaniment often stretches interpretation far beyond the photographs' visual content, and careful editorial control allows for the emphasis of visual aspects that correspond to his ideological point-of-view and the omission of otherwise contradictory material. Take, for example, Schauwecker's comparison of nationalism to a plant sprouting from the soil of destruction, or the idea that war is a necessary cleansing of "the rotten spirit of the past" from which a "new responsibility" is wrought.[3] The analogy of birth through destruction is visually anchored in the photographs of explosions that comprise a third of the images found within the volume.[4] While the war's destruction certainly is evident in those views of violence, Schauwecker contextualizes these documents as supporting a future-oriented, nationalist vision, as he predicts a time when those who sacrificed the most—"our generation"—will awaken to create their own reality.[5]

So war der Krieg! typifies the connection between the visual depiction of the First World War and the contested field of memory surrounding the conflict during the Weimar Republic, Germany's postwar parliamentary democracy from 1918 to 1933. Schauwecker's volume is just one of many German-language picture books from the period concerned with crafting interpretations of the war that were inherently bound to societal questions in the present. The picture book genre represents a rich microcosm of postwar memory contests in Germany, what historian Benjamin Ziemann has called in the context of veterans' groups "contested commemorations."[6] Analysis of text and image in picture books reveals an effort to shape how the war was visually remembered in order to influence public opinion on myriad matters in the war's wake, including notions of German guilt and responsibility, the very legitimacy of the republic, and the political future of the German nation. The highly visible and protracted nature of memory contests ensured that the picture books addressed in this study can be scrutinized as interventions in a contentious dimension of Weimar public life. Analysis here underscores notions that Germany enjoyed neither uniform understanding of the war's meaning nor shared national commemorative practices. Furthermore, they are proof that the Weimar Republic's political dynamism cannot be neatly

3. Schauwecker, *So war der Krieg!*, 8.
4. Apel, "Cultural Battlegrounds," 77.
5. Schauwecker, *So war der Krieg!*, 8.
6. Ziemann, *Contested Commemorations.*

circumscribed by a telos of collapse into the Third Reich, as Peter Fritzsche argues:

> At the end of World War I, previously authoritative instructions about law, legitimacy, and community no longer seemed applicable; new blueprints and experiments filled in the empty space and gave the German future of the 1920s its uncertain and promiscuous aspect. The common note to the political and cultural history of the period is the widespread conviction that the material world could be designed.[7]

War picture books, which freely combined the past, present, and future tenses, were exactly the type of cultural experiment that reinforces the idea that in Weimar public life "nothing was certain and everything possible."[8] They embody what Kathleen Canning calls "the contingency and undecidability of the Weimar Republic . . . , the simultaneous inhabitance of distinct time zones of past (the traumatic past of total war and defeat), present, and a sense of futurity that was both promising and unnerving."[9] The "photographic fix" comprises the effort to define past, present, and future along a stable trajectory through means of photographic representation.

In technical terms, photographic fixer is the mix of chemicals used in the final step of the gelatin silver printing process. The fixer removes any remaining silver halide from the photograph's surface, so that the print can be taken from the darkroom without being further exposed to light and risk becoming murky or completely obscured. The fixer stabilizes the image. The photographic prints that appeared in postwar picture books were, of course, already developed; they were merely selected for publication from an existing archive of images. Yet while they were physically stable as objects, the meaning of their visual information was highly unstable. The "fix" at hand refers to the attempt to establish the war's meaning through the selective sorting, sequencing, framing, and, at times, manipulating of images in picture books. In some regards, it was an attempt to "correct" or preempt other undesirable visual presentations of the war, such as Ernst Friedrich's early and shocking pacifist picture book *Krieg dem Kriege!* (*War against War!*; 1924). "Fix" also retains further colloquial connotations relevant to this proj-

7. Fritzsche, "Did Weimar Fail?," 633.

8. Fritzsche, "Did Weimar Fail?," 633.

9. Canning, "The Politics of Symbols, Semantics, and Sentiments in the Weimar Republic," 572–73.

ect. To "fix" an animal, such as a pet dog, informally means to spay or neuter it, to prevent it from sexually reproducing. Following this line, picture books "fixed"—to varying degrees of success—individual photographs and general visual motifs from the war by restraining their otherwise promiscuous meanings from multiplying. And to "get a fix" (made explicit in the German slang word *Fixer*, or drug addict) entails the satiation of sensuous bodily cravings. Published during the "photo-boom" of the 1920s, war picture books appealed to a popular audience increasingly eager to consume photographs of all kinds. The "photographic fix" in this sense, then, the satisfaction of such visual appetites, was likely for many reader-viewers the hook that initially drew them into engaging with constructed memories and ideological interpretations of the war. This "fix" was not simply intellectual, but like a drug could elicit intense affective responses, such as is the case with images of highly disfigured faces in *Krieg dem Kriege!* or in the sensational explosions of *So war der Krieg!*

The Photographic Fix traces the rhetorical strategies used by picture-book authors and editors to determine the meaning of the Great War through photographs as part of a larger effort to shape Germany's collective memory and the Weimar situation. This introduction begins with a consideration of photography theory in order to problematize the rhetorical claims of picture-book authors and to understand the framing strategies used as part of the "photographic fix." The assertion of photographic realism is quickly complicated by attention to how the status of photography itself is historically and culturally constructed and the ways in which connotation procedures, such as text and image combinations, can alter the significance of a photograph. The "photographic fix" entails the use of such strategies—both rhetorical and technical—for making meaning of the past. Therefore, the introduction moves then to memory studies to explore the role photography has in not merely reflecting collective views of the past but in shaping subjectivities in the present as a media of memory. The analysis of photo albums and picture books in this book seeks to understand how visual representations sought to shape war memory, both at the private level of individual soldiers (photo albums) and at the collective level of the public at-large (picture books). Consideration of the former category reveals how a vast archive of photographs actually came to be during the war and how individuals visually organized their lived experience and personal memories by fixing photographs into the pages of an album. It serves as an advantageous foil to the latter category, composed of published works by authors of oftentimes radically different worldviews who nevertheless share the same principal goal: to craft specific visual accounts of the war and its legacy in order to fix opinion among a broad reading public.

The Photobook, Photographic Realism, and Text and Image

That photographs were used widely in postwar picture books in the first place is not trivial, and the fact points to the rich historical connection that exists between photography and the First World War. Photography came into its own as a widespread practice in the hands of both amateur hobbyists and official record-makers during the First World War, following steep reductions in price, camera size, and the technical know-how required to participate in image making. Furthermore, postwar picture books were part of a "photo-boom" in the mid to late 1920s that saw a rapid proliferation in the quantity of images and in new types of photography practices, such as illustrated magazines, traveling exhibitions, and photographic books.[10] In the last category alone, over 5,000 German-language volumes have been identified from the period between 1918 and 1945.[11]

Recent scholarly work by Daniel Magilow (*The Photography of Crisis*, 2015), Pepper Stetler (*Stop Reading! Look!*, 2015), and Patrizia McBride (*The Chatter of the Visible*, 2016), alongside Manfred Heiting and Roland Jaeger's monumental two-volume *Autopsie: Deutschsprachige Fotobücher 1918 bis 1945* (Autopsy: German-language photobooks; 2012 and 2014), has deepened our understanding of the photobook, a foremost category of the Weimar "photo-boom." Although the term *Fotobuch* was present in the late 1920s, it did not dominate then as it does now to define a unique genre practiced by German and German-adjacent modernist artists in the 1920s, such as August Sander, Werner Graeff, Helmar Lerski, Karl Blossfeldt, László Moholy-Nagy, and Albert Renger-Patzsch.[12] The writings and photographic production of these artists and theoreticians worked to delineate the ontology of the photographic image and its construction of meaning. At the heart of many modernist photobooks—beyond their varied thematic content—was a grappling with photography's ability to offer new forms of visual representation and experience, to create forms of visual communication that could supplant text entirely, and to train viewers to respond productively to such modern phenomena. As Stetler explains, "One of the most prevalent aims of Weimar

10. Lugon, "'Photo-Inflation,'" 220.
11. Heiting, "Autopsie: Anschauung, Information und Analyse," 9.
12. Jaeger, "Die Fülle der neuen Bilderbücher," 24.

photographic books was to teach their audience various strategies of photographic meaning."[13] Although their books were produced and consumed in a bustling consumer economy for a popular audience,[14] they engaged (and are received today) largely in art-historical terms, with reference to broader debates on *Neues Sehen* (new vision), *Neue Sachlichkeit* (new objectivity), and physiognomy.[15] Contemporary reviewers of late 1920s photobooks understood the genre's twofold programmatic claim: the photobook asserted photography's primacy over text and insisted on the use of the new medium as a uniquely artistic endeavor.[16]

While they are richly illustrated with photographs and published in book form, photographic volumes from the 1920s dealing with the First World War exhibit neither of these two important facets of the modernist *Fotobuch*. They confront the status of photography at times—especially in its documentary mode—but evince far less theoretical rigor and inventiveness; naïve, if not intentionally misleading understandings of the photographic image and its ability to impart meaning prevail in the war picture books. They also refuse to foreground the primacy of photographs over text and instead include lengthy sections of explanatory commentary to guide the reader—a key component of the "photographic fix." The war "picture books" were also titled and subtitled as such, with *Bilderbuch* or *im Bild* and *in Bildern* appearing as typical affixations. It is for these reasons that the term "picture book" has been used consciously throughout this study instead of "photobook."

Nevertheless, while their aesthetic program may be less characteristically "modern," war picture books share with their more avant-garde counterparts a desire to create and contain new visual experiences through photographs. War picture books fit generally into the broader category of "photo essays" that Magilow describes as "a distinctly modern, technologically inflected vehicle used by writers and photographers to participate in crucial aesthetic, political, and cultural debates."[17] Their claims about photography and realism also establish war picture books as productive grounds for sounding the status of the medium at the time, both among theoreticians and practitioners as well as the general public. In a scholarly landscape that has elevated the modernist photobooks of Graeff, Moholy-Nagy, and Renger-

13. Stetler, *Stop Reading! Look!*, 12.
14. Magilow, *The Photography of Crisis*, 8.
15. For an overview of physiognomy, see especially Long, "Faces."
16. Jaeger, "Die Fülle der neuen Bilderbücher," 24.
17. Magilow, *The Photography of Crisis*, 6.

Patzsch, more overlooked vernacular forms of photography stand ready to reveal diverging beliefs on photography at the time—in addition to their powerful testimony of how the memory of the war was represented and contested for ideological projects in the Weimar era. If nothing else, the differences between the war picture books handled here and their modernist photobook counterparts point toward what Stetler calls the "incoherency of the medium" that complicates attempts to define and categorize its diverse and often contradictory elements in the Weimar era.[18]

The quotation from Franz Schauwecker at the start of this chapter exemplifies a shared assertion among authors and editors of war picture books from the 1920s that photography was technically impartial and therefore purely objective in generating meaning. Even Ernst Friedrich, a left-wing pacifist at the opposite end of the political spectrum from Schauwecker, found common ground with the right-wing nationalist in this belief about photography. Friedrich wrote at the start of his own war picture book, *Krieg dem Kriege!*, of the "inexorable, incorruptible photographic lens" that would present a "picture of war, objectively true and faithful to nature."[19] But, as will be shown more extensively in later chapters, neither author allows photography to "speak for itself." Both Friedrich and Schauwecker supplement their chosen photographic sequences with introductory comments, textual interludes, and captions, thus confirming the suspicions of their contemporaries, such as Siegfried Kracauer, Kurt Tucholsky, Walter Benjamin, and Bertolt Brecht, who were highly skeptical of claims made for photography's inherent transparency. These misgivings are captured most succinctly by Brecht in his essay "The *Threepenny* Lawsuit" (1932): "A photograph of the Krupp works or the AEG reveals almost nothing about these institutions."[20] Tom Kuhn describes Brecht's critical view of photography here as "nothing more than a model of impotent mimetic realism."[21] According to Kuhn, this view echoed Kracauer's earlier critique of the medium found in his 1927 essay "Die Photographie," which criticized photography for capturing reality in a superficial way that prevented the viewer from understanding the pictured reality historically or conceptually.

In the following decades, photography theory has developed more thorough arguments against photography's supposed objectivity. They must be

18. Stetler, *Stop Reading! Look!*, 8.
19. Friedrich, *Krieg dem Kriege!*, 21.
20. Brecht, "The *Threepenny* Lawsuit," 164.
21. Kuhn, "Early Brechtian Perspectives on Photography," 265.

outlined here, as assumptions of photography's objectivity are key to the eventual "photographic fix" attempted by war-picture-book authors. Highlighting the ways poststructuralist and postmodern theory has questioned the transparency of the photographic image will work to quickly destabilize the rhetorical arguments of authenticity set forth in the 1920s war picture books and make clear why those picture-book authors—more or less consciously—strove to guide the meaning of their photographic compendiums in ways that went beyond the individual photograph.

A photograph's index (following the tripartite semiotics of Charles Sanders Peirce),[22] its causal relationship to reality (a photograph can only exist as a result of the physical imprint of photons on a chemically sensitive plate), stirs temptation to see the image as a direct reproduction of a predetermined reality, reliable and objective. Roland Barthes describes this as the denotative status of the photograph in his 1961 essay "The Photographic Message." For Barthes, the photograph is a perfect "analogon" of reality, entailing a "message without a code."[23] But authors and practitioners, such as Allan Sekula, Abigail Solomon-Godeau, and John Tagg, have increasingly interrogated photographic realism by drawing attention to the discursive systems, institutional relations, and power positions throughout history that have determined photography's changing status and that exceed any inherent ontological qualities of the photograph. They call into question the category of documentary and evidence as historically contingent and relative. Sekula derides the "myth" that accompanies the documentary genre as the "folklore of photographic truth" and asserts that "the only 'objective' truth that photographs offer is the assertion that somebody or something . . . was somewhere and took a picture. Everything else, everything beyond the imprinting of a trace, is up for grabs."[24] Solomon-Godeau emphasizes the need to see documentary projects as "themselves products of distinct historical circumstances and milieus, [which] 'speak' of agendas both open and covert, personal and institutional, that inform their contents, and to a greater or lesser extent, mediate our readings of them."[25] An investigation into the "photographic fix" in Weimar Germany, which highlights the use of photography and claims about photography to sway opinion in postwar contests of collective memory, follows Solomon-Godeau's invocation: "It is properly the

22. Atkin, "Peirce's Theory of Signs," n.p.
23. Barthes, "The Photographic Message," 17.
24. Sekula, "Dismantling Modernism," 56–57.
25. Solomon-Godeau, "Who Is Speaking Thus?," 182.

work of historians and critics to attempt to excavate these coded and buried meanings, to bring to light those rhetorical and formal strategies that determined the work's production, meaning, reception, and use."[26] In tracing the documentary projects of American New Deal photographers, Tagg writes of a similar "historical 'rendezvous' of means, rhetoric and social strategy," in which the documentary form exerted power "not as the evocation of a pristine truth but as a politically mobilised rhetoric of Truth, a strategy of signification, a cultural intervention aimed at resealing social unity and structures of belief at a time of far-reaching crisis and conflict."[27] It is the contention of this book that in the crisis years following Germany's war defeat, a similar interest in marshaling photography rhetoric for social impact is clearly evident, albeit—in comparison to the New Deal projects—in greater diverging manners and intents. In carefully excavating these strategies, this book aims to fill gaps in the history of photography and Weimar cultural studies alike.

"'The thing itself' is never just out there in the world waiting to be framed by the photographer's Leica," according to Solomon-Godau, "rather, it is something dynamically produced in the act of representation and reception and already subject to the grids of meaning imposed upon it by culture, history, language, and so forth."[28] Uncovering the aesthetic strategies that create these "grids of meaning" guides the present analysis of the "photographic fix" attempted by war-picture-book authors. Barthes calls these procedures "connotation," or the "imposition of second meaning on the photographic message proper" that is not strictly part of the photographic structure, but codes the photograph's denotation.[29] Barthes points to various techniques for image manipulation, such as trick photography and posing, which comprise connotation procedures. Within the realm of war picture books, the obvious alteration of individual photographs across publications is just one example of a connotation procedure that widens the gap between "reality" and truthfulness in the war's visual mediation.[30]

Barthes also recognizes that the addition of accompanying text to images is a significant connotation procedure. Writing with some apparent resignation, he asserts an "important historical reversal" in which "the image no longer illustrates the words; it is now the words which, structurally,

26. Solomon-Godeau, "Who Is Speaking Thus?," 182.

27. Tagg, *Burden of Representation*, 13.

28. Solomon-Godeau, *Photography at the Dock*, xxviii.

29. Barthes, "The Photographic Message," 20.

30. See examples in Schneider, "Narrating the War in Pictures," and Apel, "Cultural Battlegrounds."

are parasitic on the image. . . . Today, the text loads the image, burdening it with a culture, a moral, an imagination."[31] For contemporaries of Weimar picture-book authors—to return to Tucholsky, Benjamin, and Brecht—this "burdening" represented positive political promise. Their interest was to enact a socially critical photographic practice that could make the conditions of reality visible while estranging the viewer so that critical reflection on that reality would be possible. For Tucholsky, this shift in thinking is evident when comparing articles like "Die Tendenzphotographie" (1925), in which he extolled the photograph as "irrefutable," "truthful," and "flawless," to later reflections on his own photographic practice in the photobook *Deutschland, Deutschland über alles* (1929), created in collaboration with the celebrated photomontage artist John Heartfield.[32] He describes in 1930 how the two crafted a "new technique for captioning" that used photography in a completely different way: as emphasis for text, as witty juxtaposition, as ornament, and as reinforcement. According to Tucholsky, the image was no longer an end in and of itself, but if one were to teach the reader to "see with our eyes" (through textual guidance), the photograph would not only speak, it would scream.[33] Benjamin similarly mentions captions in three separate essays as a productive technique for renewing the political function of photographs. He asks in the essay "Little History of Photography" (1931): "Won't inscription [*Beschriftung*] become the most important part of the photograph?"[34] He answers the question in two later essays: in "The Author as Producer" (1934), he insists that "what we require of the photographer is the ability to give his picture a caption that wrenches it from modish commerce and gives it a revolutionary use value";[35] and in "The Work of Art in the Age of Its Technological Reproducibility" (1935), he notes that accompanying text has become "obligatory" for the successful political reception of photographs.[36] Brecht, too, found text and image a productive strategy for avoiding both naturalist realism and abstraction and for overcoming the free-floating contemplation of photographs encouraged by art photography in the 1920s.[37] Brecht engaged later in his career in his own photographic practices through his *Kriegsfibel* (*War Primer*, 1955), model books for stage

31. Barthes, "The Photographic Message," 25.
32. See Mayer, "Aktiver Pessimismus."
33. Tucholsky, "Auf dem Nachtisch," 140.
34. Benjamin, "Little History of Photography," 527.
35. Benjamin, "The Author as Producer," 775.
36. Benjamin, "The Work of Art," 108.
37. Kuhn, "Early Brechtian Perspectives on Photography," 278.

productions, and extensive work journals,[38] but he was already lauding the text and image work of others in 1926. He recommended Friedrich's *Krieg dem Kriege!* alongside Erich Mendelsohn's photobook *Amerika: Bilderbuch eines Architekten* (America: Picture book of an architect) to the periodical *Das Tage-Buch* in 1926 as two of the six best publications of the year, apparently drawn to the way text and image could compel viewers to engage in political interpretations of pictured historical processes.[39]

Unfortunately for these German theorists, oriented as they were on the socialist and Marxist left, renewing the political potential of the photograph through text and image did not preordain any specific leftist political message. With few exceptions—Ernst Friedrich foremost among them—the war picture books of the 1920s worked in an opposite direction, to reestablish and reify traditional, conservative societal orders, such as Wilhelmine militarism, and to subject the masses to a naturalized view of the war that could underwrite right-wing legends concerning the past.

In addition to the connotation practices of text and image, the "photographic fix" entails the ways that photographs of the First World War were created, distributed, and received in various contexts, thus undergoing a shapeshifting of meaning. Vilém Flusser calls this photography's "channeling," and he points to the way photographs can slip between channels to take on new significance. "The division of photographs into channels is in no way simply a mechanical process but rather an encoding one: The distribution apparatuses impregnate the photograph with the decisive significance for its reception."[40] Such slippage among channels was exceedingly common among photographs from the First World War. Photographs were produced by a wide swath of creators, from paid officials reporting for the German government to soldiers capturing personal memories with amateur cameras, and photographs ended up in state archives, newspaper holdings, and personal collections, all of which were mined for postwar publications. Even soldiers who created their own photographs and collated them into albums appropriated additional photographic material, such as purchased postcards, newspaper clippings, and commissioned portraits, into their collections, thus imbuing them with their own personal significance. Reconstructing the entire universe in motion of war photographs would be an insurmountable task, but tracing the trajectory of individual photographs

38. See Imbrigotta, "Framing Brecht."
39. Kuhn, "Early Brechtian Perspectives on Photography," 271 and 278.
40. Flusser, *Towards a Philosophy of Photography*, 54.

that crossed channels will draw out fruitful examples of this phenomenon later. For now, the simple recognition of the myriad differences in the creation, distribution, and reception of mass-market picture books and personal photo albums serves to highlight how channeling comprises a significant feature of the "photographic fix."

Memory, Media, Photography

If analysis of the strategies employed by postwar photographic projects reveals how meaning was layered onto photographs, the framework of memory is useful for understanding how those meanings were intended as interventions in a dynamically contested realm of Weimar culture and society, namely remembrance of the war and its impact on present and future German society. Paying attention to the cultural processes of memory, especially as it unfolds in media practices, makes obvious the commemorative functions of personal photo albums in the private realm, the intended influence of mass-market picture books on social questions, and the salient differences in mode, purpose, and reception between the two genres.

Although their subject matter was obviously historical, the mass-market picture books under analysis here do little to interpret the war as a product of historical development or to seriously debate its cause and effects. The views offered are often kaleidoscopic and attend to diverse aspects of the war but are rarely totalizing in any historiographical manner. Instead, explanation is firmly concentrated on meaning-making in the present. In other words: What slivers of insight can be carved from the war experience that are worthwhile for the present? What should and should not be remembered about the war and to what ends? Refracted against the personal photo albums of soldiers, in which the processes of remembering and commemoration are more overtly subjective, the memory projects in mass-market picture books reveal themselves as dubious and bound to bias. The picture books analyzed in this study mobilize the asserted impartiality of photography to present the war naturalistically and authoritatively, as a rhetorical strategy to legitimize ideological interpretations of the war's meaning.

The effort to "fix" the public's understanding of the war, both its shape in the past and its bearing on the present and future, can best be understood through reference to foundational ideas of collective memory. Writing in *Les Cadres sociaux de la mémoire* (*The Social Frameworks of Memory*; 1925) Maurice Halbwachs was the first to posit the idea of collective memory to explain how prevailing societal attitudes and frames of thinking guide how a shared vision of the past emerges.[41] The concept of "collective memory" does not explain the biological or psychological processes of memory per se but serves as a frame of reference for the ordering of individual memories into a group's sum notion of the past. These frames are not always "true" to history, and reconstructions of the past often entail a distortion of that past to meet the present needs of the group in asserting its desired shared identity.[42]

One salient example of such a distortion of collective memory from the context of post–First World War commemoration is what historian George Mosse calls the "Myth of the War Experience." Despite the massive loss of human life and countless individual experiences of extreme violence, those concerned with the reputation of Germany and its military worked to construct a myth that downplayed the war's meaninglessness to embolden the nation in whose name the war had been fought.[43] Indeed, the experience of mass death is a central concern of the Weimar-era picture books, whether they soften the experience of death by focusing on orderly gravesites, present gruesome facts but transform their meaning into something of a higher symbolic nature, or display it in plain detail as a shock to the viewer meant to motivate aversion to war. Photographs of death and destruction abound in the larger photographic archive of the war, and paying attention to the ways in which book editors and authors deal with such images (including outright avoidance) helps to discern the ideological motives that undergird their projects. Death becomes a foremost intersection of visuality, memory, and ideology in postwar picture books.

From one typical contemporary notion of the First World War that focuses on the conflict's futility,[44] it is difficult to grasp how war memory could have been spun for positive political purchase at all. In short, how could so many instances of personal suffering be transformed into any affirmative collective experience? Although the effects of "shell-shock" were experienced widely among frontline soldiers during the First World War, the sort of trauma at hand when considering postwar memory contests is better understood if the difference between personal and collective trauma is delineated. Halbwachs's idea of collective memory has been refined and devel-

41. Halbwachs, *Das Gedächtnis und seine sozialen Bedingungen*, 22–23.

42. Halbwachs, *Das Gedächtnis und seine sozialen Bedingungen*, 381.

43. Mosse, *Fallen Soldiers*, 6–7.

44. However, as Dan Todman seeks to show in *The Great War: Myth and Memory*, the notion of the First World War as a "fight about nothing" is itself a layman's perspective supported more by decades of modern myth-making than accurate historical interpretation (xii–xiii).

oped in the almost 100 years since its first formulation, but one of the earliest objections to the term, coming from Marc Bloch in 1925, concerned Halbwachs's transposition of terms and concepts from individual psychology to a collective level.[45] Jeffrey Alexander mounts a similar critique in his more recent book *Trauma: A Social Theory* (2012). He notes the significant difference between a popular understanding of trauma to the individual (the real psychosomatic effects that plague a person subjected to extreme violence) and the ways in which a large-scale event, such as war, is written as *collectively* "traumatic." The first lay notion of trauma is often falsely transcribed to a collective, so that violent events or cultural ruptures are thought to automatically inflict a "trauma" on a community of people. Alexander pushes back against the "naturalistic fallacy" of trauma espoused by Enlightenment and psychoanalytical approaches to trauma, represented foremost by Arthur Neal and Cathy Caruth, respectively, to claim that "events are not inherently traumatic. Trauma is a socially mediated attribution. The attribution may be made in real time, as an event unfolds; it may also be made before the event occurs, as an adumbration, or after the event has concluded, as a post-hoc reconstruction."[46] "Trauma," in Alexander's social theory, becomes a shorthand for expressing how groups do or do not remember violent pasts and the extent to which they incorporate them as foundational to their collective identities.

For Alexander, the process of attributing trauma to collective events relies on cultural representations, thereby echoing the way memory studies is deeply entangled with media studies:

> For traumas to emerge at the level of the collectivity, social crises must become cultural crises. Events are one thing; representations of these events are quite another. Trauma is not the result of a group experiencing pain. It is the result of this acute discomfort entering into the core of the collectivity's sense of its own identity. Collective actors "decide" to represent social pain as a fundamental threat to their sense of who they are, where they came from, and where they want to go.[47]

45. Erll, *Kollektives Gedächtnis und Erinnerungskulturen*, 110. The methodological debate has persisted long after Bloch's criticism, as Wulf Kansteiner's 2002 essay "Finding Meaning in Memory: A Methodological Critique of Collective Memory Studies" attests.

46. Alexander, *Trauma: A Social Theory*, 13.

47. Alexander, *Trauma: A Social Theory*, 15.

Which cultural representations are successful in shaping a collectivity's sense of identity is in turn "a matter of cultural power in the most mundane, material sense: Who controls the means of symbolic production?"[48] In contrast to other nations, such as Britain and France, which developed consistent forms of remembrance and mourning that bound the nation together, Germany enjoyed no unanimously accepted commemorative practices or even a common semantic or language to speak about the war.[49] Political, social, and economic upheaval in defeated Germany, coupled with continued antagonisms over questions of war guilt and reparations, meant that any move to enshrine an interpretation of the war was tied up with rancorous questions of contemporary politics and society. The disputed nature of postwar memory in Germany is therefore stimulating ground for investigating the contest of cultural power through media representations, in this case photography and its extended applications.

Following Alexander's understanding of collective trauma as a social construct, the "Myth of the War Experience" can be understood in other terms: not as a myth consciously crafted with unified intent by a coordinated set of actors but as interrelated moments of resistance reacting to the prospect of a cultural narrative of trauma crystallizing around the war. For forces on the ideological right, the Treaty of Versailles, which apportioned full guilt to the Germans, and the accompanying feelings of national betrayal, which came to be understood under the notion of a *Dolchstoß* (stab in the back), signified the real cultural trauma. Efforts in popular culture perceived as inscribing a traumatic account of the war itself—including Ernst Friedrich's picture book *Krieg dem Kriege!* (1924) and Erich Maria Remarque's bestselling novel *Im Westen nichts Neues* (*All Quiet on the Western Front*; 1929) alongside its 1930 American film adaptation—were treated not only as threats to positive war memories but as casting unfavorable light on the German nation at large. The well-documented cultural flashpoint of *Im Westen nichts Neues* exemplifies how collective memory is shaped, circulated, and negotiated in the reception of media, a central concern of this book.[50]

More so than the psychological processes by which individuals remember and forget and how those functions might translate to a group scale, collective memory is a matter of the means of representing the past. Analyzing how media representations attain collective relevance by being structured

48. Alexander, *Trauma: A Social Theory*, 36.
49. Hirschfeld, "Das historische Erbe," 161.
50. See, for example, Müller, *Der Krieg und die Schriftsteller.*

for social settings provides the best information about how collective memories develop.[51] Prominent memory-studies theorist Astrid Erll differentiates between *Gedächtnis* ("memory") and *Erinnerung* ("remembrance") to define collective memory from a "cultural semiotic" approach that assumes an understanding of culture as a system of signs in which collectives relate to the past via symbols, codes, texts, media, and so forth. In this way, only *acts* of collective memory are truly observable, and the emphasis is placed on media, such as images or writing, as the connection between the mental and social levels of collective memory.[52] It follows that collective memory is impossible without media, and studies of memory are by nature studies of media constructs, which are never neutral bearers of memory and always reveal traces of their own modality. Media do not function as mere storage for the organization of information; rather, they act as vehicles that create their own "worlds" of memory aligned with their media-specific processes.[53] In this sense, individual photographs do not contain memories in and of themselves, but they can acquire memorial significance when fixed into a larger apparatus, like a photo album or a picture book, that creates a frame for meaning-making.

Erll writes that media are "producers" of memory not because of any inherent qualities, but because they speak to the social conditions surrounding their production. Historian Alon Confino makes a similar argument for memory as the outcome of the relationship between a distinct representation of the past and the "full spectrum of symbolic representations available in a given culture."[54] However, Confino cautions that the extrapolation of "memory" from a representation of the past runs the risk of circular argumentation through "cultural" reading. In other words, the significance of visible signs is taken for granted unless the *reception* of those signs is systematically studied.[55] Wulf Kansteiner issues a similar warning that an overreliance on the media of memory in pursuit of past collective identities invites a troubling disregard for proof: "The formal and semantic qualities of historical representations might have little in common with the intentions of their authors, and neither the object's characteristics nor the authors' objectives are good indicators for subsequent reception processes."[56] To address this methodolog-

51. Kansteiner, "Finding Meaning in Memory," 190.
52. Erll, *Kollektives Gedächtnis und Erinnerungskulturen*, 114–17.
53. Erll, *Kollektives Gedächtnis und Erinnerungskulturen*, 138.
54. Confino, *Germany as a Culture of Remembrance*, 173–74.
55. Confino, *Germany as a Culture of Remembrance*, 180.
56. Kansteiner, "Finding Meaning in Memory," 192.

ical hurdle, this book seeks to provide, where available, a reception history of the picture books discussed—including, variously, reviews in newspapers and journals, official memoranda detailing production, reported sales figures, and general public reaction. These moments in historical reception help understand how publications not only responded to but also gave shape to the contested field of postwar memory. Reconstructing the impact of private photo albums within the family collective must remain more speculative. However, taken as a whole, postwar photographic projects point to a highly heterogeneous collective memory of the war. Confino notes that a problem of method with memory, its multiplicity, can be useful to draw attention as a heuristic device to the "commingling of reception, representation, and contestation" so that the interaction between a given memory and the context of society can be articulated.[57] In this way, the photographic projects discussed in this project are not analyzed to ascertain their end effect on the identity of various collectivities, such as veterans' groups or political parties. Rather, the project looks to situate the reckoning with the First World War through its visual representation within broader sociopolitical debates of the Weimar period, and vice versa.

The enticing visual aspects of picture books sets such memory projects apart from many others of the era, including the hugely popular war novel. Foremost among the attractions of mass-market picture books was the promise of seeing the war "as it was," made explicit to reader-viewers in titles like *So war der Krieg!* (This is what the war was like) and *Der Krieg in seiner rauhen Wirklichkeit* (The war in its harsh reality). Photography, which combines—again, following Peirce's semiotics—the index (the physical trace of the past, literally the capturing of light on the photosensitive plate that attests to the pictured object's existence in the past) and the icon (the resemblance between image and referent), has a privileged status in memory construction for the way it connects firsthand experience with secondary witnessing. According to Daniel Sherman, "Sight is the only sense powerful enough to bridge the gap between those who hold a memory rooted in bodily experience and those who, lacking such 'experience,' nonetheless seek to share the memory."[58] Alison Landberg's concept of "prosthetic memory" follows a similar line of thinking to explain how people can embody memories that are not their own through experiential encounters with visual mass media. The encounter does not just entail the comprehension of a

57. Confino, *Germany as a Culture of Remembrance*, 182–83.
58. Sherman, *Construction of Memory in Interwar France*, 14.

past historical event but also the assumption of a more deeply felt, personal memory. “The resulting prosthetic memory,” Alison Landsberg concludes, “has the ability to shape that person’s subjectivity and politics.”[59] The concept is valuable here for conceptualizing how photographic accounts of the war could have shaped reader-viewers’ subjectivities in the present through an experience with the past in its visual representation. In other words, the vision of war crafted in a picture book and offered to reader-viewers as an experiential encounter could influence the way a person remembered the war—even if they did not experience it firsthand—and shape their attitude toward the war’s legacy in the present.

Landsberg calls such memories prosthetic because they are not the product of lived experience; they are worn on the body as sensuous experience; they are interchangeable (underscoring their commodified form); and they are useful.[60] Postwar picture books follow this pattern: they compiled from a larger archive of images specific encounters with “the war,” sometimes inspired from actual firsthand accounts, more often amalgamations of common themes and typical experiences; they offered visual excitement meant to stir the viewer’s emotions through photographs; they were circulated broadly to a reading audience as mass cultural products (the only barrier was the price of acquisition); and they were useful for articulating subjectivities about the present vis-à-vis the war’s contentious legacy in Germany.

Landsberg’s concept of prosthetic memory implicitly entails large historical and at times geographical distance between past object and the subject assuming new memories, so that “remembering” is divorced entirely from lived social context. Even though the picture books analyzed in this book were published within a decade after the war’s end, and it is likely that all but the youngest reader-viewers experienced the war’s effects to some degree, it is still productive to think of the memories presented by the war picture books as artificial constructs that, although inspired by lived experience, offered a surplus of meaning that nonetheless could alter subjectivities. For one, due to the vast number of participants in the war, the breadth of its global stage, and the duration of the conflict, it is impossible to speak of *the* essential war experience (although the trenches of the Western Front have certainly been written as such in cultural memory). The personal photo albums compiled by soldiers underscore the fact that soldiers’ lived experience and memories deviated considerably from those of their peers and even more so from what popular picture-book editors interpret as “The War.”

59. Landsberg, *Prosthetic Memory*, 2.
60. Landsberg, *Prosthetic Memory*, 20–21.

Further evidence suggests a German public eager not only to engage with war memory but adopt war memories not their own. For example, many participants of the Freikorps campaigns following the war were of a younger generation that were eager to act out and partake through paramilitarism ideals left over from the war, such as manliness, camaraderie, and service to the nation.[61] In this light, picture books can be seen as an enticing and powerful supplement to lived experience, expanding the scope of who remembered the war to include those who took on memories not their own. The "photographic fix" retains the possibility that even those who experienced the war firsthand could have their actual memories supplanted by the ones offered in photographs. And while Landsberg positions prosthetic memory in contrast to collective memory, as the former reaches across national or other collective boundaries, it is equally productive to think about the cultural, ethnic, political, and even linguistic divisions of the relatively young German republic, especially in the upheaval of the post-1918 era, as fertile ground for media projects to construct a new and different, more cohesive "imagined community."[62]

The promise of picture books was to reveal the war to viewers; "revelation" understood both in terms of making the war visible and unmasking its secret meaning. Such revelation, and the subsequent production and appropriation of prosthetic memory, relies on a sensuous encounter with visual representations. Although film and experiential museum exhibitions are Landsberg's main objects of study, photography and the sometimes supernatural beliefs commonly ascribed to it is further territory for considering how memories might be adopted by those to which they do not naturally belong. Photography's affect, its ability to stir emotions through visual signs, has indeed been a perennial concern of theory, from Kracauer and Benjamin, through Barthes and Sontag. Summarizing the long tradition of both embrace and skepticism toward the power of visual representation, W. J. T. Mitchell describes an abiding "double consciousness" toward images—the vacillation between "magical beliefs and skeptical doubts, naïve animism and hardheaded materialism, mystical and critical attitudes"—as a "deep and abiding feature of human responses to representation" that is not diminished when one "grow[s] up, become[s] modern, or acquire[s] critical consciousness."[63] There is a seemingly mystical connection between a photograph and the past, by which photographs are popularly said to keep the

61. Rusinek, "Der Kult der Jugend und des Krieges," 183.
62. See Anderson, *Imagined Communities.*
63. Mitchell, *What Do Pictures Want?*, 7–8.

past alive. It is no mistake that photography has been called *the* medium of memory for the twentieth century.[64] War picture books frequently engage this rhetoric of mysticism as part of the "photographic fix," eliding critical reflection in order to construct mythic pasts and to undergird the claim that photography will stir, shock, and move in the present.

One of the most striking features of the pursuit to uncover photography's mystical connection to memory has been to untangle what it means to look at the dead in photographs, perhaps nowhere better exemplified than in Barthes's *Camera Lucida* (1980), in part a eulogy to his mother and a reckoning with how viewing a photograph of her as a young child wounds him. The dead similarly haunt all photographic projects of the First World War in one way or another, even if death is elided through metonyms like the honorable gravesite or through symbolic transfiguration, as in the case of the popular motif of the village crucifix intact among ruins.[65] The shock of seeing the dead in photographs is a rhetorical maneuver present only in Friedrich's *Krieg dem Kriege!* The absence of similar photographs of naked human destruction in other works suggests their editors were also aware of their shocking affect but did not find the appropriate frame to fix its meaning. (The one exception being the rare photographs of enemy dead, which hide gruesome details and are contextualized as merely necessary for German success.)

The primary power bestowed upon photographs by picture-book editors is the apparent unparalleled access to reality they afford, a rhetoric of affect in and of itself: to encounter "the real" in the past means to transform one's subjectivity in the present. The presentation of the photographic index (even if they do not employ the term) as unassailable seeks to tie visuality to memory in an apparently seamless bond. The naturalistic style—"see the war is it really was"—serves as a productive veil for more dubious persuasion as editors sort, sequence, and contextualize photographs with text in order to tie their visually constructed "reality" to distortions of collective memory.

Outline of Chapters

Due to their publication successes and wide reception,[66] picture books should be considered no small part of the broad struggle of ideas to cement the war's

64. Gerstner, *Das andere Gedächtnis*, 9.

65. See Dewitz and Hoffmann, "Christus in aktualisierter Gestalt."

66. Despite its high price, which made it something of a luxury good during the years of high unemployment, *So war der Krieg!*, for example, was a large success for its publisher (Hüppauf, "Zwischen Metaphysik und visuellem Essayismus," 233–34).

meaning in the Weimar era. As Benjamin Ziemann notes, "Every act of war commemoration in Weimar Germany had—directly or indirectly—political implications."[67] Whether it be a peaceful future without war (Ernst Friedrich), an affirmation of the fighting German spirit and a return to Wilhelmine ideals (Walter Bloem, George Soldan, and the Reichsarchiv), or a visionary new nation under the leadership of soldiers transformed at the front (Franz Schauwecker), picture-book authors envisioned a different present and a prospective future by remembering the past through specific frames. These efforts extended beyond the lines of party politics and at times the more general polarization between left and right but must nevertheless be considered part of the highly politicized memory contests that tied the war legacy's to contemporary life.

Although the majority of this study is concerned with mass-market picture books, analysis in the following chapters begins with the private photo albums of soldiers. Chapter 1 outlines the role of amateur photography during the First World War and considers how soldiers fixed their war memories into personal photo albums. Attention to what soldiers pictured and how they organized their experience for posterity highlights how the depiction of war in Weimar-era picture books was markedly different from the one constructed by the average soldier. The chapter also draws immediate attention to the different processes of memory that inhere in private photo albums, processes that stand in stark contrast to the aim of mass-market picture books to intervene in ongoing public memory contests.

Chapters 2 through 6 analyze a variety of picture books that instrumentalized war memory for various ideological and political purposes. These chapters draw out the visual strategies authors and editors used to ascribe specific meaning to the war through photographic and textual representation, while investigating their contrasting motivations for doing so. Because the archive of picture books from the Weimar era is rich, this study focuses on those volumes that most clearly draw connections between the war experience and the war's enduring legacy in an array of contemporary societal controversies, from the shape of the German nation and its place in the world, to questions of war guilt and commemoration.[68] They are presented

67. Ziemann, *Contested Commemorations*, 139. See also Schumann, *Politische Gewalt.*

68. Other war picture books that evince less concern for Germany's present and future status as it relates to the war have received due scholarly attention, foremost among them Ernst Jünger's *Das Antlitz des Weltkrieges* (1930). See Encke, *Augenblicke der Gefahr*, Horstkotte, "Inkongruente Bilder," Long, "From *Das Antlitz des Weltkrieges* to *Der gefährliche Augenblick*," and Hüppauf, "Kriegsfotografie." For a contemporary

in order according to a loose ideological spectrum stretching from left to right, although none of the projects can be matched definitively to Weimar party politics. The order also neatly corresponds to their chronological publication dates. Although the German public was most receptive to critical assessments of the war in the early 1920s, the structure should not be misconstrued as reinforcing a teleology of collapse into the Third Reich. On the contrary, the relatively close publication dates between 1924 and 1928 point to a highly unresolved discourse about war memory; even among projects that might be lumped together as belonging to the political right, there were many diverging understandings of the war.

Chapter 2 presents the case of Ernst Friedrich, a radical pacifist who decried the horrific material and psychological costs of war in his picture book *Krieg dem Kriege!* (*War against War!*; 1924). Friedrich offers a broadly leftist critique of the entanglement between war and profit at the same time he shocks readers by displaying the war's most gruesome photographs. He uses the juxtaposition of text and image to generate sarcasm intended to incriminate militaristic mentalities and to inspire broad societal resistance to war. Friedrich's book, however, likely inspired more action among his opponents than it did among its intended audience. It is presented first in this study not only because it is one of the first postwar picture books chronologically but also because it came under explicit attack in right-wing picture books that followed and tried to "fix" its horrific vision of war. With just a few insignificant exceptions, *Krieg dem Kriege!* stands alone against a mountain of positive interpretations of the war in right-wing, nationalist, and patriotic picture books.

Chapter 3 considers the patriotic picture book *Deutschland: Ein Buch der Größe und der Hoffnung in Bildern, 1914–1924* (Germany: A book of greatness and hope in pictures; 1924) and its author Walter Bloem. Although published in the same year, the tenth anniversary of mobilization, Bloem's account stands in plain contrast to Friedrich's. He looks to restore military prestige by focusing on the fighting German spirit and the nation's technological and economic superiority. Unlike the stark horrors of Friedrich's books, Bloem's visual presentation entails a certain whitewashing of the war's visual record, as it excludes most signs of violence in favor of showing the military's reach across—and implied supremacy in—the world. Death is similarly erased, appearing only in the tidy graves of "heroes." Bloem, a self-described nation-

review of Jünger's book that addresses questions of realism and ideology, see Iblher, "Photographie und Wirklichkeit."

alist proud of his lengthy military service, provided a patriotic vision of the war that sought to rejuvenate the *Volk* in a turbulent postwar era by turning back toward the guiding principles of the old Wilhelmine military elite.

The same holds true for the military-affirming political history championed by George Soldan and other ex-military men at the Reichsarchiv (imperial archives). Chapter 4 explores how military historians working for the German General Staff handled the relegation of military historiography to the civilian Reichsarchiv at war's end. Concerned with writing and endorsing positive war accounts, Soldan and others articulated a form of popular history writing that sought to maintain the military's monopoly on war history and to edify the public with uncritical patriotism. Reichsarchiv book series, such as "Schlachten des Weltkrieges" (Battles of the World War) and "Erinnerungsblätter deutscher Regimenter" (Commemoration papers of German regiments), were intended to educate broad audiences about the war in a manner that defended the actions of the old military elite and created positive myths about the war experience. The two-volume picture book *Der Weltkrieg im Bild* (The World War in pictures; 1926–28), produced with cooperation from the Reichsarchiv and introduced by Soldan and popular war author Werner Beumelburg, extends myths about the sacrifice of Germany's youth for the nation to a new interpretation of the war: the "birth by fire" of the frontline soldiers, who now rise to assume the nation's mantle.

This *Frontkämpferlegende*, the legend of the frontline soldier's metaphysical transformation into a breed of future leaders, reaches its zenith in the self-styled *soldatischer Nationalismus* (soldierly nationalism) of Franz Schauwecker. Chapter 5 considers how his picture book *So war der Krieg!* (This is what the war was like; 1927) attempts to re-create the front's sensatory experience in order to claim political authority for the transformed soldier in the postwar era. For Schauwecker, the front was the breeding ground for a new nationalism that sweeps away old social orders and governs the future. More so than all other authors treated in this study, with the exception of Ernst Friedrich, Schauwecker ties his interpretation of the war experience to a political agenda for the present. This is most obvious in the sequel to *So war der Krieg!*, which is treated in chapter 6. *So ist der Friede* (This is what peace is like, 1928) extends Schauwecker's positive war account and its new brand of nationalism to rail against the Weimar Republic as a failed system of government unworthy to bear the spirit of wartime Germany. He understands the war as a struggle between nationalism and liberalism, personified in static portraits of the Weimar Republic's political elite, and looks to countries across the globe to define the type of governance Germany sorely needs. The answer lies in strong, charismatic leaders like Benito Mussolini who harness the people's will with decisive action. Along with a screed against liberalism, *So ist der Friede* decries rearmament around the world as Germany falls behind due to the unfavorable terms of "peace."

However stark their ideological differences and political goals may have been, the competing visions in Weimar-era picture books shared the mission of fixing—both stabilizing and correcting—the collective memory of the war. To do so, they offered visually sensuous encounters with "the war," prosthetic memories to influence postwar subjectivities. While soldiers turned to their photo albums to remember the war experience in private, picture-book authors looked to gain broad influence among the public with curated visions of the war that were concerned just as much with the past as with the present and future.

CHAPTER ONE

Private Memory and Mourning
The Photo Albums of German Soldiers

George Soldan begins the first volume of *Der Weltkrieg im Bild* (The World War in pictures; ca. 1926) with the assessment that "untold millions of images have come into being in the titanic struggle of our human race, the first great European war in the age of amateur photography."[1] Improved photographic technology, spurred by demand among soldiers and in many cases marketed specifically to them,[2] made cameras affordable and portable for the average war-participant in a previously unparalleled way. Photographs taken by German soldiers alone comprise an immense visual archive of the war. Indeed, at the outbreak of war, the military press department turned immediately to their very own soldiers to picture the war. While other nations like England and France placed harsher restrictions on amateur soldier-photographers and relied on a small number of official war photographers, the German military press department claimed to have collected over 75,000 images from amateur photographers by November 1915 alone.[3] The military favored soldiers, with their cheap, handy, and easy-to-use cameras, who did not need to be paid or organized like their professional counterparts.[4]

This chapter considers the figure of the amateur soldier-photographer and his role in the creation of the visual archives on which all postwar picture-book editors relied. By paying attention to the way soldiers contextualized their own war experience in their photographs and photographic albums, this chapter sheds a different light on the "fixes" that took place

1. Soldan, "Zum Geleit," *Der Weltkrieg im Bild* 1, n.p.
2. Dewitz, "Schießen oder fotografieren," 51.
3. "Die Photographie als Hilfsmittel im Krieg," 70.
4. Dewitz, "German Snapshots," 154.

within the visual archive of the war in mass-market picture books of the 1920s, a process that had begun already during the war, as will be shown later in this chapter through a handful of publications that predate the war's end. Far removed from the ideological or political projects of postwar memory contests, the narrative of war that emerges from photographs created by soldiers themselves reveals photographic practices that were motivated by individual meaning-making, by familial affiliation and fraternal companionship, and by personal self-reflection and self-assertion.

A rich archive of newspaper reports from trade and hobby periodicals on photography confirms the central facts about amateur soldier-photographers during the war. Already in October 1914, the weekly paper *Die Photographische Industrie: Fachblatt für Fabrikation und Handel aller photographischer Bedarfsartikel* (The photographic industry: Trade journal for the fabrication and sale of photographic consumer goods) was suggesting to its readership of industry insiders that the sale of small-format cameras to "unsere 'Feldgrauen'" (our boys in gray) could boost business. The editors explain that "our soldiers naturally have a large interest in capturing for posterity various moments and situations from the front lines in pictures and, due to the high wages of wartime, they have enough cash to get themselves a small camera."[5] W. Weißermel, writing "from the field" for the *Photographische Rundschau und Mitteilungen: Zeitschrift für Freunde der Photographie* (Photographic review and communications: Magazine for friends of photography), describes the different types of cameras that soldiers at the front could spend their pay on. He regrets having brought along a bulky 9 × 12 camera that takes up precious space in an already full pack, so therefore recommends the more easily transportable small formats that use roll film instead of plates or packaged film: "I therefore consider a 6 × 6 roll film camera to be the ideal field camera. I must admit, though, that the images are quite small. But they are not meant to be mere images, rather memories; and they serve that purpose perfectly, as I have been able to convince myself with more than 200 shots so far."[6] Besides the preserving of memories that Weißermel regards as the foremost function of taking photographs—more important than their intrinsic aesthetic quality—Lieutenant Max Schiel explains that amateur photography offers soldiers the opportunity "to engage on quieter days in a stimulating and distracting activity that refreshes mind and

5. "Der Verkauf kleiner Apparate an unsere 'Feldgrauen.'"
6. Weißermel, "Die Feldkamera," 181.

spirit."[7] Schiel reports on what cameras and film types he prefers, and gives advice for jerry-rigging a simple dark room with materials available in the field, such as a flashlight or candle, cigarette boxes, and packing cord. "Even though working in the field requires a certain practical know-how, you can still bring great joy to yourself and your comrades with simple means."[8] Similar articles printed in the *Photographische Rundschau* provide more thorough advice on setting up a portable darkroom,[9] and give ratios for chemical mixes composed of materials available to soldiers for use in developing film and making prints.[10]

The high level of interest in photography among soldiers had immense influence on the German photography industry: the realization that the photographic plate format, although providing higher-quality images, was less favorable than its smaller, quicker, sturdier, and more transportable counterpart, roll film, meant many factories shifted their production lines to meet demand. Existing cameras most suitable for transport into the field were quickly sold out and new designs were commissioned to fill production gaps. Although it initially lagged behind in meeting the sudden shift in demand toward small-format, roll-film cameras, the photographic industry blossomed.[11] Realities of war, such as interrupted trade routes and a lack of materials, added further stress to the photographic industry. But even a "Filmnot" (acute lack of film), as *Die Photographische Industrie* called it, was still used by commentators to spur producers into inventing cheaper, alternative products to meet the demands of professional photographers and amateurs alike: "But we must act quickly, because when the time comes, our customers in the field will want to take more photographs than before."[12] Despite complaints about bans on exports to combatant countries and the censorship of amateur photographers in public places on the home front, *Die Photographische Industrie* cites the war's positive role in an economically flourishing industry: "It is undeniable that photography in the field has contributed significantly to popularizing the medium, and in particular amateur photography, so that the trade is not wrongly hoping for good business in the future."[13]

Soldiers not only reaped the benefits of the photography industry reor-

7. Schiel, "Photographische Arbeiten im Feld," 219.
8. Schiel, "Photographische Arbeiten im Feld," 221.
9. "Photographische Behelfe im Felde," 202–3.
10. Weißermel, "Entwickeln des Amateurs im Felde," 161–62.
11. Eyermann, "Die Lichtbildkunst und Krieg," 190–91.
12. "Die Filmnot," 130.
13. "Die photographische Industrie im dritten Kriegsjahr," 4–6.

ganizing to meet their consumer demands, but they also enjoyed favored treatment in terms of censorship in comparison to civilians on the home front. *Die Photographische Industrie* reported throughout the war on various state and military-led efforts to ban amateur photography, both in the field and at home, whose purpose was to relieve some of the strain on factories and free up resources for professionals. Reports from the newspaper exhibit the confusion that such controversial efforts created, as not all policies were communicated clearly or enforced uniformly across local, state, and national government or military departments.[14] No general ban of amateur photography seems to have been passed, but civilians were forbidden from photographing military installations or other government buildings, such as the king's parks and palaces, for security reasons,[15] and they had to apply for special permits from the military if they wished to take photographs when visiting the front.[16] Soldiers were not subject to such rules and were allowed to photograph freely—if their immediate superior permitted it. Rules forbade the photographing of active combat, but the photographs and written testimonies alike attest to the frequent noncompliance with this rule.[17] Even a widely known literary work like Ernst Jünger's memoir *In Stahlgewittern* (*Storm of Steel*; 1920) provides testimony to this small fact, as the figure of Kius is said in passing to have taken pictures during the company's storming of a railway embankment.[18] Despite a general permission for the act of taking photographs, images created by soldiers that were sent willingly to military authorities underwent strict censorship before being allowed to appear in newspapers and magazines. The Photographic Association of Berlin even created a Central Office for the Censorship of Photographs so that those interested in submitting their photographs for publication would send it to the correct military department, ensuring that their images would not get lost and then delayed in a flood of photographs.[19] Censorship rules and the convoluted bureaucracies that accompanied them, however, could not reach the images kept in the private possession of soldiers.

---

14. See, for example, the following articles in *Die Photographische Industrie*: "Warnung vor dem Photographieren?" (July 14, 1915, front page), "Photographierverbot im Feld?" (December 22, 1915, front page), "Über Photographierverbote" (November 15, 1916, front page), "Photographier-Verbote" (January 3, 1917, front page), and "Beschränkungen der Amateurphotographie?!" (July 4, 1917, p. 514).

15. "Aufhebung der Photograhie-Verbote," title page.

16. Dewitz, "German Snapshots," 154.

17. Dewitz, "German Snapshots," 154.

18. Jünger, *In Stahlgewittern*, 262.

19. "Kleine Mitteilungen: Zentralstelle für die Zensur von Photographien," 303–4.

In addition to the aforementioned reasons that soldiers were interested in photography—to remember their service, to fill their downtime, or to find purpose by contributing to official archives—the editors of the *Photographische Rundschau* described in 1914 the amateur soldier-photographer's "tasks": (1) out of security concerns, any prohibition on photographing military positions or installations should be strictly followed; (2) service to local police or security services in photographing and identifying suspects should be offered freely; (3) soldiers should continue to take advantage of portrait-sittings at professional studios and could even lend a hand where studios have been affected through loss of personnel; and (4) when it is not possible to visit a professional studio, amateur photographers should happily make portraits of fellow soldiers that they can send back to family members. The editors summarize these efforts as both an important logistical and spiritual component of the overall war effort: "Everyone should do what is in their power, to the best of their knowledge and ability, to alleviate the difficult task of the army command, to strengthen the spirit of deploying troops, and to support and comfort those who remain behind."[20] A. Eyermann, writing from the field a year later in the same paper, adds that the amateur photographer plays a vital role in creating "irreplaceable documentation . . . , evidence that is more effective than many words, silent witnesses who speak when the mouth is silent."[21] Eyermann's claim that photographs are not only documents of unique expressiveness, but that they also attest to the spirit of the age from which they were created, evinces the layman's mythos of photography as an accurate and meaningful transcript of reality at the same time that it anticipates the positive claims made for war photography in the popular picture books of the Weimar era.

The actual photographs created by the soldiers reveal similar motivations to the ones described by contemporary hobby and trade photography journals. Cultural historian Bodo von Dewitz, who surveyed over 30,000 images in researching amateur German photography during the war, estimates that over two-thirds of photographs taken by soldiers were of other soldiers.[22] Portraits and group shots were not only popular for soldiers to send back home to their families, but functioned as tools for "self-assertion" and "self-affirmation" and as "survival strategies."[23] It seems to be no coincidence, then, that most photographed soldiers stare directly into the camera,

20. "Der Krieg und der Amateurphotograph," 242.
21. Eyermann, "Die Lichtbildkunst und der Krieg," 191.
22. Dewitz, "German Snapshots," 154.
23. Dewitz, *So wird bei uns der Krieg geführt*, 263.

as if to declare themselves present for eternity,[24] either in candid snapshots taken by comrades or in the popular staged studio. The commemorative function of photography that Weißermel described in the *Photographische Rundschau* was therefore imbued with a far more significant personal meaning than the simple remembering of events. It is uncertain whether many soldier-photographers rendered their service to police or security authorities for the sake of identification procedures, but an abundance of touristic snapshots and of ethnographic-like portraits, especially from those mobilized on the Eastern Front, display typical aspects of the war experience that were centered on a sense of adventure and seeing the world, aspects that exist separate from prevalent notions of war.[25] The picture of war that did appear in amateur photographs commonly included desolate landscapes with low horizons, mirroring the entrenched perspective on the Western Front; views of ruins or other signs of destruction that fascinated soldiers, such as the large smoke clouds that followed explosions; or objects that signified war successes, such as broken tanks or shot-down airplanes.[26] While soldiers shared the fascination for destruction that is common to postwar picture books, the heroic views of battle that are used to excite Weimar-era reader-viewers are far less common than the small, hard-to-decipher pictures of battlefields that abound in amateur soldier photography. There is also a marked absence in postwar picture books of photographs that evince soldiers' main preoccupation with asserting their individual identity and place in history.[27]

Photographs of self-assertion and self-affirmation that are legion in the visual archive created by amateur soldier-photographers fulfill a function not unlike another common medium of memory preservation: the diary. A 1918 article in the newspaper *Photographie für Alle* (Photography for everyone) notes that many soldiers carry small journals with them, "which serve as documents for the combatant's later memory and bear witness to Germany's high times for relatives and descendants."[28] Like photographs of other soldiers, the war diary unites the double impulse for personal recollection and historical self-assertion. The two media—photography and textual chronicling—come together in the popular photo album format, for which *Photographie für Alle* provides recommendations on size, format, composition, and even strategies for ensuring that one's album lasts as long as pos-

24. Dewitz, "German Snapshots," 157.
25. Dewitz, *So wird bei uns der Krieg geführt*, 264.
26. Dewitz, *So wird bei uns der Krieg geführt*, 263–65.
27. Dewitz, *So wird bei uns der Krieg geführt*, 287.
28. E., "Kriegstagebücher," 132.

sible, such as using a clean ink and not writing directly on images.[29] The same article also notes that photo albums are a useful repository for all sorts of mixed media, including photographs taken with one's own camera, shared by comrades, or taken in professional studios, postcards, newspaper clippings, reports from the German General Staff, maps, and illustrations of received medals.[30] War albums therefore extend the photographic practice of self-representation among soldiers to a wide range of visual, textual, and graphic material, allowing soldiers to create, collect, and curate their memories and their sense of self in a meaningful way that fixed present experiences for the future.

Soldier photo albums offer a rich array of material to the cultural historian looking to understand the experience of soldiers, but individual photographs remain their main component. Individual photographs provide evidence of how soldiers pictured the war and what they deemed worthy of being pictured, including aspects that may be neglected in or even written out of the narratives presented in postwar picture books. But when taken alone, individual photographs provide only superficial information on the context and motivation behind their creation. John Tagg warns:

> One cannot "use" photography as an unproblematic "source." Photography does not transmit a pre-existent reality which is already meaningful in itself. As with any other discursive system, the question we must ask is not, "What does this discourse reveal of something else?" but, "what does it do; what are the conditions of its existence; how does it inflect its context rather than reflect it; how does it animate meaning rather than discover it."[31]

In the case of the First World War, photography found many highly varied uses that are well documented, including the first widespread use of photography to enhance battle reconnaissance.[32] However, as the indiscriminate selection of photographs in postwar picture books reveals, the semantic openness of photography was taken advantage of by editors to craft their own meanings. A very basic example of this in patriotic or nationalist picture books are photographs of unidentified soldiers or groups of soldiers meant to

29. E., "Kriegstagebücher," 132–33.
30. E., "Kriegstagebücher," 133.
31. Tagg, *Burden of Representation*, 119.
32. See Jäger, *Erkundung mit der Kamera*.

represent the idea of the *Frontkämpfer* (frontline warriors), a unified group forged mystically at the front, ready to take on the mantle of the new nation. In the postwar picture books, photographs from a wide variety of sources are selected to fit predetermined meanings, with their original purpose, context, and creator erased.

Tagg states that "photography as such has no identity. Its status as a technology varies with the power relations which invest it."[33] By paying greater attention to the photographic collections of individuals, such as those fixed into photo albums, the way the photographic practice inflects its context becomes more fully revealed than in individual photographs. We can understand what Tagg calls the "terms of [photographs'] legibility, and the range and limits of their effectivities," determined "across the images, in what they do and do not do, in what they encompass and exclude, in the ways they open on to or resist a repertoire of uses in which they can be meaningful and productive."[34] Photographs are often less realistic than they seem, and those who do not take account of an image's variety of possible meanings may be misled to a distorted view of "reality." However, as Peter Burke claims—and as later chapters will show in the analysis of picture books—"the process of distortion is itself evidence of phenomena that many historians want to study: mentalities, ideologies and identities. The material or literal image is good evidence of the mental or metaphorical 'image' of the self or of others."[35]

The greater clues that photo albums provide—above all, extended contexts and sequential narratives that stretch beyond single images—are able to both illuminate and circumscribe some of the inherent problems in using photographs as a "source" of history, whether that entails a tendency toward mere illustration or an active distortion of the past. For one, photo albums exist as reconstructions of experience and must be read as the product of an individual's version of events. That is to say, their individualism resists the definitive readings of "History," whether ideologically motivated or not, and even draws attention to their own shortcomings through comparison with the larger events they reflect. While their unavoidable ambiguities and gaps in representation must be recognized, photo albums offer a more thorough look into mentalities of the war experience as it was visually structured and remembered by individual soldiers. They represent "an intersection between

33. Tagg, *Burden of Representation*, 118.
34. Tagg, *Burden of Representation*, 119.
35. Burke, *Eyewitnessing*, 30.

war experience and war memory," and—perhaps most akin to memoirs—serve as objects in which the complicated process of memory inheres.[36] This makes any photo album a potential point of entry for understanding not only what the war actually looked like but how it was remembered visually by its participants. Along with letters, postcards, and diaries, all once "unorthodox" historical sources that are now commonly utilized for approaches to history "from below,"[37] photo albums offer a counterweight to the sensationalized, ideologically laden, and often dubiously selective "picture" of the war that was presented to the German public in the late 1920s.

At the same time, many contemporary thinkers have drawn attention to the seeming silence of such photo albums. Martha Langford underscores a photo album's potential as a cue for conversation, an "instrument of social performance" in which it serves as a "mnemonic device for storytelling" in a realm of orality. Once removed from the private sphere, a photo album's "performative cord" is cut.[38] Gillian Rose echoes this idea by defining the genre of family photography, among which soldierly photo albums must be counted, not by the content of images but by the sort of communicative and commemorative practices in which they are embedded within the familial group. Likewise, Marianne Hirsch writes about the "unconscious optics" of family photographs that, if they are to be deciphered, rely heavily on surrounding narration. Addressing memory more generally, Aleida Assmann contends that visual documents become mute witnesses to history when their corresponding stories and memories are lost.[39] How soldiers' albums from the First World War functioned in the familial sphere or among friends would therefore require supporting documents, such as diaries or letters, if they exist. But even this assumption is complicated by a case like that of German soldier "Otto H.," whose photo album and war diary bear few direct connections.[40] No matter their limitations, photo albums also represent an intersection between the private and the public. Originally made for and

36. Stiftung DHM, *100 Objekten*, 106. Taylor reminds us: "The 'war' was not a fixed physical or psychological entity for the individual soldier. It was something that was experienced and re-experienced on a continuing basis; it was something that was interpreted and reinterpreted as time passed and the war was viewed from differing vantage points" (*Memory, Narrative and the Great War*, 40).

37. Crew, "*Alltagsgeschichte,*" 395. For issues concerning military historiography "from above" and "from below," see Wette, "Militärgeschichte von unten."

38. Langford, *Suspended Conversations*, 223–24, 227.

39. Rose, *Doing Family Photography*, 14; Hirsch, *Family Frames*, 119; Assmann, *Der lange Schatten der Vergangenheit*, 57.

40. See Krase, "Aber die armen Kerle."

sometimes showing a familial context, they are nevertheless a representation of the war, a phenomenon that transcends the realm of an individual and his social group. In other words, soldiers' albums contain private experiences that can be *partially* deciphered with public knowledge. But if historical knowledge only goes so far in "reading" private albums, how can a photo album's apparent silence be broken and what can be gained by doing so? These questions are explored in the following examples.

The Special Collections of the University of Wisconsin–Madison Library holds an album of First World War photographs made by the German soldier Jakob "Jako" Sitzmann.[41] "Aufnahmen aus den [*sic*] Weltkrieg: 1914–1918" (Pictures from the World War) assembles photographs from Sitzmann's four years of service with the Royal Bavarian Infantry Lifeguards Regiment. "History" tells nothing about Sitzmann as an individual but reveals that his company was deployed as a highly mobile unit that reacted to the fluctuating personnel needs of the larger German military forces. This meant that his regiment was constantly shifting positions between the Western Front in France, the Eastern Front in Serbia, Romania, and Hungary, and the mountain wars in northern Italy. Because Sitzmann served during the entire war, his photo album reflects all the locales to which the regiment was deployed, including more notorious ones such as Verdun. The soldiers who served in Sitzmann's regiment were from Bavaria, and although the album does not state where Sitzmann came from in Bavaria, reference to two childhood friends—war casualties—who were both from Rottenburg an der Laaber suggests that this was also his hometown. Sitzmann's military records, which exist separately from his photo album, confirm that he was born in Weiherhof (Landkreis Kelheim), not far from Rottenburg an der Laaber. He was born in 1891, meaning he was 23 years old at the war's start, although he had entered the military before 1914. Military records for his brothers, who are pictured lovingly in the album, confirm their participation in the war and provide some additional details to the story left out of the photo album, including their regiments and the locations where they served. Missing basic information like this foregrounds the potential gaps in a photo album if longer textual description is absent, as is the case throughout Sitzmann's album. While these gaps represent frustrating obstacles to the viewer's historical understanding today, they would have been easily bridged by shared oral testimony or other written accounts when the album was passed around the family living room.

---

41. The full album has been digitized and is accessible to the public on the website of the UW-Madison libraries: https://search.library.wisc.edu/digital/A4UE3ELHF7LOLF86

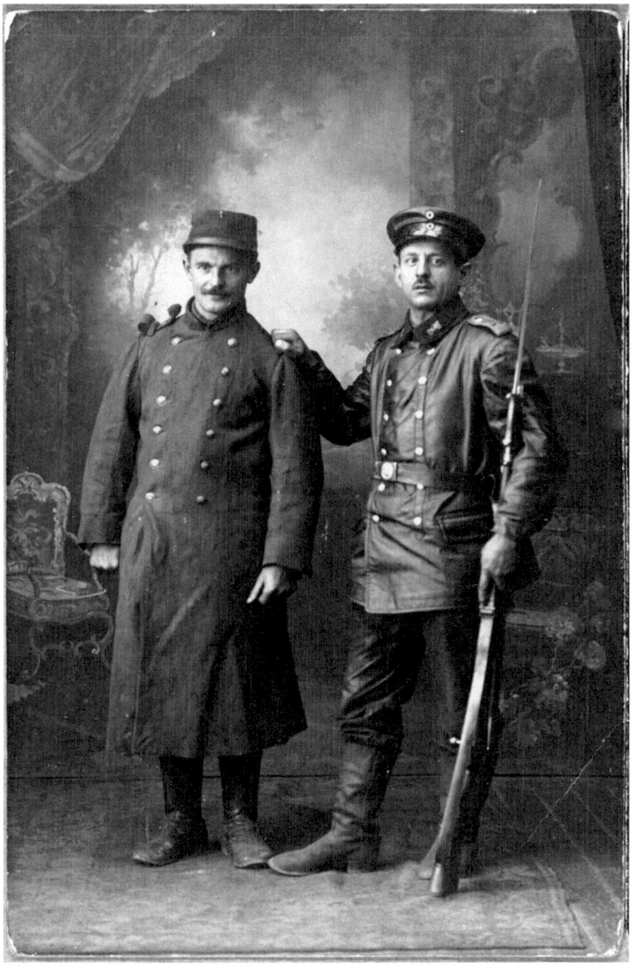

Fig. 1. "Vali verkleidet als Gefangener" (Vali dressed up as a prisoner), *Jako Sitzmann, Photo Album, 1914–1918*, MS 411 no. 10. Courtesy of the Department of Special Collections, Memorial Library, University of Wisconsin–Madison.

Despite obvious withholdings, Sitzmann's album offers a rich view into the perspective of a soldier from the First World War, and one can tell from the very first pages that that perspective is centered squarely on the personal. The album's inside cover contains portraits of Jako's three brothers, "Wendl," "Vali," and "Schorsch." Even though such commemorative photographs were wildly popular among soldiers and their families during the war,[42] such images rarely—if ever—appear in mass-market war picture books from the Weimar era; their intimate charge remains untranslatable for public audiences. The portrait of Wendl is staged in a studio; the backdrop's edge shows on the right and bottom of the image. The portrait of Vali (fig. 1) is similarly staged; curiously, the caption states that he is wearing the costume of a prisoner, although he is standing in a studio on an ornate rug and in front of an elaborately painted backdrop. The apparent model standing next to him, tightly gripping the shoulder of Vali's uniform, looks bored, while Vali, despite a clenched right fist, displays a slight grin, as if to divulge that he is in on the photograph's joke. Vali makes a second appearance later in the album in a commemorative portrait as an ambulance driver—the image's corners are rounded and the photograph is larger than the ones taken by Sitzmann. The third brother, Schorsch, is pictured standing naturally in a garden for what appears to be a spontaneous portrait. While these photographs could never be construed to relay the experience of individual soldiers during the war, the three portraits highlight the centrality of picturing personal relations among soldiers and establish for the viewer an empathic connection with the Sitzmann family. One cannot help wonder about the four brothers' fate. This question is compounded when the viewer sees later in the album the image of a fifth (!) Sitzmann brother in uniform, "Sepp," posing casually with Schorsch in a snapshot portrait.

Beyond the initial pages, even a cursory look through Jakob Sitzmann's album shows just how central a role other soldiers, friends, and family alike played in the photographs that he took himself and collected from other sources. More than half the pictures in Sitzmann's album are of his companions marching, resting at camp, or posing for the camera, as Hans Gruber, Ernst Toni, Jacob Kessner, Hans Kellringer, and many others do. One figure, another Hans, makes four appearances in the album, and each time he has a differently spelled surname: Hans "Dünzel" relaxes with Sergeant Mitterer, Hans "Dünel" poses with a donkey in St. Pierre, Hans "Dünzl" sits exhaustedly with his knees to his chest, and Hans "Düzel" reclines against a building dressed as a Macedonian (fig. 2). Again, these four photographs do not convey Hans's complete war experience (or even his actual name), but they attest to the manifold experiences of individual soldiers—not just the "Soldier"—during the war.

Sitzmann's album is certainly not alone in its attention to fellow sol-

42. Riha, "Den Krieg photographieren," 148–49, and Moriarty, "Though in a Picture Only," 36.

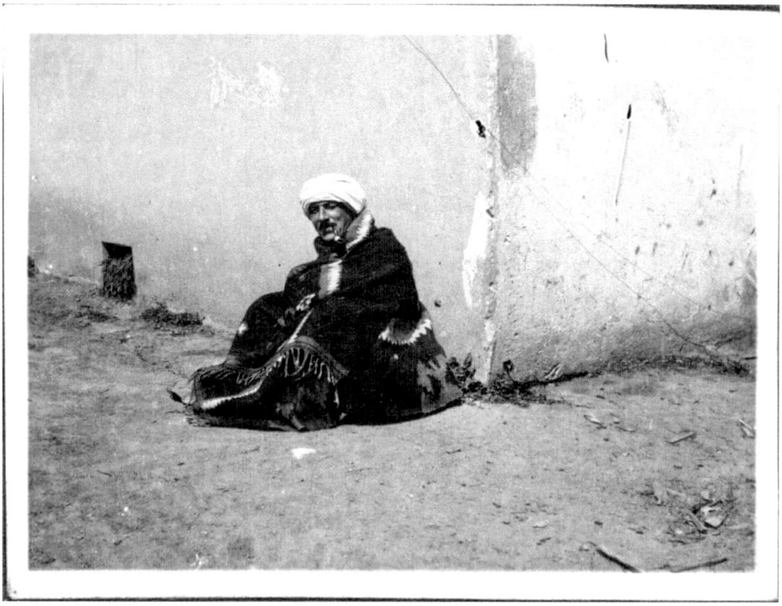

Fig. 2. "Hans Düzel als Mazadonier" (Hans Düzel as a Macedonian), *Jako Sitzmann, Photo Album, 1914–1918,* MS 411 no. 10. Courtesy of the Department of Special Collections, Memorial Library, University of Wisconsin–Madison.

diers and their range of shared experiences. An amateur photo album in the archives of the Deutsches Historisches Museum simply labeled "Weltkrieg 1914–1918" includes 59 photographs of soldiers in various formations (commemorative portraits, posed group shots, candid pictures in the field, and so forth) out of a total of 81.[43] Although the anonymous creator of this album provides scarce captions throughout the album (mainly dates and locations), the attention to shared memories, such as "Christmas 1917 (Russia)," reveals not only the importance of camaraderie among soldiers but the variety of lived experience during the war. Another album documents various company celebrations (beer included), such as "Forest Festival in Livercourt, June 1918" and a performance for the troops by "Clown Müller."[44] Dan Todman summarizes that "laughter, drunkenness and camaraderie were as much a

43. "Album mit Fotos aus dem 1. Weltkrieg vom Kriegsschauplatz an der Ostfront."

44. "Fotoalbum aus dem Ersten Weltkrieg mit zahlreichen Aufnahmen von Kriegszerstörungen in Frankreich, Belgien und Polen."

part of the war, for many men, as terror, violence and obedience." These, and many other experiences, including those of civilians, are "obscured in our modern understanding by the concentration on the horrors of combat."[45] The same holds true for the representation of war in many Weimar-era picture books, with their emphasis on destruction, either as a negative terror (in Ernst Friedrich's *Krieg dem Kriege!*) or as a positive metaphysical transformation (in Franz Schauwecker's *So war der Krieg!*). Even when postwar picture books stress a positive aspect of the war experience, their ideologically minded authors often heighten its significance to assert political claims. Camaraderie, for example, was co-opted in service of the "front generation" mythos that posited an elite community of soldiers forged in the sacrifices at the front.

One largely neglected aspect of First World War historiography, the Eastern Front and beyond,[46] comes alive through some soldiers' albums. The visual potency of trench warfare on the Western Front or the excitement of new technologies, such as airplanes, has caused other views from what was truly a *world* war to fade from (dominant Western) memory. Anton Holzer claims that, in Germany and Austria, "memory of the war is characterized by pictures that everyone knows: most of the time this means photographs from the Western Front that show the trenches, the effects of attrition warfare, the pockmarked landscape. In picture books and TV documentaries, these photographs represent 'the' First World War."[47] While Holzer is concerned with the present, the trend toward consolidation of the First World War's visual representation around images of the Western Front is already evident in the postwar picture books, where it is not uncommon for introductions to state openly that everything but the Western Front is purposely ignored. The same does not hold true for the photo albums of German soldiers, whose actual experiences stretched far beyond the trenches of northeastern France.

In comparison to the trench warfare in the West, the Eastern Front was longer, stretching across most of eastern and central Europe, and more sparsely defended, ensuring that trenches rarely developed and front lines

45. Todman, *The Great War*, 5, 4.

46. Jay Winter calls the ten million men who fought on the Eastern Front "the largest group of unknown soldiers in the twentieth century" in *Remembering War*, 80–81.

47. Holzer, *Das Lächeln der Henker*, 9. One recent example from popular entertainment, the film adaptation of Vera Brittain's memoir *Testament of Youth* (published 1933; film 2014), speaks to this elision: the time Brittain served on Malta and her visits to the battlefields of northern Italy to visit her brother's grave are excised in the film script in favor of longer attention to the horrors of the field hospitals on the Western Front.

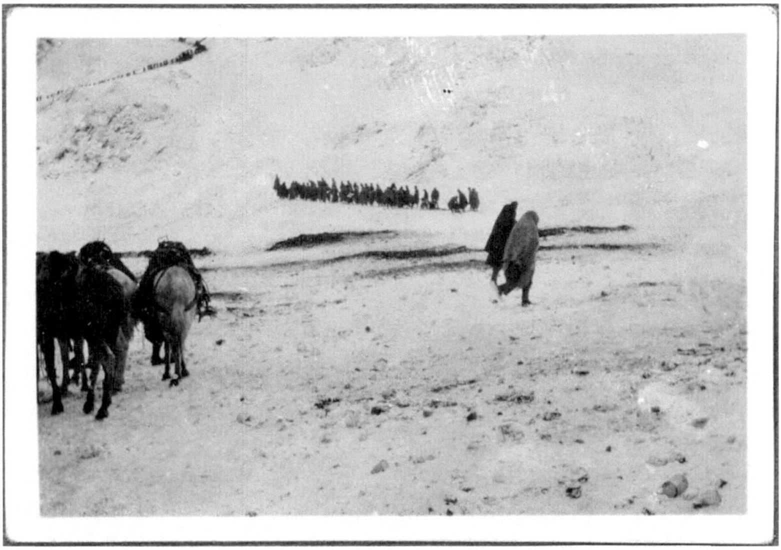

Fig. 3. "Bei grimmiger Kälte u. heftigen Schneesturm auf den Moscovul" (In the bitter cold and snow on the Moscovul), *Jako Sitzmann, Photo Album, 1914–1918,* MS 411 no. 10. Courtesy of the Department of Special Collections, Memorial Library, University of Wisconsin–Madison.

fluctuated more rapidly. The pictures of soldiers from the Eastern Front attest to this difference: instead of flat, cratered landscapes, mountain vistas and forests prevail; instead of bombed French churches, shots of Eastern Europe's capital cities; instead of prisoners of war, locals dressed in traditional ethnic garb.[48] The excitement among soldiers at "seeing the world" was part of the enthusiasm with which Europeans greeted the war in general. Historian Rudy Koshar asserts that "soldiers took advantage of their chance to see parts of Europe they might never have experienced were it not for war. In effect, they made up vast armies of part-time tourists."[49] And like any well-prepared tourist, many soldiers came outfitted with cameras: Sitzmann, for example, took the opportunity to snap a photo of the main train station in Budapest and another of that city's old Elizabeth Bridge. These views, too, were significant enough to be fixed into his photo album.

48. This "foreign gaze" is often aimed at eastern Europe's Jewish populations. Antisemitism in some albums from the Eastern Front hints at the First World War's consequences for later European history (Stiftung DHM, *100 Objekten,* 106).

49. Koshar, "What Should Haunt Us about World War I?"

The variety of experience occluded from popular memory of the First World War in postwar picture books can be seen in Sitzmann's album alone. As stated above, he served in a regiment that transitioned back and forth between the different war fronts. Accordingly, his album reflects various locales, and the differences between them are striking. The wasted landscapes around Verdun and Douaumont stand in contrast to the natural beauty of the Roter-Turm-Pass (Romanian: Pasul Turnu Roșu), where heavy fighting occurred in fall 1916, and the Moscovul Massif, a location in Carpathia that was part of the Battle of Sălătrucu. Despite the well-documented horrors of the Western Front, Sitzmann's only emotional qualification of his war experience in the album's captions is in reference to the Eastern Front: two pictures mention his company's bivouac "after a very cold night," and a picture of the Moscovul is labeled "in the bitter cold and snow" (fig. 3). Among all the captions that matter-of-factly label the many depressing locations Sitzmann visited during the war, including Verdun, only these few short remarks could be construed either as complaint or as manly assertion of lived experience.[50] The terror of the Western Front served as the epitome of the war experience in both the negative and positive interpretations of Weimar-era picture books, but survival for soldiers meant something much more comprehensive than living under the threat of enemy fire: it included enduring the cold, boredom, lice, and so forth, of daily life, both at and more typically away from the front line.[51]

The experiences of soldiers in prisoner-of-war camps are among the most ignored aspects of the war's retelling in popular picture books of the Weimar Republic. Several photo albums held by the Deutsches Historisches Museum attest to the manifold experiences of POWs often elided from the war's "Big Show."[52] One soldier, a doctor and officer in the army, compiled an album of photographs that traces his experience from his initial training in Germany, to the far eastern Siberian POW camps of Stretensk and Krasnoyarsk, back to Europe through stays in Swedish and Danish hospital camps, and finally home to Germany.[53] His album provides many clues to the

50. Rudy Koshar writes that "not only travel, but also rugged interaction with nature was an element of the experience. . . . soldiers' letters reveal a sense of vigorous physical accomplishment in addition to their fear and homesickness. Soldiers lucky enough to return home without serious injury were often tan, had gained weight, and had the general appearance of health" ("What Should Haunt Us").

51. Todman, *The Great War*, 4–5.

52. Hynes, *The Soldiers' Tale*, 75.

53. "Album mit Postkarten, Fotos und Dokumenten zum Leben deutscher Kriegs-

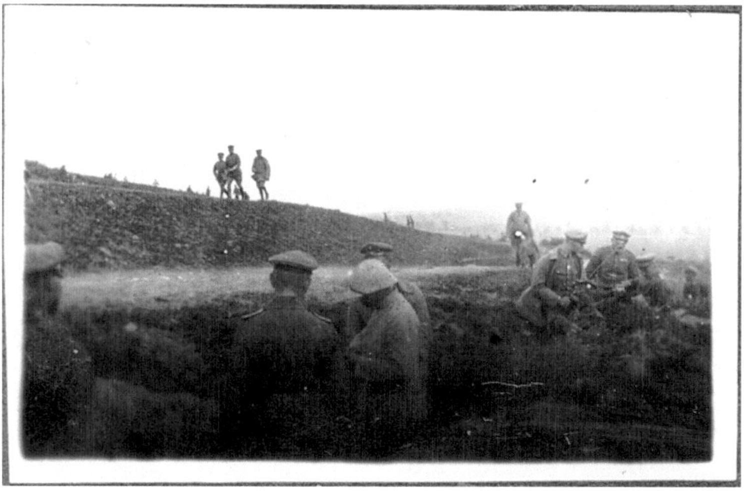

Fig. 4. "Verdun," *Jako Sitzmann, Photo Album, 1914–1918*, MS 411 no. 10. Courtesy of the Department of Special Collections, Memorial Library, University of Wisconsin–Madison.

mix of misery and comradeship experienced in POW camps. One picture of the camp's theater group, well supplied with costumes, musical instruments, and stage props, is captioned: "Humor sometimes also shows itself in hard times, especially when the Russian camp commander is a reasonable person and has already heard bullets whistling in the field." Such leisure activities are perhaps unassimilable to expectations of how a prison camp would function, but prisoners were ultimately still subject to the whims of their Russian captors. A happy picture from the same album of a tennis game between German officers is tempered by its caption: "For about 14 days officers and men were able to enjoy the sport, then the Russians suddenly destroyed everything again—probably out of anger over a suffered defeat." Loss of privileges, however, is the least serious concern, as the presence of death pervades the album. References to mass graves, forced labor, and widespread outbreaks of typhus are evidence of the suffering experienced in POW camps. Alon Rachamimov details how the POW story did not find resonance in the war's popular historiography: "Despite the ubiquity of ex-prisoners in post–World

gefangener in russischen Lagern." The name "Dr. med. Walter Heinze / Naumburg–Saale" is penciled on the back of the album's front cover, but it is not entirely clear if he is the album's creator.

War I Europe (one out of every eight veterans to reenter civilian society after the war had been a POW), despite the activities of ex-POWs organizations and despite the publication of scores of POW memoirs, the story of captivity never became part of what had been termed the Memory (or the Idea) of the Great War."[54]

In comparison to an emphasis on the violence of war in some postwar picture books, soldiers rarely thematized violence in their personal photo albums. In Sitzmann's album, for example, there are only eight photographs (out of about 175) that show signs of destruction, and even these show only destroyed buildings; there are no corpses. Battlefields are pictured in around ten photographs, but always from a spatial and temporal distance; there are no explosions or soldiers crouching in trenches. However, some of the most striking moments of Sitzmann's album are still related to the recognizable battlefields that have become synonymous with the horrors of war. Verdun, for instance, lurks throughout the album's pages as a reminder of the grim reality Sitzmann and his companions faced (see fig. 4). The album thus reminds viewers of more brutal experiences through the side door, by soberingly linking the private war experience pictured in the album to common knowledge of the war's destruction; in short, the album places Sitzmann at the scene of the action, without actually showing the action. This visual representation offers a more contemplative viewing of war that bypasses the excitement of violence (explosions, trenches, corpses) and draws attention to the ambiguity and blank spaces in the representations of other people's lived experience.[55] It does so in a way that does not make claims about representing "The War" or the idea of war in general, as postwar picture books often do—despite sometimes their acknowledgment of the inability to attend to the entire visual archive of the war. Instead, photo albums expand the possible frames for picturing the war by avoiding totalizing interpretations. By focusing attention on individual experience, photo albums evoke a deep sense of the war with even the shallowest amount of personal information.

This is certainly the case with the attention given to fallen comrades in many of the photo albums of German soldiers. The precise identification of the dead and their graves is frequently even more careful than that afforded to the living. The only soldier explicitly named in one anonymous

---

54. Rachamimov, *POWs and the Great War*, 4. Alon Rachamimov considers the "familiar" nature of this type of misery one reason for the disinterest in the POW experience; all twentieth-century wars have inflicted similar hardships on soldiers and civilians alike (225).

55. See Langford, *Suspended Conversations*, 18–19.

photo album held by the German Historical Museum (Deutsche Historische Museum) is Fritz Malisius, who is visually denoted by the cross that stood above his grave. Another album devotes two entire pages to the depiction of a funeral procession;[56] this amounts to an unusual instance of an album-maker grouping photographs in a fashion that creates a short yet cohesive visual narrative. The viewer can easily trace the "story": a casket is loaded onto a horse-drawn carriage under the supervision of men in uniform, wheeled from the camp to a neighboring cemetery, and prepped for being lifted into an open grave as a priest in white robes supervises. Although the deceased is not identified, the attention to this series of events—out of all the possible things that could be or are included in the album—contributes to the moment's emotional poignancy. Two further albums made by former prisoners of war show the simple yet elegant memorials built for fallen comrades in POW camps. In one album, the caption "A memorial for fallen comrades, self-made by prisoners of war" accompanies a photograph of a short, thick concrete obelisk sitting on a basic brick plinth surrounded by a short fence, and in the second album, the photograph of a similar memorial—"our grave monument in Radolnoje"—is given a carefully hand-drawn border of draped, ornate curtains, all topped with the gravitas-lending Roman numerals "MCMXVI."[57] By photographing gravesites, surviving soldiers incorporated personal and emotional acts of commemoration into their photo albums and, as was surely true in some cases, provided some small solace to grieving families. Such memento mori bridged the often great distance to the final resting place of their loved ones through the photograph's perceived visual immediacy.

The commemoration of fallen soldiers goes beyond private remembrance and pervades the picture books published in 1920s Germany. Private photo albums, however, are best able to attest to the emotional impact of death on a personal scale. The example of Sitzmann's album is again telling here. On the final page of his album, he includes two portraits of Max and Josef Müller (fig. 5), a personally motivated inclusion that indicates his reckoning with the death of his friends. Sitzmann writes under the portraits their years of death (1916 and 1918) and their occupations (plumber and locksmith).

56. "Album mit Fotos aus dem 1. Weltkrieg vom Kriegsschauplatz an der Ostfront"; "Album mit Fotos, Postkarten und Theaterprogrammen deutscher Gefangener in englischen Lagern."

57. "Album mit Postkarten, Fotos und Dokumenten zum Leben deutscher Kriegsgefangener in russischen Lagern"; "Album mit Fotos und Kunstexponaten aus der Kriegsgefangenschaft in Sibirien im Ersten Weltkrieg."

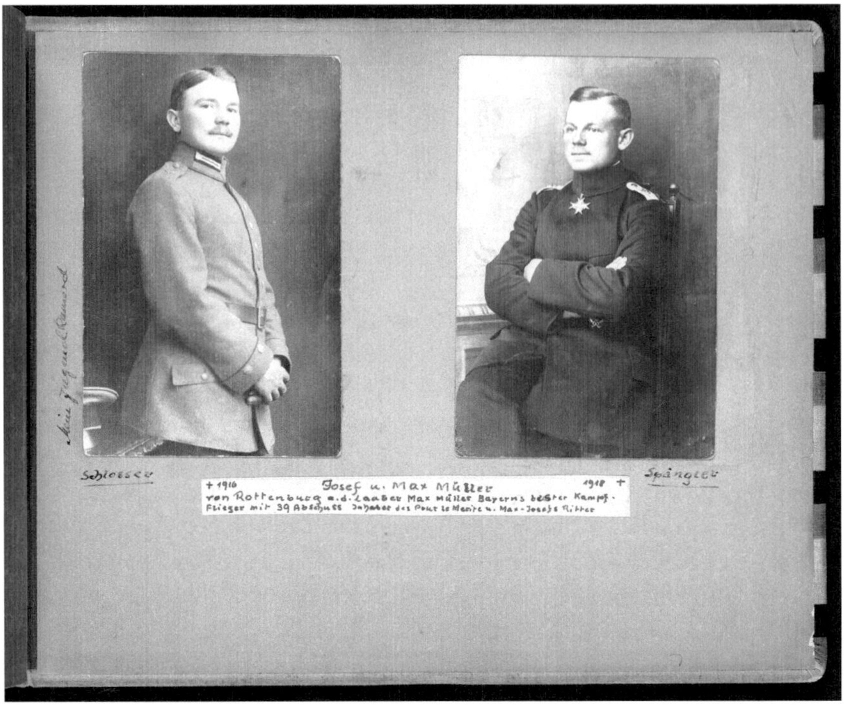

Fig. 5. Inside of back cover, *Jako Sitzmann, Photo Album, 1914–1918*, MS 411 no. 10. Courtesy of the Department of Special Collections, Memorial Library, University of Wisconsin–Madison.

Next to the portrait of Josef, he wrote "my childhood friend." He notes that Max Müller was "Bavaria's best fighter pilot with 39 victories; recipient of the *Pour le Merite* and *Max-Josefs Ritters*"—heroizing information used to cast Max's death as a meaningful sacrifice. An earlier photograph in the album is a professional photograph of Josef's funeral (fig. 6), and another shows Max standing next to his airplane. These personal narratives, although admittedly quite basic, still forge strong empathic connections with the viewer via the bond between Sitzmann and his friends. They evince processes of grieving that are separate from commemoration of heroes ("Heldengedenken"), which elevates war sacrifice to collective memory for national symbolism, and the cult of the dead ("Totenkult"), which keeps memory of the dead alive by erasing the boundaries between life and death.[58] (The former is characteristic of

58. Haas, "Im Schatten," 203.

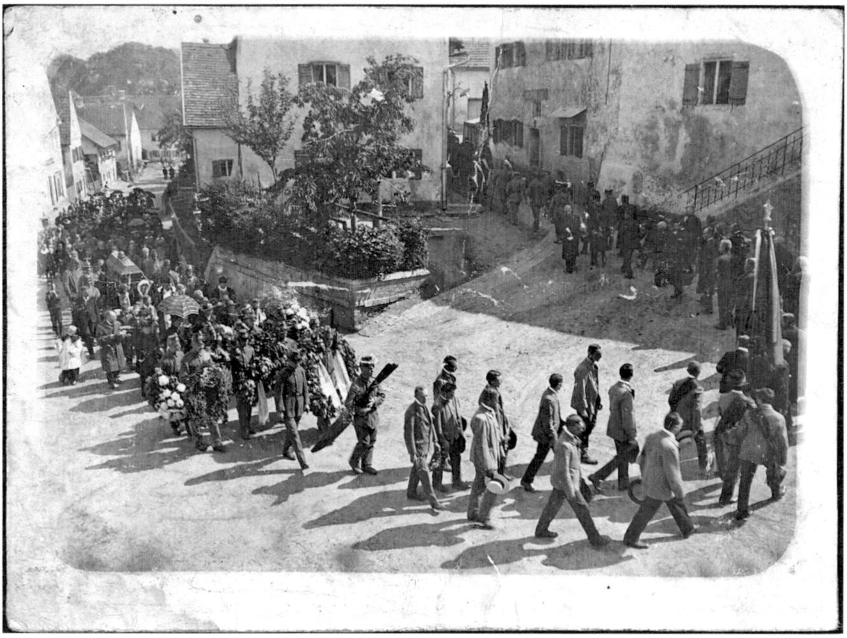

Fig. 6. "Die Beerdigung des Kameraden Josef Müller" (The burial of comrade Josef Müller), *Jako Sitzmann, Photo Album, 1914–1918*, MS 411 no. 10. Courtesy of the Department of Special Collections, Memorial Library, University of Wisconsin–Madison.

the publications affiliated with the Reichsarchiv analyzed in chapters 3 and 4, while the latter is typical of Franz Schauwecker's interpretation of the front experience and its legacy examined in chapters 5 and 6.) In other words, pictures of the dead are presented in Sitzmann's photo album as more than just representations of a national sacrifice; they are placed into the context of the photo album in which the process of memory and mourning inheres and others are bidden to take part. In comparison to the appeal made upon viewers to mourn the fallen soldier in nationalist, patriotic picture books, or the appeal to mobilize to prevent future depersonalized death in pacifist interpretations of the war's visual archive, the mourning process in Sitzmann's photo album remains politically uncharged and focused on a personal reckoning with the meaning of war and death that may not be by nature entirely apolitical but is devoid of predetermined interpretations.

The very act of viewing a photo album, whether for a creator's contemporaries or those who followed, is also deeply intimate. Even without the preexisting empathic bond of familial affiliations that would have generated their own worlds of memory in communicative exchange, a certain aura surrounds the album as an object. This is due in no small part to its vulnerability as a unique object, beset by the consequences of time and its amateur means of production. Most albums have quite unexceptional, if not fragile physical characteristics. Sitzmann's album, for example, is simply crafted in an unremarkable book with orange, black, and gray stripes on a plush front and back cover. Four or five photographs are glued onto each page of thick, green construction paper, which are separated by sheets of preservation paper. Most pictures in the album are taken by Sitzmann and are small, at around 5.5 cm × 8 cm. Captions are handwritten on cut pieces of ruled notebook paper pasted into the album.

Although these properties may initially seem secondary to the visual contents of the photographs found within the album, they determine the encounter with the album as a unique object.[59] Geoffrey Batchen describes photo albums as "tactile objects with moveable parts, and to be experienced fully, they . . . demand that we add the physical intimacy of touch to the more distanced apprehension of looking."[60] In the age of mechanical (and now digital) reproducibility, viewing such an album anchors the enclosed photographs to a specific context in a way that mass-market picture books could not. Although pages can be skimmed over or even skipped, the album's physicality predetermines a mode of viewing that becomes more focused and contemplative through touch. And as explained above, photo albums include much more than photographs. Postcards, official documents, and even objects like dried flowers become part of assemblages that draw attention to an album's mediated construction; in short, dimensions of physicality invite emotional investment. In one album, a picture of "Stretensk [a POW camp in Siberia] on a beautiful summer day" has a dried flower glued next to it, a "Siberian Edelweiss / picked 5.6.1916."[61] The object's physicality introduces an example of what Batchen terms "doubled indexicality": along with the photograph, the flower places the soldier in a specific place and time, creating a heightened emotional effect that reminds the viewer how

59. Holger Brohm warns that the contemporary digitization of soldier photographs and letters alike, although it makes the documents available to a wider audience, risks a loss of their particular materiality and the corresponding signs that animate their meaning ("From *Erlebnis* to *Erinnerung*," 40).

60. Batchen, *Forget Me Not*, 49.

61. "Album mit Postkarten, Fotos und Dokumenten zum Leben deutscher Kriegsgefangener in russischen Lagern."

"the passing of time that makes memory possible and necessary is also what makes memory fade and die."[62]

Addition of text to family photographs, like the short captions in Sitzmann's album, "can enliven images and enhance their capacity to arouse emotions," as Batchen details.[63] This is true of the way Sitzmann identifies soldiers briefly by their names, thereby erasing their potential historical anonymity and humanizing them. It is noteworthy here that almost no soldiers are mentioned by name in postwar picture books unless they count among the top military brass. Other examples of short texts in Sitzmann's album—none longer than a few truncated sentences—add personal dimensions to the included images, as in the captions mentioning the terribly cold winter nights in the mountains of Romania. Drawn or written additions complement the personalized representation of the war. For example, in photographs that he did not take himself, including official group portraits, Sitzmann always draws an arrow to identify himself. In general, soldiers' albums often avoid lengthier exposition—in contrast to postwar picture books—but they offer enough tantalizing details to keep the viewer mentally and emotionally engaged. The results, although dependent on a certain amount of contemplation and piecing together of visual clues, have the potential to be emotionally stirring in a way that the anonymous death often central to mass-market picture books—no matter the ideological spin—cannot achieve.

Photo albums encourage, as Batchen explains about other mixed-media photo objects, "both speculation and an empathetic, phenomenological style of historical writing that seeks to bridge the temporal and emotional gap between them and us."[64] The soldier albums testify at once to a specific past and its historical events, the First World War, while they evoke the immediacy of death, loss, and grief at the time of viewing. Batchen writes: "Such shifting from past to present (and back again), and from third to first person, might begin to register the complexity of the identity we witness in [such an] object." This demands a new type of historiography that transforms the subjects of photographs "from somebody merely seen to someone really felt, from an image viewed at a distance on the wall into an emotional exchange transacted in the heart."[65] Photo albums, with their intersection between

62. Batchen, *Forget Me Not*, 75, 78.
63. Batchen, *Forget Me Not*, 49.
64. Batchen, *Forget Me Not*, 93.
65. Batchen, *Forget Me Not*, 93, 94.

private memory and public history, reveal this tension, and therefore are significant not only for what they reveal about the war but also for how that process works, namely how visual representations can determine the very relationship viewers take to the past.

The pronounced differences in structure and meaning-making between private soldier photo albums and mass-market picture books, which will reach its highest contrast in the publications of the late 1920s, analyzed in later chapters, comes into focus already during the war. In addition to photo albums created by individual soldiers and newspapers produced in the field,[66] soldiers worked together to remember their war experience as it unfolded in properly published photographic compendiums. One such book, *Zwischen Arras und Peronne* (Between Arras and Peronne; 1916), includes 311 photographs from the Western Front.[67] Members of a reserve corps deployed in France conceived and edited the book, and members of the unnamed division(s) supplied their original photographs for the volume. The final product is intended as a memory book (*Erinnerungsbuch*) of places and people, a counteragent to the fading of individual memories that will occur over the course of the war.[68] Not intended for a wider public, it should serve as "a book purely of views without the addition of text" that can be appreciated only by members of the reserve corps.[69] The photographs selected for inclusion in the book from among the more than 700 apparently submitted show the areas and locales where the division was stationed, and which should hold special significance for the troops who spent the war in and around those places. But save for a few markers of war—troops in uniform, the occasional ruined building, orderly military graveyards—the picture that the volume presents of the war is tame, if not outright idyllic (see, for example, figure 7). For the uninitiated viewer, the photographs are a cryptic representation of war, as they appear more like an ethnographic study of the French countryside than a documentation of any violent conflict. Picturesque views of quaint villages, rural manors, and country lanes dominate the volume. Simple captions, which list only the location of origin and the photographer by military rank and last name, highlight the personal tone. Familiarity with

66. See Nelson, *German Soldier Newspapers.*

67. Among many others, titles include Habbig, *Eine deutsche Division zwei Jahre im Weltkrieg* (1917), *Zwei Jahre an der Westfront* (1917), and *Das 41. Reserve-Korps von der Somme zum Pripjat* (1918). These and other similar volumes have been digitized by the Staatsbibliothek zu Berlin and can be viewed for free online.

68. *Zwischen Arras und Peronne*, "Geleitwort des Herausgebers," n.p.

69. *Zwischen Arras und Peronne*, "Geleitwort des Herausgebers," n.p.

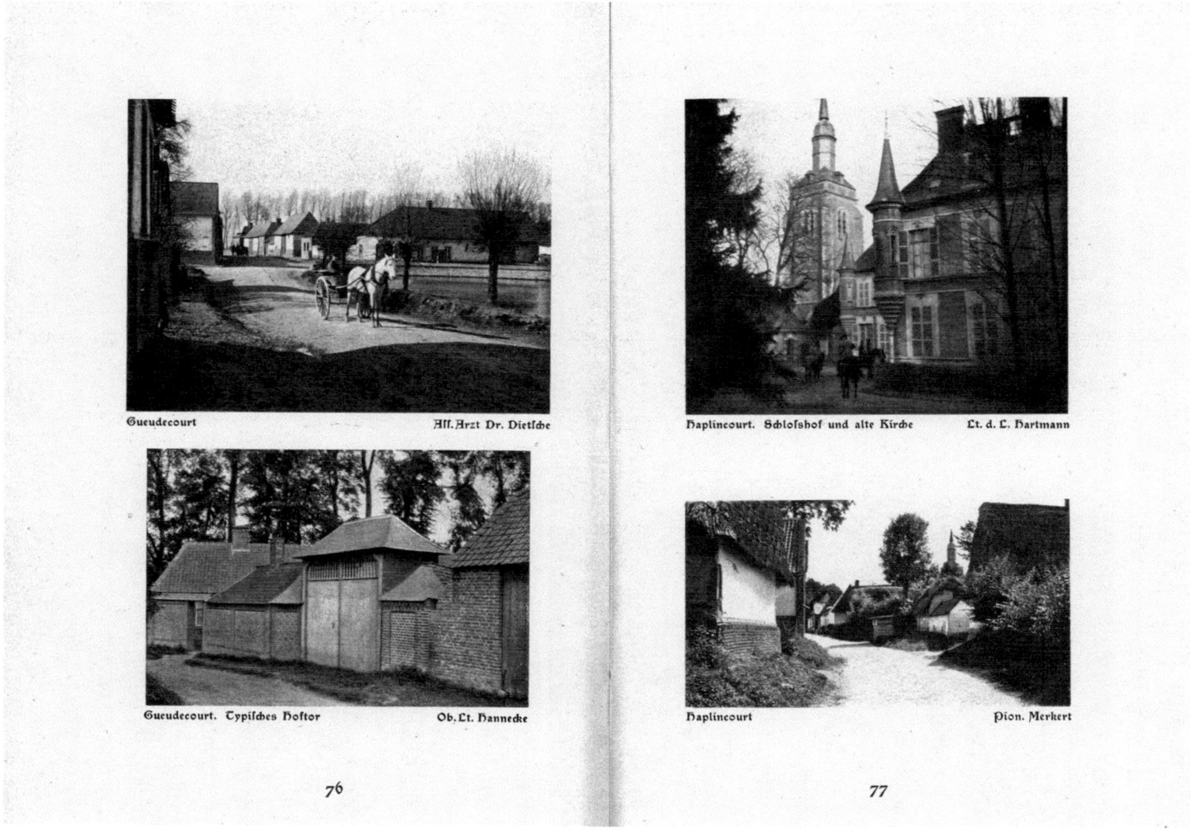

Fig. 7. *Zwischen Arras und Peronne. Herausgegeben von einem deutschen Reservekorps. 311 Lichtbilder zur Erinnerung an die Zeit des Stellungskampfes und der Abwehr der englischen Offensive* (Between Arras and Peronne. Published by a German reserve corps. 311 photographs to remember the time of trench warfare and the defense of the English offensive), Korps-Verlagsbuchhandlung Bapaume 1916, pages 76–77.

these provincial areas and abbreviated names serves as the only point of entry to the volume, and it is impossible to trace the experience of individual soldiers with any sort of significance. In contrast to a single photo album, group publications like these are paradoxically more expansive in scope yet even more constrained in their ability to aid individual memory processes, as is the stated goal, or to offer a meaningful encounter with the past for viewers today. The effort to preserve a group's collective memory unintentionally obscures the individual, thereby predating but reflecting the generalized, panoramic view of the war found in postwar picture books.

Newly established periodicals during the war intended for the public at home also leveraged photographs collected from soldiers but for the different purpose of reporting and guiding public opinion on the war as it developed. The weekly magazine *Der Krieg in Wort und Bild* (The war in words and pictures; 1914–19), published by the Deutsches Verlagshaus Bong und Co. in Berlin with collaboration from top military officials of the German General Staff, promised a general overview of the war alongside detailed descriptions of specific battles. The editors set their objective in the first issue: "We long to see the battles and movements of our armies and fleets in their entirety, as they unfold before the eyes of our generals, and to follow in spirit our German and Austro-Hungarian compatriots and share their warrior life with them."[70] To these ends, the editors requested the submission of photographs from the front, alongside soldier's letters, drawn illustrations, and textual descriptions of battles. Nevertheless, a look through the journal's more than 200 issues shows the predominance of stylized war paintings and drawn illustrations to provide the picture of war. Photographic spreads are largely limited to mundane topics, such as portraits of officers or touristic views of landscapes—a symptom perhaps both of the magazine's carefully curated message aligned with German military leadership and the established popularity of the illustrated history genre that predated the war.[71] Nevertheless, *Der Krieg in Wort und Bild* represents an initial foray into the use of text and image to explain the war in a totalizing way and it anticipates the ideological agenda of the postwar picture books.

Perhaps the most impressive photographic compendium created during the war is the *Großer Bilderatlas des Weltkrieges* (Large picture atlas of the World War), which appeared from 1915 to 1919 in three 400-page volumes divided into individually released installments of 40 pages, each retailing

70. *Der Krieg in Wort und Bild* 1 (1914): 27.

71. See Fox, *The Image of the Soldier in German Culture.*

for two marks, or about one-tenth of the average industrial worker's weekly wages.[72] It is most similar to the 1920s war picture books in its fullness of photographic images—6,000 in total—and its claims of photographic objectivity to serve an ideological position. The editors' goal is to show every war arena through the "true to reality" medium of photography: "The countless pictures created with imagination that we encounter even today are strictly banned."[73] The editors make an exception to their own rule, however, for drawn or painted illustrations if they convey a sense of "the hate-filled attitude of our enemies . . . , testimonies therefore of conscious lies and slander."[74] Such sentiments are evidence of the wartime mentalities that pervade the volume and mark the difference in purpose for looking at the war in photographs from soldier photo albums. Beyond satisfying the public's curiosity of what the war looked like as it happened, it is intended to gratify "an inner compulsion" of wartime to have publications that resonate "with the prevailing mood,"[75] in this case, the wave of enthusiasm that gripped Germany in 1914. The introduction speaks in a highly patriotic manner, calling the war "our newest *Nibelungen* distress" and Germany's "heavy fate," an "onslaught" of enemies comparable to the "stampede" ran against Friedrich the Great's Prussia: "Hail to the people who were good Fritzians in the years 1914/15!" The book's ideological horizon is centered on the hurrah-patriotism of the initial war period, and its editors recognize that the volume offers little more than that: "And even if today, after one and a half years of war, it is premature to speak of the dawn of that golden age in which there will be no more sounds of gunfire, the sentence that the Chancellor uttered soon after the outbreak of fighting is indelibly recorded in the eternal book of human history: 'Germany will not be destroyed!'"[76]

The editors thematize the matter more explicitly, claiming that the time for history writing and interpretation will come later as "we are still standing too close to the terrific events."[77] The focus of such a report in pictures (*Bilderbericht*) now should be to train the eye to perceive and come to know the war: "Internal connections to images are established solely through looking, observing, and enjoying; this process should also be repeated in the

72. In 1913, the closest year for which exact data exists, the average industrial worker in Germany earned around 25 marks weekly (Bry, *Wages in Germany*, 51).

73. Konsbrück, *Großer Bilderatlas des Weltkrieges* 1, v.

74. Konsbrück, *Großer Bilderatlas des Weltkrieges* 1, v.

75. Konsbrück, *Großer Bilderatlas des Weltkrieges* 1, v.

76. Konsbrück, *Großer Bilderatlas des Weltkrieges* 1, v.

77. Konsbrück, *Großer Bilderatlas des Weltkrieges* 1, vi.

present picture atlas, in which the incorruptible camera lens has captured facts in perfect form, which our strongest sense, the eye, can also clearly read and enjoy later."[78] Textual guidance is explicitly limited to identifying captions and section headings, but what "facts" viewers should take away from a consideration of the photographs is defined by the introduction's patriotic tone and interpretation of the war: despite the Kaiser's great efforts to keep peace through diplomacy, the world attacked Germany, which must defend itself; any enthusiasm for war among the population was merely "the recognition that life was in jeopardy."[79] The book's presentation as an "atlas," an impartial compendium of facts about the world, belies its patriotic bent, but *Großer Bilderatlas des Weltkrieges* lives up to its title by presenting a far-reaching yet organized view of the war, capped off with a name and place index—an anomaly among other postwar picture books. The first volume alone covers all fronts equally and even gives special attention in one installment to topics related to the war effort on the home front, including civilian food distribution in Berlin, the increase of women in the work force, and the collection of raw materials to be repurposed for war. In this way the volume not only depicts a general population mobilized for war but stresses to its audience, civilian and soldier alike, the important role they play in the ongoing war effort.

The first volume's overt patriotism remains intact in the third volume, published in the fall of 1919, but the tone has shifted from active encouragement to resigned defeat. The editors maintain the frustrated mentalities of wartime, asserting that the war was a "defensive war," that Germany was dishonorably portrayed as aggressor to the world through its enemies' "poisonous lies," and that German soldiers remained "undefeated."[80] The editors again claim that it is too early for a proper evaluation of the war but suggest that above all the other reasons for the war loss was the English hunger blockade, a violation of human rights that starved civilians and led indirectly to the nation's inner collapse. Also complicit is the foreign press, without whose lies America would have remained neutral. The final section in the entire series is devoted to this critique: a collection of illustrations, including sentimental paintings, satirical comics, and propaganda posters, from Germany's enemies attest to the extravagant lies told about the apparent savagery of the German military and the singular criminality of its kaiser.

78. Konsbrück, *Großer Bilderatlas des Weltkrieges* 1, vi.
79. Konsbrück, *Großer Bilderatlas des Weltkrieges* 1, v.
80. Konsbrück, *Großer Bilderatlas des Weltkrieges* 3, v.

These offenses are deeply upsetting to the editors, who sardonically dub them evidence for the "high domestic culture and fine taste of Germany's enemies."[81] And although the editors limit their critique of the postwar political and societal situation in the volume's introduction—they wish only that Germany becomes strong again, no matter the form of government—their assessment of the war's end in the series' final pages is telling for the place of controversy that the war would later hold in the Weimar Republic. The third volume ends with a short and simple textual chronicle of the Treaty of Versailles, what the editors call the "peace of shame and disgrace, a monstrous document of the hatred and fear of our enemies."[82] Despite its earlier publication date, the third volume of the *Großer Bilderatlas des Weltkrieges* previews already in 1919 the cultural and political flashpoints of the Weimar Republic, such as the "stab-in-the-back" myth, that are central to the war picture books of the late 1920s. The view of the war that unfolds in text and image is therefore already in the year after its end burdened by the sense that war memory will be a contentious issue of politics and cultural life.

Nevertheless, due to its generally positive and widely acceptable patriotic take on the war, *Großer Bilderatlas des Weltkrieges* is not scrutinized by reviewers according to the provocative questions about the war's actual course or its social, economic, or cultural meaning, as is the case for later war picture books. Instead reviewers focus on the richness of its illustration and the unique and objective look into the war that the photographic work affords. The atlas was praised as "exquisite" and "gorgeous" by the *Blätter für Volksbibliotheken und Lesehallen* (Journal for public libraries and reading rooms),[83] and the review in *Die Umschau* (Survey) calls it a "magnificent work," "the most beautiful of its type that we have seen."[84] According to the reviewer in *Das größere Deutschland: Wochenschrift für deutsche Welt- und Kolonialpolitik* (Greater Germany: Weekly for German international and colonial politics), the "execution of the images is impeccable," and the photographs themselves are "moving" and "splendid." Despite initial hesitations about such a book's ability to show in photographs the "extraordinary times in which we are living," the reviewer is convinced of its visual power in capturing the enthusiasm of 1914 and recommends it to every family, for

81. Konsbrück, *Großer Bilderatlas des Weltkrieges* 3, 396.

82. Konsbrück, *Großer Bilderatlas des Weltkrieges* 3, 400.

83. "Neue Eingänge bei der Schriftleitung" 1916, 138, and "Neue Eingänge bei der Schriftleitung" 1917, 221.

84. "Neue Bücher," 236.

children and adults alike.[85] It seems at one point in his review for the Social Democratic newspaper *Die neue Zeit* (The new age) that Edgar Steiger might veer into a criticism of the war itself when he draws attention to the book's portrayal of the war's horrible destruction, but in the end such photographs of destruction just exemplify for him the *Bilderatlas*'s unique and wide scope of visual material that makes it—in his view—"without doubt the best" pictorial work on the war.[86] Steiger assesses the book as an invaluable and objective source for the postwar historian in the same way that the reviewer in the *Kunstgewerbeblatt* (Journal for the decorative arts) calls the book "a fine document of the war" that was produced with the "greatest technical perfection."[87] Questions about the truth-telling capability of photography are therefore ignored just like those about the volume's patriotic tone.

Reviews of *Großer Bilderatlas des Weltkrieges* point toward the early and positive reception of war picture books that will continue into the 1920s. The variety of journals, magazines, and newspapers that reviewed the book is evidence itself of the broad and diverse audience that was interested in seeing the war in photographs. Although the ideological motives of later war picture books would be more obviously focused on swaying opinion on contentious questions of memory and politics, even an early work like *Großer Bilderatlas des Weltkrieges*, published between 1915 and 1919, makes clear the strong impact that picture books could have on the formation of a collective view of the war—in stark contrast to any individual soldier's photo album. Even among diverse reviewers, the shared belief in photography's objectivity meant that the war's meaning, even the very "facts" about it, as the editors of the *Bilderatlas* wrote, could be determined through its visual representation. While soldiers constructed personal meaning through photographs in the pages of their albums, the picture-book genre was a far-reaching public channel already during the war for collective memories to form, for the public to decide what was important to see about the war, determine exactly what that looked like, and contest what it all should mean. Susan Sontag maintains in *On Photography* that ideology defines this naming process:

> Though an event has come to mean, precisely, something worth photographing, it is still ideology (in the broadest sense) that determines what constitutes an event. There can be no evidence, photographic or other-

85. "Literatur," 1127.
86. Steiger, "Aus unserer Bücherei," 474–76.
87. "Großer Bilderatlas des Weltkrieges. Band I [Rezension]," 200.

> wise, of an event until the event itself has been named and characterized. And it is never photographic evidence which can construct—more properly, identify—events; the contribution of photography always follows the naming of the event. What determines the possibility of being affected morally by photographs is the existence of a relevant political consciousness.[88]

It is the very premise of the "photographic fix" that the postwar contestation of memory through photographic representation sought to name and characterize only those events that would support a given political consciousness, established in picture books largely through accompanying textual explanation. With a bit of circular reasoning, picture-book editors constrained the surplus meanings of photographs to existing ideologies, while claiming that the photographs were themselves exact proof of such ideologies. It will become even more obvious over the next chapters that the events that were named by soldiers and fixed into their private photo albums followed a vastly different logic from those appearing in mass-market picture books.

Photo albums ultimately do not provide more historical objectivity than other mediated forms of memory, like memoirs, or other forms of historiography, like illustrated compendiums, although the examples in this chapter have shown how much subjectivity is at stake in the different presentations of the war. Viewing a personal photo album like Sitzmann's opens up alternative perspectives on the war that reference popular narratives at the same time as they complement and refract them. They invite a type of contemplative viewing that stirs both past and present viewer into thinking about the war without falling into the sensationalism or ideological bias that is typical in mass-market picture books from the Weimar era. As shown in the following chapters, those works, although they exhibit at times radically different worldviews, are united in their efforts to transform the collective memory of the war in a way that private photo albums cannot. Personal photo albums remain limited to the visual horizon of their creators and therefore evince aspects of individual experience, whereas postwar picture books gather freely from a general archive of war images (created principally by amateur photographers) to craft interpretations of the war meant to sway broad public opinion. Private photo albums are firmly rooted in a backwards-looking mode that looks to organize and secure individual experience for personal meaning-making, whereas picture books reorganize any number of indi-

88. Sontag, *On Photography*, 18–19.

vidual experiences of the past into general claims meant to influence Germany's course forward. Both categories work together to comprise the war's visual representation as a whole, but how and why they employ images to fix memory is fundamentally different. Private photo albums from the First World War are therefore not just a significant and perhaps underutilized source for understanding the historical war experience, they are also a useful analytical foil to postwar picture books, whose efforts to fix collective memory of the war are motivated as much by remembering the past as they are by ideological visions of the present and future.

CHAPTER TWO

Horror Unmasked

The Pacifist Plea of Ernst Friedrich's *Krieg dem Kriege!*

The picture books that followed the war's end and reached their broadest audience in the late Weimar era must be situated in the trajectory of pictorial practices established by photographic representations from 1914 to 1918. Not only does the public's general fascination with seeing the war that is evident in the midwar projects remain strong a decade or more after the war but the understanding of the actual relationship between photography and "reality" is left undeveloped for a general public, by author and reviewer alike, despite a growing body of theoretical work on photography in the late Weimar era. As the editors of the *Großer Bilderatlas des Krieges* astutely noted, the task of historical interpretation fell to those who came later; but their assertion that photographs served as ironclad documents that capture the war's truth, "facts" for a postwar era, is naïve at best. The vast ideological differences in assessments of the war's meaning, which were crafted after all from the same archive of war photographs, not only hints at the nature of photography's malleability in the service of interpretation but reveals just how contested the basic facts were in postwar Germany.

The history of postwar picture books and the contest of memory, that is, how the war was to be viewed literally and figuratively, begins most markedly with the publication of Ernst Friedrich's controversial picture book *Krieg dem Kriege!* (*War against War!*) in 1924, the 10-year anniversary of the war's beginning. The book is the most radical visual denunciation of Germany's war involvement and a screed against war in general. And as comments from other picture-book authors directed at Friedrich's pacifist message and rhetorical strategies suggest, it was not a small factor driving the publication of patriotic or nationalist picture books that sought to correct the damning message of *Krieg dem Krieg!* It is likely Friedrich whom Ernst Jünger calls out in the introduction of his own book *Das Antlitz des Weltkrieges* (The face of the World War; 1930) when he asserts that a representation of war cannot solely rely on images of the "misery of war,"[1] and it is Friedrich whom Franz Schauwecker implicitly derides in *So war der Krieg!* as someone who can see in war only "senseless slaughter." Schauwecker dismisses pacifists: "Whoever becomes a pacifist like that, only proves that merely staying alive is the most important thing for him. I admit, I find such people trivial."[2] *Krieg dem Kriege!* earned its notoriety through photographs showing the worst horrors of war—dead soldiers, military executions, mutilated faces—that no other war volume presents in as great a number or with such graphic intensity. Friedrich also makes liberal use of captions, which are often playfully sarcastic and biting, to connect the photographs of horror to wide-ranging accusations about war, capitalism, and national honor that present an especially damning representation of Germany in war.

Krieg dem Kriege! evinces Friedrich's deep-rooted pacifism, his progressive ideas about a pedagogy of nonviolence, and his disillusionment with all forms of government that lend his political ideas anarchistic tones. Although the book's publication is an event in itself, it is just one of the many moments of activism in Friedrich's life. His biography reveals an endless idealism for peace that placed him in contact with leading political activists on the left, but the self-imposed purity of that idealism meant his mission of peace remained a singular effort largely removed from the fray of party politicking.

As a young man, Friedrich founded the Breslauer Arbeiter-Jugendbewegung, a youth organization of the Social Democratic Party, but left in disgust when the party voted to support the war effort with bonds. His own experience with the war was limited to short tours he made as an actor with the Potsdam Theater, during which he traveled to the front to perform for the troops. Later he was incarcerated in an observation clinic for the mentally ill after he refused his own draft call as a conscientious objector; he spent further time in a prison in Potsdam for his involvement with an anarchist group's act of sabotage against the military. Freed by revolting soldiers during the November Revolution, Friedrich was an active fighter during the Spartacus uprising, earning himself the nickname of "Barricade Friedrich." He joined the short-lived Free Socialist Youth, founded by Karl Liebknecht and Rosa Luxemburg, and was asked to take on the editorship of *Die junge*

1. Jünger, *Das Antlitz des Weltkrieges*, 10.

2. Schauwecker, *So war der Krieg!*, 7. See also Apel, "Cultural Battlegrounds," 70–76, for an analysis of the patriotic and nationalist photobook *Der Krieg in seiner rauhen Wirklichkeit* (1926) by Hermann Rex as a corrective response to Friedrich's damning portrayal.

Garde (The young guard), the party paper for the Young Communist League of Germany, but he rejected the offer and formed his own group, Die Freie Jugend (The free youth), a group that supported "non-authoritarian socialism" and the cessation of violence through the dismantling of the military and police. Forty young people, members of Die Freie Jugend, lived together with Friedrich and his family in a commune that rejected the demands of organization and other bourgeois ideals as they sought to enact on a microscale the utopia of a collective free from state violence. Friedrich used his training as an actor to achieve moderate popularity—although financial stability eluded him throughout his life—by giving artistic recitations of the works of Leo Tolstoy, Maxim Gorki, and Heinrich Heine, along with impassioned speeches for peace to proletarian parties and youth groups upwards of 30 times a month. He organized the first workers' art exhibition in Berlin to showcase "proletarian" art, including the works of Käthe Kollwitz, Heinrich Zille, Hans Baluschek, and Otto Nagel, and the two newspapers he edited, *Freie Jugend* (Free youth) and *Die Waffen nieder* (Lay down your arms; named after the famous 1889 antiwar novel by Bertha von Suttner), became important mouthpieces for his unique blend of youth engagement, pacifism, and anti-authoritarianism.[3] Over the course of the Weimar Republic, Friedrich went to prison at least 12 times for sedition and slander against the military,[4] cases for which he often received legal defense from his close friend Erich Mühsam, prominent lawyer, writer, and anarchist. The cases left him in financial ruin by 1929.[5]

The exceptional—and controversial—nature of Friedrich's mission to eradicate war and violence is best embodied by the culmination of his life's work, the Anti-Kriegs-Museum (Anti-War Museum) that he opened in 1923 and for which the book *Krieg dem Kriege!* served as a type of companion catalogue. Friedrich purchased a derelict house in Berlin's Parochialstraße and renovated it on his own into the first "international" antiwar museum that combined pacifist displays of war objects and photographs in the front with space in the back for a small stage used for a variety of events. Writing from his Swiss exile in 1935, Friedrich reflected on the impetus for the museum:

> There is no country in the world that is so full of memorials to emperor and war, of battle [*read:* slaughter] paintings, of flags and uniforms and medals—as "peaceful" Germany! . . . Why not a house of peace that

3. Spree, *Ich kenne keine "Feinde,"* 7–33.
4. Krumeich, "Ein einzigartiges Werk," xviii.
5. Spree, *Ich kenne keine "Feinde,"* 65, 67.

> teaches our children from an early age how terrible war is and how beautiful life could be if people would finally stop hating and killing each other.[6]

Reports indicate that the museum did have a special draw for children and, like Friedrich's literary projects *Proletarischer Kindergarten: Ein Märchen- und Lesebuch für Groß und Klein* (Proletarian kindergarten: A fairy tale and reader book for young and old; 1921, cover design by Käthe Kollwitz) and his series *Kinder-Bibliothek* (Children's library), addressed children directly with a warning about war and offered an alternative, peaceful vision of the world.[7] In *Krieg dem Kriege!*, the first series of illustrations is dedicated to showing how pervasive war is in the world of play. It shows military-themed board games, puzzles, paper dolls, toy soldiers, and children's books that are evidence of "how children are educated for war."[8] Erasing such objects and signs of war from a child's perspective of the world has an important pedagogical motive in preventing future wars. Friedrich pleads with parents to not give their children toy soldiers nor sing them soldiers' songs so that, although capitalism may be the cause of all wars, they refuse to make the conduct of war possible. "Bring up your children so that they may later refuse to render military and war service," he urges in the introduction to *Krieg dem Kriege!* "How very many overlook the fact that in one's own home, in the family, war is being spontaneously prepared!"[9] Friedrich's pedagogical mission extended to his own leadership of "pacifist play groups" that modeled alternative modes of play. For example, he led large groups of Berlin children in the Friedrichshain Volkspark in a not unproblematic game of "Indians" that stressed their peaceful disposition and intimate connection to nature.[10]

Alongside the display of toys that were said to be habituating children to war, the Anti-Kriegs-Museum openly exhibited shocking photographs from the war that focused solely on the horrific physical effects of the fighting on the human body. The same photographs that would later cause a sensation when published in *Krieg dem Kriege!* were hung in the museum's front window for all passersby to see. The police objected quickly to the images, deeming them offensive to the nation and obscene for public display, and, when Friedrich refused to take them down, entered the museum by force

6. Quoted in Spree, *Ich kenne keine "Feinde,"* 41.
7. Krumeich, "Ein einzigartiges Werk," xlviii.
8. Friedrich, *Krieg dem Kriege!*, 37.
9. Friedrich, *Krieg dem Kriege!*, 25.
10. Spree, *Ich kenne keine "Feinde,"* 17.

and tore them down.[11] The personal cost of running the provocative museum included numerous legal suits for treason and slander of the military and accompanying time spent in prison. Friedrich wrote later of his efforts: "This cost a lot of sweat and money, and even more nerves. Over time, this required two offices for the director: one in the museum and one in prison!"[12]

The price paid only increased as the Weimar Republic entered its twilight years. In 1932 the museum became a favorite target of Nazi street terror, keeping patrons away and the director in fear for his life. The museum's windows were smashed so frequently that insurance companies refused further coverage, and Friedrich was attacked and beaten by members of the SA, the Nazi paramilitary organization, in November 1932.[13] Friedrich's use of *Stahlhelme* (steel helmets) as flowerpots on the museum's outside façade and the international pacifist symbol of two hands breaking a weapon in half displayed above the front door especially offended the National Socialists. The symbols were evidence—according to the *Völkischer Beobachter*, newspaper of the Nazi Party—of Friedrich's perverse desire "to systematically poison the mind and soul of the honest German worker with Jewish-Marxist ideologies." The broken gun symbol represented for them "a sign of cowardice and the will to deprive our people of even the smallest means of defending themselves against any foreign infiltration and against any theft of their national [*völkischen*] goods."[14] Friedrich was arrested and placed under protective custody on the day of the Reichstag fire, the SA ransacked the museum for a last time, and the building was soon converted into a barracks for SA members. After his release, Friedrich gathered the remaining archives and photographs of the Anti-Kriegs-Museum and fled with his family first to Czechoslovakia, where he published a series of joke books aimed at Nazi Germany, and then to Switzerland, from which he was deported—"for insulting a friend of the state"—for his 1935 memoir *Vom Friedens-Museum zur Hitler Kaserne* (From peace museum to Hitler barracks).[15]

Friedrich arrived in Belgium in 1936, where he used the archives he smuggled from Germany to open a second antiwar museum with support from labor unions and the Belgian Socialist Party. The museum attracted much public interest, but its existence was short-lived; it was quickly destroyed by German troops advancing into Belgium in May 1940. During

11. Spree, *Ich kenne keine "Feinde,"* 43.
12. Spree, *Ich kenne keine "Feinde,"* 43.
13. Spree, *Ich kenne keine "Feinde,"* 77, 79.
14. Quoted in Spree, *Ich kenne keine "Feinde,"* 45.
15. Spree, *Ich kenne keine "Feinde,"* 95.

the Second World War, Friedrich was imprisoned in a Vichy-run internment camp, from which he escaped just weeks before the remaining prisoners were sent to concentration camps in Eastern Europe. He briefly joined the French Resistance and narrowly survived the war. Friedrich continued his peace activism and pedagogical mission after 1945 by using reparation money from the West German government to found an "Isle of Peace" in the Marne River north of Paris where French and German youth groups gathered to better understand each other and foster reconciliation among the nations. After his death in 1967 and at the height of the peace movement of the 1980s, Friedrich's grandson founded a third Anti-Kriegs-Museum at a new address in Berlin-Wedding that remains open today.

The picture book *Krieg dem Kriege!* reflects many of the important strands of Friedrich's singular antiwar mission embodied in his prized Anti-Kriegs-Museum and the other literary and journalistic output of his time: it is grounded in a leftist critique of capitalism, albeit one unconcerned with party politics, pedagogically minded toward stemming any glorification of the nation, war, and militarism, and equally unapologetic in its display of horrors as it is blunt in its message. Extended analysis is not needed to ascertain the ideological standpoint or intent that influences Friedrich's editorial choices. The volume's style reflects Friedrich's tendency toward agitation and away from intellectual reflection. Historian Gerd Krumeich explains that Friedrich

> knew exactly that people are, as he so aptly put it, "forgetting machines" [*Vergeßmaschinen*] and he looked for ways to get his truth across to the public. He did not shy away from repetition and brute force emphasis. He underlined almost everything he wrote and added exclamation marks, sometimes several in a single sentence. He had no sense for the stylistics and aesthetics of words.[16]

The introduction to *Krieg dem Kriege!* is a broadside manifesto against the elite who direct war and the world order of international capitalism that prospers from war. Although he does not mention anything in particular, it is likely that Friedrich was alarmed by contemporary events in the lead-up to the book's 1924 publication. Hyperinflation, the question of reparations, and the Ruhr occupation, among other events that forebode further international conflict, must have weighed heavily on his mind as he tried to warn

16. Krumeich, "Ein einzigartiges Werk," xvii.

the masses about the entanglement of war and economics. Despite these assumptions, however, nuanced analysis lies beyond the scope of Friedrich's production. He presents his arguments in short, declamatory sentences, such as "All wars arise for the possession of wealth" and "Fight against capitalism within yourselves!"[17] Such slogans are akin to those found on posters in their rhetorical simplicity, and Friedrich's dynamic page design, which utilizes varying font sizes, spacing, and typefaces, often mirrors that of a poster. The book's overall aesthetics are inspired to some degree by the Dada and expressionist movements that reached their heights in the lead-up to the publication of *Krieg dem Kriege!*, and Friedrich's black-and-white messaging was part and parcel of Weimar political culture, characterized broadly by energetic sloganeering and agitation. "In Friedrich's work, the argumentative differences are washed away in the emphasis of screaming," according to Krumeich.[18]

Central to the book's appeal to a broad audience is its simultaneous use of four languages: German, French, English, and Dutch. Every piece of text in—to give the book's full title—*Krieg dem Kriege! Guerre à Guerre! War against War! Oorlog aan den Oorlog!*, including the introduction and picture captions, is repeated in each language to reach as wide a readership as possible, at least among the combatant nations of Western Europe. This reflects a further aspect of Friedrich's larger mission: however grounded in the German situation his attacks on militarism and nationalism were, his peace activism was always oriented beyond a domestic audience. He indeed had personal connections to socialist and pacifist movements across Europe and received financial support from the international labor movement. *Krieg dem Kriege!* was funded in part by the Swedish pastor Per Gyberg and his congregation,[19] and an abridged version was published as a pamphlet by the International Federation of Trade Unions in 1929—with a cover motif by Käthe Kollwitz. It circulated 50,000 copies across Europe by 1930. The internationalism of Friedrich's mission extended to a second project: he remodeled a small yacht on Berlin's Müggelsee with the goal of turning it into a mobile antiwar museum that he could pilot from port to port around Europe, spreading a message of peace and reconciliation. The refinished boat never fulfilled its purpose; it was confiscated in 1933 and—with the same twisted symbolism that befell the Anti-Kriegs-Museum—was repurposed as a police

17. Friedrich, *Krieg dem Kriege!*, 23–24.
18. Krumeich, "Ein einzigartiges Werk," xxvi.
19. Spree, *Ich kenne keine "Feinde,"* 47.

boat. The boat had been a target since Friedrich's earlier arrest in 1930, when he was charged with agitation against the state and the planning of high treason for secretly printing the communist newspaper *Die Rote Fahne* (The red flag) aboard the vessel out of sympathy with the enemies of Hitler.[20]

Although the use of multiple languages in *Krieg dem Kriege!* is a significant aspect of the broad reach intended by Friedrich, the photographs carry the pathos of his message. He utilizes primarily two rhetorical techniques to present a damning view of the war through photographic representation: first, he juxtaposes two disparate images on opposite pages, whose critical message is reinforced by sardonic or satirical captions; second, he relies on the inherent horror contained in graphic photographs of the war, including close-up images of dead bodies and mutilated faces. This choice aggressively broke societal taboos as well as official state pictorial policies about representing the war, which used sanitized views of the conflict to reassure and moralize to the home front.[21] These shocking rhetorical strategies, Krumeich writes in the introduction to the book's 2015 facsimile edition, "were undoubtedly the achievement of Ernst Friedrich, who wanted to portray the horrific reality of war in such a way that truly everyone could clearly understand the message."[22]

Friedrich's critical message is most obvious in the juxtapositions he creates in *Krieg dem Kriege!*, both between single images and between image and caption. Like the writing style of his introduction, the message of such arrangements is intended to be immediately impactful and does not strive to offer nuanced arguments. Friedrich's entrenched ethical position vis-à-vis war entails a black-and-white view sustained throughout the volume. The horrors of war not only undermine any attempt at its justification but are inextricably tied to the unjust world order that caused the war and profited from it. An introductory example shows two images of dead soldiers positioned on opposite pages, the first labeled "For the interests of Capital . . ." and the second ". . . and the glory of the Monarchy." The set of images tie the anonymous war dead to a broadside attack against capitalism and the idea of monarchy. The nationality of the pictured dead remains unknown to the viewer, as it is unimportant to Friedrich's criticism of militarism and war of any type. He admits in an afterword to *Krieg dem Kriege!* that the book may unfairly present a picture of German soldiers as criminals, but that is just a coincidence of his being German and having access to associ-

20. Spree, *Ich kenne keine "Feinde,"* 70–73.
21. Ramsbrock, "The 'Face of War' in Weimar Visual Culture," 59–61.
22. Krumeich, "Ein einzigartiges Werk," xxv.

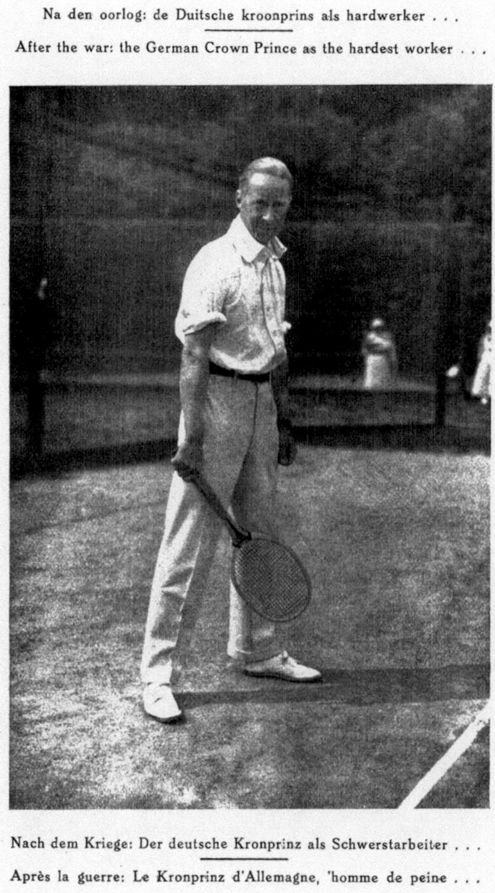

Fig. 8. Ernst Friedrich, *Krieg dem Kriege!* (*War against War!*) (1924; rpt, Berlin: Christoph Links, 2015), page 186.

ated photographs; in truth, all combatant nations are equally culpable for the war's horrors, as militarism and capitalism are crimes of international scope.[23] The images rely on the unquestioned power of seeing dead bodies to create an emotional arousal of disgust that is then layered with a societal critique through the captions. Whether or not the created connection between the anonymous images and Friedrich's message is convincing depends on

23. Friedrich, *Krieg dem Kriege!*, 238.

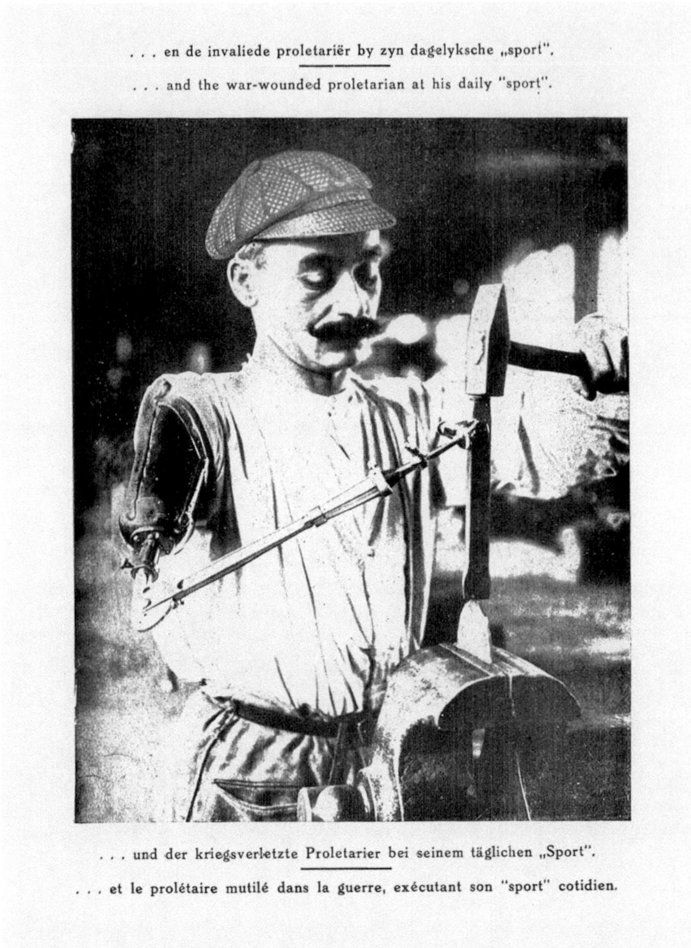

Fig. 9. Ernst Friedrich, *Krieg dem Kriege!* (*War against War!*) (1924; rpt, Berlin: Christoph Links, 2015), page 187.

whether or not the viewer is already predisposed to Friedrich's view of war or can be swayed by such rhetorical maneuvers.

The critique of monarchy is extended to two other pairs of images that juxtapose the life of luxury enjoyed by the nobility after the war and the daily drudgery of the injured veteran. The first pair (fig. 8) combines a snapshot of Crown Prince Wilhelm playing tennis—"After the war: the German Crown Prince as the hardest worker . . ."—with an image of a veteran working in the factory with his prosthetic arm—". . . and the war-wounded proletarian at his daily 'sport'" (fig. 9). The tennis racket of the crown prince, an object purely of leisure, is visually mirrored in the metal prosthetics of the laborer at work, which seem to have been fitted for the specific task he is performing. Both accessories extend at an angle from rolled-up white shirt sleeves yet serve drastically different functions. How the opposing tasks should be assessed is written on the faces of the two men, with the playful smirk of the crown prince juxtaposed against the deep bags under the eyes of the exhausted veteran. The indictment is continued on the following two pages, which show King George of England skippering a yacht across from a "proletarian" putting on a sock with a prosthetic forearm, his contorted pose and focused concentration showing the apparent struggle of such a task.[24] These and other class-based critiques should have resonated with the far left of Weimar politics, but instead elicited mostly ambivalence. *Die Rote Fahne* (The red flag), party organ for the Communist Party of Germany and the same paper that Friedrich would later get arrested for secretly printing on his boat, maintained that *Krieg dem Kriege!* lacked a fundamental understanding of Marxism and a "clear direction." Although she praised "the first great picture book [*Bilderbuch*] of the war" as "an indelible testament," Berta Lask deemed the book useless for the proletariat, as Friedrich's broadly antiwar stance necessarily precluded advocacy of a (civil) war against capitalism (although she may have forgotten or not been aware of Friedrich's active role during the Spartacus uprising). "Unfortunately, since Ernst Friedrich lacks any clear Marxist way of thinking, his laborious work is robbed of the significance it could have had for the proletariat. Instead of calling for action and whipping people into motion, it will only frighten off the weak-nerved."[25] The review not only evinces the type of intellectual and ideological objection to which Friedrich's uncomplicated argumentative style subjected him, it also questions the rhetorical strategy of presenting the war's horrors as an effective way to sway public opinion, a stance problematically assumed by Friedrich.

The strategy of juxtaposing callous monarchs with the soldiers they sent to war is repeated in a related critique of the officer class as being favorably provisioned and safely removed from the dangerous combat to which they freely sent others. Three pairs of images in *Krieg dem Kriege!* echo the idea of the *Etappensumpf* (the morass of the *Etappe*, the area behind the front lines) that resonated with those critical of the war in the immediate postwar

24. Friedrich, *Krieg dem Kriege!*, 188–89.
25. Berta Lask, "Das wahre Gesicht des Krieges."

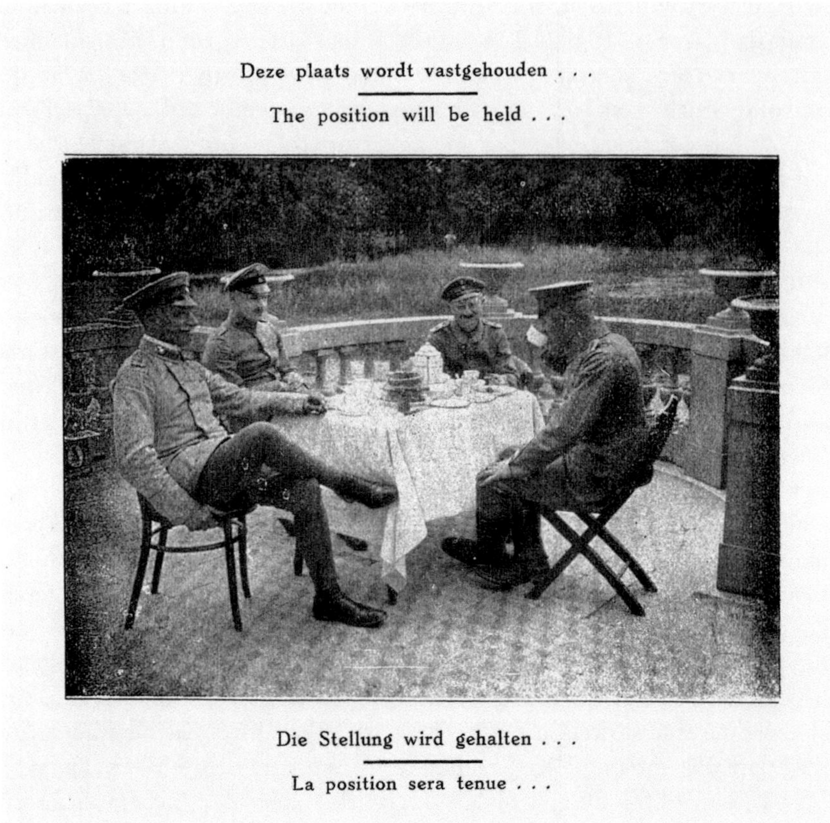

Fig. 10. Ernst Friedrich, *Krieg dem Kriege!* (1924; rpt, Berlin: Christoph Links, 2015), page 78.

years, such as the pro-republican and Social Democratic Party–affiliated veterans' group, the Reichsbanner.[26] The first pair of photographs combines a snapshot of the crown prince "behind the front" with his many greyhounds in tow—a sign of the privilege he enjoyed—with a photograph taken of dead soldiers at the front. The first caption says that the crown prince liked to use the expression "Immer feste druff" (keep hammering at it), while the second caption states "At the front: the Crown Prince is not present."[27] The idea that the officer class was detached from the reality of the front lines is continued

26. See Ziemann, *Contested Commemorations.*
27. Friedrich, *Krieg dem Kriege!*, 60–61.

. . . tot aan den laatsten man toe.

. . . to the last man.

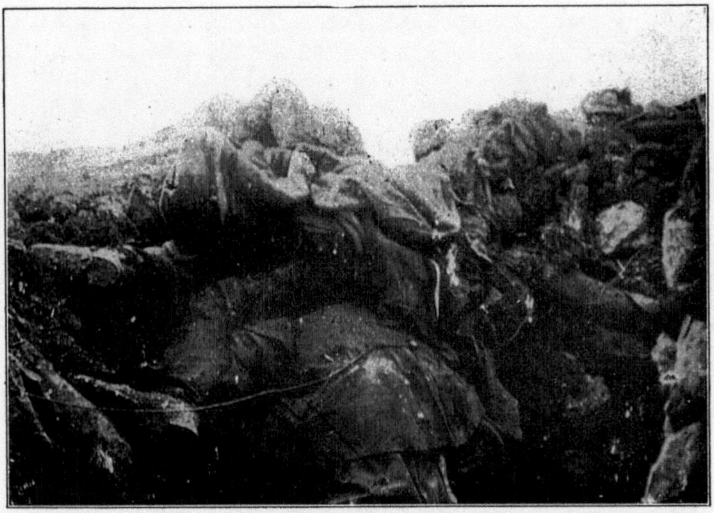

. . . bis zum letzten Mann.

. . . jusqu'au dernier homme.

Fig. 11. Ernst Friedrich, *Krieg dem Kriege!* (1924; rpt, Berlin: Christoph Links, 2015), page 79.

in the second pair of images, which shows a group of officers having tea (fig. 10) juxtaposed with an image of an indiscriminate number of bodies lumped together in what appear to be the trenches (fig. 11). The officers in the first image smile as they sit at a table, decked with a white tablecloth and proper tableware, on the decoratively adorned terrace of what was likely a French villa near the front that the military commandeered to house its headquarters or officers. It is captioned "The position will be held . . . ," while the second image of dead soldiers is labeled ". . . to the last man." Friedrich extends his critique of the officer class to include the special burial treatment they received in the third juxtaposition of images. The respectable military funeral for "a general who passed away softly in slepp [*sic*] behind the front" (fig. 12) is paired with a gruesome photograph of dead soldiers at the front

Hoe een generaal, die in de etappe gestorven is, begraven wordt . . .

How a general who passed away softly in slepp behind the front was buried . . .

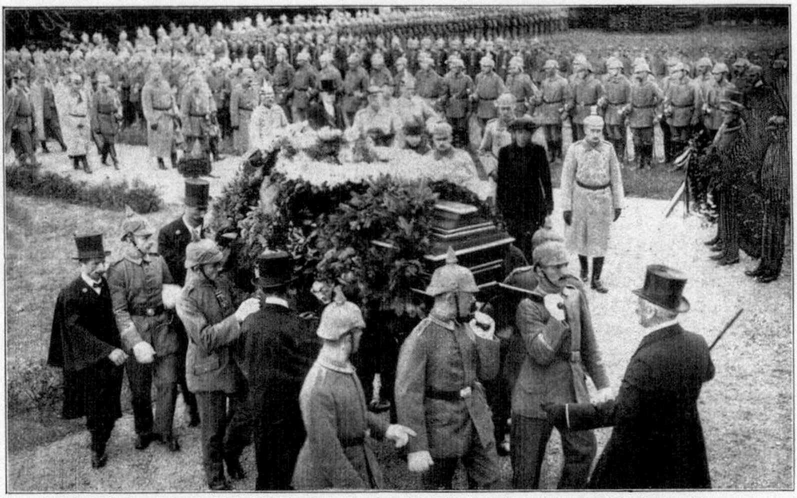

Wie ein in der Etappe sanft entschlafener General beerdigt wurde . . .

De quelle manière on enterre un général, doucement expiré à l'étape . . .

Fig. 12. Ernst Friedrich, *Krieg dem Kriege!* (1924; rpt, Berlin: Christoph Links, 2015), page 120.

being loaded onto a horse-drawn cart that is captioned ". . . and how the proletarians massacred at the front were dispatched"[28] (fig. 13). Unlike the first two sets of photographs, in which the juxtaposed images share no connection beyond the one that Friedrich asserts in his incriminations, the images in the third set share a theme and even obvious visual signs that point more convincingly to the disparity between the higher-ups and the enlisted: rows and rows of orderly arranged soldiers accompany the funeral procession of the general who "died in his sleep," while the fallen of the battlefield die in anonymity surrounded only by rows of trees; ceremonial wreaths and flowers drape the general's coffin, mirroring the casual draping of bodies onto the cart at the front; military men in clean and pressed uniforms and civilians with formal top hats and cloaks carry the general's coffin with care and organized pomp, while a few comrades in stained uniforms load the battlefield dead unceremoniously onto the wagon; and the white-gloved hands of the

28. Friedrich, *Krieg dem Kriege!*, 120–21.

. . . en hoe de aan het front geslachte proletariërs verstuwd werden.

. . . and how the proletarians massacred at the front were dispatched.

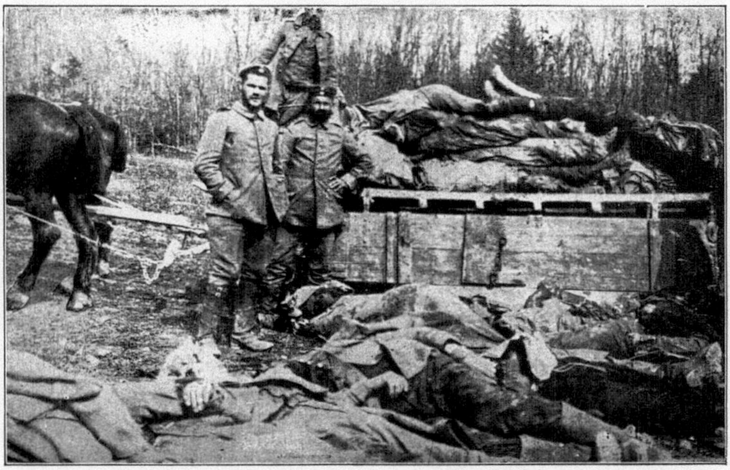

. . . und wie die an der Front abgeschlachteten Proletarier verladen wurden.

. . . et de quelle manière on expédiait les prolétaires, égorgés au front.

Fig. 13. Ernst Friedrich, *Krieg dem Kriege!* (1924; rpt, Berlin: Christoph Links, 2015), page 121.

men who carry the general's casket contrast with the bare hands of the men who take a break while loading the nameless dead onto the cart.

The juxtaposition between the treatment of the general and the anonymous war dead contributes to a main argumentative thread that runs through *Krieg dem Kriege!*: according to Friedrich, the pictures in the book should reveal the many lies told about the war, especially the way mass death during the war came to be falsely inscribed in glorifying terms, such as *Feld der Ehre* (field of honor), *Heldentod* (heroic death), *Tapferkeit* (bravery), or sacrifice for the *Vaterland.* Many of the pictures point to the war's horrors, but a series of before-and-after juxtapositions that contrast the supposed positives of war service—honor, national pride, camaraderie—with the reality of undignified death in the field exposes the naïveté of the belief in heroic death. To do so, Friedrich imagines connections between photographs that show soldiers before and after their deaths. For example, an enthusiastic group of men mobilizing in August 1914 in one image is reduced to a jumble of corpses on the "'Feld der Ehre'" in a second image on the opposite page.[29] Along the same lines, an image showing a group of soldiers enjoying a drink in relative comfort, captioned "German soldier's song: In victory we shall vanquish France . . ." is juxtaposed with a close-up image of a dead soldier, captioned ". . . to die like a hero."[30] Friedrich takes the before-and-after to an extreme in two further pairs of images by proposing literal connections between the pictured "before" soldiers, happy and alive, and the dead "after" soldiers. A photograph of a smiling man in uniform that is labeled "Papa as 'hero' in the enemy's country (Picture for the illustrated Family Journal)" is paired with an image on the opposite page that shows a medic examining corpses in the field with the caption "How Papa was found two days later (Picture not published in the Family Journal)."[31] The same literalism is used with a staged portrait of a soldier (fig. 14)—"The pride of the family: (An 'interesting' arranged photograph)"—and of a dead soldier in the field—"The pride of the family: (The other side of the picture, a few weeks later)"[32] (fig. 15). Although it is largely inconsequential to Friedrich's rhetorical strategy, there is no easy way to ascertain whether the subjects in these image pairs are actually matches. The task is complicated by the fact that credits for photographs do not appear anywhere in the volume, and the corpses in the "after" photographs are mangled beyond recognition. It is likely that Friedrich, who collected his visual material from wherever he could find it and even sent out a request at the end of the book for more images to be sent to him, does not mean for these pictures to have an actual literal connection, and his captions are merely meant to be evocative if not satirical, although the naïve reader may make false assumptions. Like all the photographs in the book, these images are freely decontextualized to work as broad signs of horror. That the "before" pictures show real people who may have been enthusiastic about their war service and who may or may not have died during the war is inconsequential to the meanings that can be layered onto their portraits to serve Friedrich's message. In a clear example of what Flusser calls "channeling,"[33] such images, especially the "before" portraits, were likely appropriated from the private realm of the amateur soldier-photographer to stand in as a visual symbol for Friedrich's hoodwinked soldier. Ironically, in trying to arouse empathy through such personal photographs, Friedrich all but erases the subjectivity of the photographed subjects.

29. Friedrich, *Krieg dem Kriege!*, 50–51.
30. Friedrich, *Krieg dem Kriege!*, 98–99.
31. Friedrich, *Krieg dem Kriege!*, 54–55.
32. Friedrich, *Krieg dem Kriege!*, 94–95.
33. See the introduction.

De trots van de familie: (Een „interessante" kiek).

The pride of the family: (An "interesting" arranged photograph).

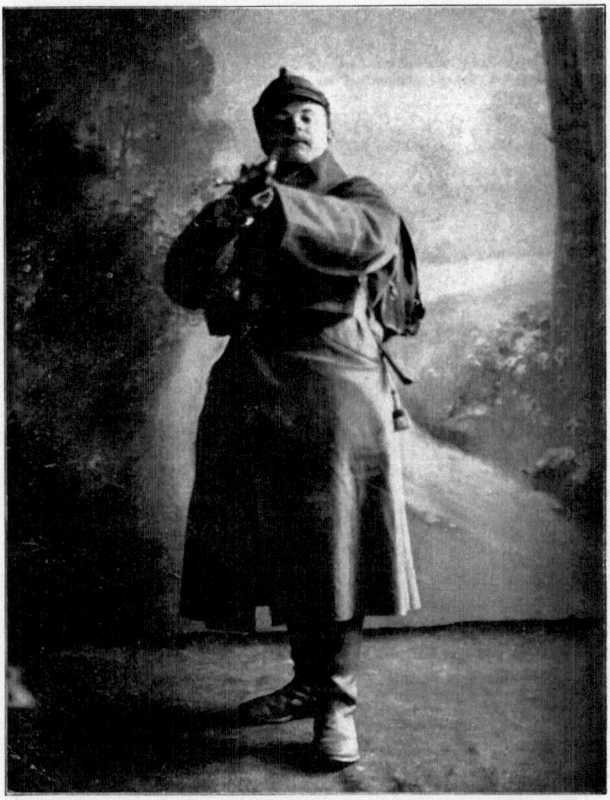

Der Stolz der Familie: (Eine „interessante", gestellte Photographie).

L'orgueil de la famille: (Une photographie "intéressante" posée).

Fig. 14. Ernst Friedrich, *Krieg dem Kriege!* (1924; rpt, Berlin: Christoph Links, 2015), page 94.

The idea of honor through war service and even death comes under further attack in a second type of juxtaposition characteristic of *Krieg dem Kriege!*: that between single image and caption. A picture of a debris- and body-strewn battle landscape is simply captioned "Das 'Feld der Ehre'" and a similar photograph of bodies in a shallow trench is titled "Forgotten . . ."[34] A 10-page series of photographs showing various mass graves in uncom-

34. Friedrich, *Krieg dem Kriege!*, 80–81.

De trots van de familie: (De keerzijde van de kiek, enkele weken later).

The pride of the family: (The other side of the picture, a few weeks later).

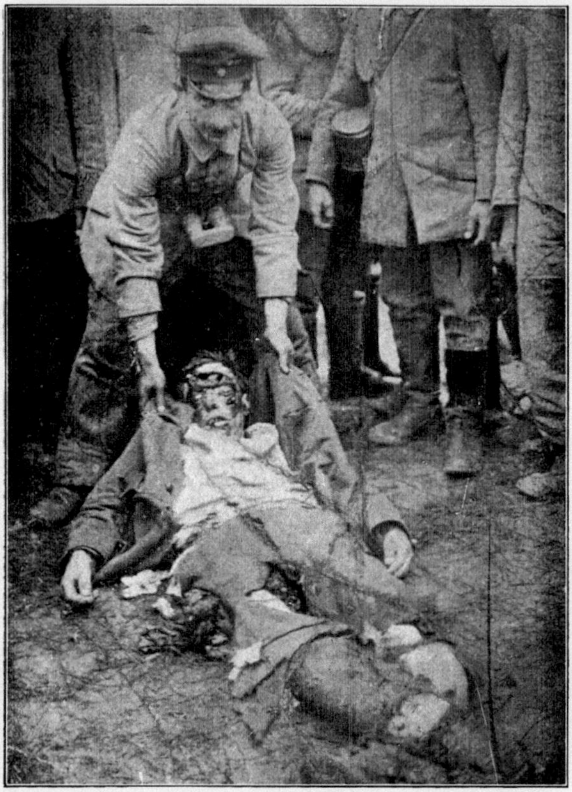

Der Stolz der Familie: (Die Kehrseite des Bildes, einige Wochen später).

L'orgueil de la famille: (Le revers de la médaille quelques semaines plus tard).

Fig. 15. Ernst Friedrich, *Krieg dem Kriege!* (1924; rpt, Berlin: Christoph Links, 2015), page 95.

fortable detail, some taken so close to their subject that individual faces and genitalia can be easily made out, are combined with sarcastic captions, such as "hero's grave" and "For the Fatherland," or simple declarations, such as "But all this 'heroism' is a lie."[35] Through such image and text juxtapositions, Friedrich invokes the patriotic rhetoric surrounding the war effort and throws it against the obvious horrors of war documented in photographs.

35. Friedrich, *Krieg dem Kriege!*, 113, 115–16.

Other positive mentalities of war come under the same scope through the combination of gruesome images and critical captions that use the very words of Germany's military elite to expose their apparent callousness. A photograph of dozens of dead soldiers is captioned with the quotation "War is an element in the order ordained by God" from Graf von Moltke, field marshal during the Unification Wars;[36] a photograph of skulls abandoned on the battlefield is captioned "Kaiser Wilhelm II.:—'I lead you towards glorious times'";[37] and a photograph of three hanged soldiers is captioned "'No war can be conducted by sentimentalities' (Hindenburg)."[38] The damning of such mentalities in *Krieg dem Kriege!* is meant as an exposé of patriotic notions that were assumed by the public without first having been able to consider the full extent of the war's destruction in its visual record. Photographs that were banned from general view during the war are meant now to fix that record. A pair of photographs showing the horrifically deformed and burned bodies of crashed airmen are given captions that highlight how the shocks of war were kept from the public through formal military euphemisms. The first image is captioned, "Newspaper announcement: His Majesty the Kaiser has been graciously pleased to confer the order of 'Pour le mérite' (for meritorious service) on our distinguished air hero . . . on the occasion of his seventh air victory" and, with sarcastic use of quotations marks, the second: "A 'meritorious' achievement."[39]

Although the sarcastic captions of text-and-image juxtapositions most clearly embody Friedrich's rhetorical and political punch, the second main strategy he uses is to let the war's horrors speak for themselves. He writes in the introduction that much ink has been spilled in both glorifying and attacking the war, "but all the treasury of words of all men of all lands suffices not, in the present and in the future, to paint correctly this butchery of human beings." In the place of words, *Krieg dem Kriege!* offers "a picture of War, objectively true and faithful to nature, . . . photographically recorded for all time." Photography's truth-telling capability is unquestioned in Friedrich's rhetoric; for him, the photographic lens is "inexorable" and "incorruptible," and "not one single man of any country whatsoever can arise and bear witneas [*sic*] against these photographs, that they are untrue and that they do not correspond to realities."[40] Beyond simply providing a more accurate or

36. Friedrich, *Krieg dem Kriege!*, 57.
37. Friedrich, *Krieg dem Kriege!*, 77.
38. Friedrich, *Krieg dem Kriege!*, 136.
39. Friedrich, *Krieg dem Kriege!*, 74–75.
40. Friedrich, *Krieg dem Kriege!*, 20–21.

revealing picture of the war than what has been offered by other accounts, the photographs in *Krieg dem Kriege!* are intended to convince the public about the raw horror of war in order to steel them for the broad work of pacifism laid out in Friedrich's introductory appeal: fighting against capitalism, raising children free from the influence of violence, and preparing for a general strike or refusing to report for military service in the event of a future war. Mere witnessing is assumed by Friedrich to lead to future action. In the face of certain conflict to come, "it lies in our hands, in our power, to prevent, to hinder, this most dreadful tragedy."[41] Although he anticipates that the photographs may convince the general public—"Show these pictures to all men who still can think!"[42]—it is clear from the rest of his introduction that his appeal to pacifism is aimed squarely at "my brothers, the proletarians . . . the class-war fighters."[43] What effect the shock photographs in the volume had on its audience was likely predetermined by the reader-viewer's worldview: those open to the rhetoric would have found confirmation of the entanglement of violence and state exploitation in the many photographs of twisted corpses and mutilated faces, while those who were either unideological or displayed the "bourgeois prejudices"[44] that Friedrich so detested would likely have been repelled by the radical breaking of taboos entailed in such a frank representation of violence and death and therefore resist the intended effect. The shock—assumed as the output of photography's apparent realism—was never actually fixed. Furthermore, as Dora Apel notes of *Krieg dem Kriege!*, Friedrich's appeal to the "humanist subjectivity of the individual" encapsulated in "idealist, moral outrage" likely doomed its capacity to create a unified collective that could counter nation-building community identities on the right.[45]

The litany of horrors presented in *Krieg dem Kriege!* with simple, identifying captions include photographs showing the effect of rigor mortis, gas warfare, military executions,[46] starved children, a violated female corpse, and views of physical destruction, including towns, forests, churches, and boats. The last group can be found in many postwar picture books and does not stand out among a larger archive of war photographs in the way the images of human injury in *Krieg dem Kriege!* do. The book reaches the zenith of its

41. Friedrich, *Krieg dem Kriege!*, 27.
42. Friedrich, *Krieg dem Kriege!*, 21.
43. Friedrich, *Krieg dem Kriege!*, 24.
44. Friedrich, *Krieg dem Kriege!*, 24.
45. Apel, "Cultural Battlegrounds," 84.
46. For a consideration of many of the same and similar execution images from the First World War, see Holzer, *Das Lächeln der Henker*.

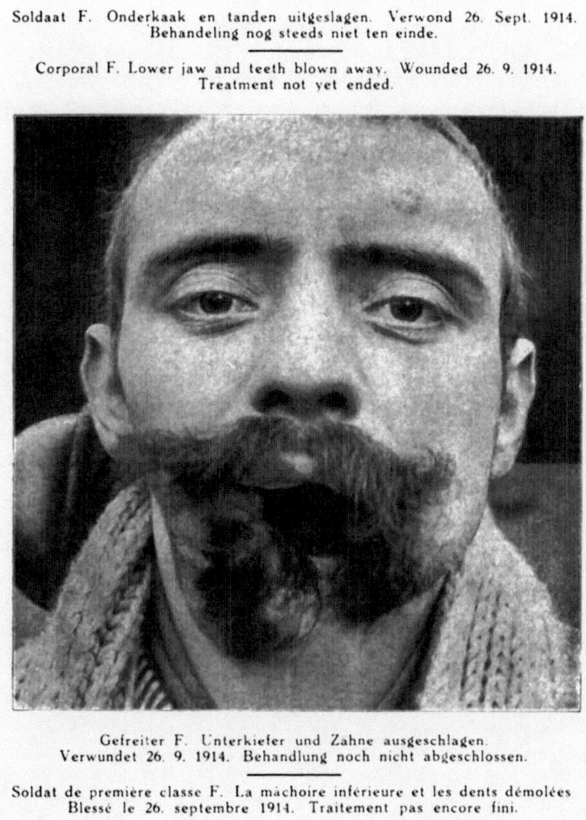

Fig. 16. Ernst Friedrich, *Krieg dem Kriege!* (1924; rpt, Berlin: Christoph Links, 2015), page 208.

intended affective shock factor in a series titled "Das Antlitz des Krieges" (The face of war) that includes only close-up portraits of soldiers whose faces were disfigured during the war, the injuries becoming more gruesome from one page to the next (see figs. 16 and 17). According to his daughter, Friedrich received the photographs from a Professor Sauerbach at the Berlin Charité hospital.[47] The medical photographs, which were taken to document

47. Spree, *Ich kenne keine "Feinde,"* 51.

Er zijn alleen in Duitschland nog altijd 48 000 verpleegden in hospitalen, die afgescheiden van de wereld, ver van hun familie, ver van vrienden en bekenden, voortleven in de hoop dut zy wellicht na jaren een eenigszins menschelyk uiterlyk zullen terugkrygen.

In Germany alone there are still 48 000 hospital inmates who are totally cut off from the world and drag on their existences far from their families and friends and relatives, in the hope that they may perhaps after years again acquire the appearance of human beings.

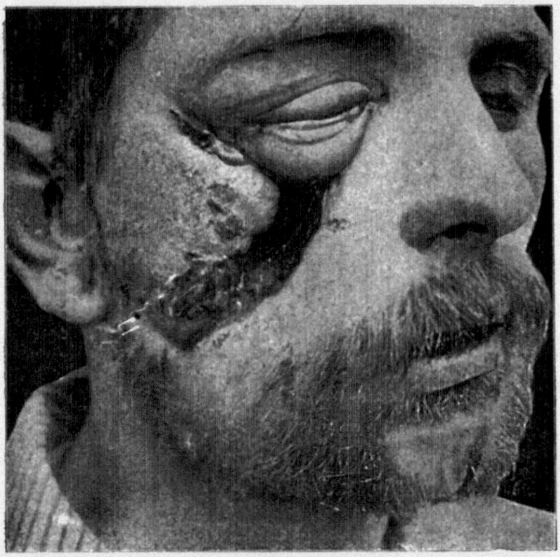

Es gibt allein in Deutschland immer noch 48 000 Lazarettinsassen, die weltabgeschieden, fern von ihrer Familie, fern von Freunden und Bekannten dahinleben in der Hoffnung, daß sie vielleicht nach Jahren ein menschenähnliches Aussehen wieder erhalten.

Rien qu'en Allemagne, il y a toujours 48 000 habitants d'hôpitaux militaires, végétant loin du monde, loin de leurs familles, de leurs amis et connaissances, dans l'espoir vague que peut-être, après de longues années, ils réussissent à regagner des dehors humainement possibles.

Fig. 17. Ernst Friedrich, *Krieg dem Kriege!* (1924; rpt, Berlin: Christoph Links, 2015), page 209.

the various stages and types of facial reconstruction treatment for the educational benefit of clinicians, are captioned with personal information (when available), offering readers names, ages, dates of injury, and details about the course of surgeries and other medical interventions. Unlike the corpses elsewhere in the volume that stand in for the horror of death generally or, as explored earlier, are sometimes connected rhetorically to mismatched living bodies, the subjects in the "Antlitz" series are treated individually and factually. The viewer does not only feel the shock of the pictured wounds but must reckon with the reality of the soldiers who not only have a name but in many cases look directly into the camera—if their eyes are still intact. The direct gaze of mutilated soldiers is a dark complement to the self-assertion and self-affirmation of soldiers found pictured staring into the camera in private photo albums as a metaphorical "survival strategy."[48] This straight-ahead gaze, which in the medical context positioned the head to be useful for clinical analysis, is redirected by Friedrich to elicit empathic responses. Apel asserts that this shift in discourse—or, following Flusser, the photographs' slip between channels—allowed the assumed neutral scientific objectivity of medical photography to elicit a "visceral and moral reaction, a felt sense of horror and victimization that implicated the state and the military for the institution of war and its consequences on the body."[49] In tracing the medical context in which the photographs were taken, Annelie Ramsbrock shows that they "conformed to contemporary notions of medical photography, and were anything but sensational."[50] It is therefore the presentation and their shift in discourse that layered shock onto the photographs.

Friedrich employs the photographs of soldier's faces not only to engulf reader-viewers into a negative affective experience that would alter their subjectivity but also as a powerful visual marker of the war's lingering effects in postwar life. The effect is compounded by the fact that the reality of crippled and injured war veterans was an unmentionable in polite Weimar society; the "Antlitz" series was therefore a breaking of a taboo.[51] The soldier's scars were not only highly personal and visible signs of the war's destruction but also marked the injured soldiers in the "Antlitz" series—unlike any other subject pictured in *Krieg dem Kriege!*—as victims caught in the limbo of life and death long after the war ended: "In Germany alone there are still 48,000 hospital inmates who are totally cut off from the world and drag on their existences far from their families and friends and relatives, in the hope that they may perhaps after years again acquire the appearance of human beings."[52] That Friedrich withholds the "after" pictures that were taken of patients who underwent facial reconstruction surgery further prob-

48. Dewitz, *So wird bei uns der Krieg geführt*, 263.

49. Apel, "Cultural Battlegrounds," 84.

50. Ramsbrock, "The 'Face of War' in Weimar Visual Culture," 65.

51. Krumeich, "Ein einzigartiges Werk," xii. See also Ramsbrock, "The 'Face of War' in Weimar Visual Culture."

52. Friedrich, *Krieg dem Kriege!*, 209.

lematizes his appropriation of photographs.[53] Nevertheless, the photographs are useful for Friedrich to throw into question patriotic ideas of heroism and the "Field of Honor" through the indignity felt by soldiers upon literally losing their face. Although Friedrich made the medical frame of reference in which the photographs were taken invisible, the approach allowed him to articulate the visible horror in an "ethics of seeing."[54] By considering the perpetually injured, who "drag on their existences," Friedrich opens up the war for contemporary scrutiny in a way that is foreclosed by other memorials, such as the war cemeteries that are pictured following the "Antlitz" series. For Friedrich, the question of how society will treat the most grievously injured in the present reflects as much an empathetic concern for victims as it does an impulse to continually agitate the public into reflecting on the unjust nature of war in general.

Considering the controversial nature of *Krieg dem Kriege!*, especially its defamation of German military honor and the images of violence it contained, Friedrich's volume generated expected scandal upon publication. Like his antiwar museum, the book drew harsh negative responses from patriotic and nationalistic groups. Most telling is the reaction from the Bavarian Veterans' League, which complained to the public prosecutor at the regional court in Munich that Friedrich's book "represents the most base and vile slander of the old army and, through intentionally denigrating juxtapositions, pursues the intention to belittle the old army and hold individual personalities within it in contempt."[55] They entreated the courts to take action to not only ban the book but also destroy extant copies. Furthermore, the book was evidence for them of a cultural divide: "The fact that this book has already reached its third edition in Berlin fits with the image that people in Germany have of the swampy atmosphere of the Reich's capital."[56] The court ignored their requests, and a second volume was even published in 1926, although it aroused little interest and is difficult to find today; Krumeich suggests the first volume was "so comprehensively and paradigmatically illuminated that further explanations were essentially superfluous."[57] Economic turnaround likely played a role, too; the "short period of insight"

53. Ramsbrock, "The 'Face of War' in Weimar Visual Culture," 66.

54. Ramsbrock, "The 'Face of War' in Weimar Visual Culture," 73. See also Evans, "Photography as an Ethics of Seeing," from the same volume.

55. Quoted in Spree, *Ich kenne keine "Feinde,"* 31.

56. Quoted in Spree, *Ich kenne keine "Feinde,"* 31.

57. Krumeich, "Ein einzigartiges Werk," xxxiii.

in which the public felt the economic misery of defeat and was willing to think critically about the war's legacy had passed after the first volume's publication in 1924.[58]

Although *Krieg dem Kriege!* elicited such strong responses, there is only limited written debate surrounding the picture book in contemporaneous newspapers and magazines.[59] It was reviewed positively in large left/liberal outlets like *Vorwärts* and the *Berliner Tagesblatt*,[60] and found a broader resonance with reviews in regional newspapers, such as the *Sächsische Volksblatt* and the *Sonntags-Zeitung* in Heilbronn.[61] But this handful of positive reviews marks the limit of the book's literary sensation. Krumeich explains that the great public stir the book aroused was not reflected in written debate.[62] Bertolt Brecht recommended it to readers in 1926,[63] and Kurt Tucholsky (alias Ignaz Wrobel) penned a review in *Die Weltbühne.* Unlike the ambivalent reviewer in the *Rote Fahne* who questions Friedrich's purpose in showing shocking images to the masses, Tucholsky affirms Friedrich's goals and rhetorical strategies with glowing praise and a plea for his readers to buy many copies of the book.[64] The audience for *Krieg dem Kriege!* should not be confirmed pacifists but those who need convincing most, their enemies—"none of them knows this horror."[65] While Friedrich makes a direct appeal to women as the bearers of a future generation disposed to pacifism, Tucholsky takes the matter to the next level and wishes that the effect of the book's difficult images will entail a physically felt shock: "And the book should also be shown to women, especially women. It is possible that one of them will faint. But it is better that she faints at the sight of a book than after receiving a telegram from the front."[66] In addition to the supposed persuasiveness of savagery, the photographs offer truthfulness and promise to reveal "the true face of the war" in a way that not even the most talented writer could.

According to Tucholsky, it is especially important that *Krieg dem Kriege!*

58. See Ziemann, *Contested Commemorations*, 56.
59. Krumeich, "Ein einzigartiges Werk," xxxiii.
60. See Apel, "Cultural Battlegrounds," n. 39.
61. Krumeich, "Ein einzigartiges Werk," xxxiii–xxxiv.
62. Krumeich, "Ein einzigartiges Werk," xxxiii.
63. Kuhn, "Early Brechtian Perspectives on Photography," 271.
64. Friedrich was surely one inspiration for Tucholsky's own picture book, *Deutschland, Deutschland über alles* (1929, with John Heartfield), which combined images and satirical text to critique late Weimar society.
65. Tucholsky, "Waffe gegen den Krieg," 312.
66. Tucholsky, "Waffe gegen den Krieg," 312.

reaches as broad a readership as possible in light of prowar publications being produced by and with support from the Reichsarchiv (explored in the next chapters):

> And because such an anti-war publication will never be found in the Reichsarchiv, which is completely in the hands of war propagandists—the worst kind of war-mongering is openly being carried out there—a counter-weapon should be employed that will paralyze the efforts of that superfluous institute, paid for by the public. Here is the weapon. Anyone who sees this and does not shudder is not a human being, he is a patriot.[67]

More so than any other aspect of his glowing review, this final argument by Tucholsky is a critical point in understanding the reception and legacy of Friedrich's picture book. In addition to a scandal instigated by shocking images—think of the police forcibly removing them from the Anti-Kriegs-Museum's windows—the book was a challenge to any and all positive war memories that were peddled by a range of personally and ideologically motivated former military men and their sympathizers. Tucholsky recognized the book's potential to offend this population: "The bad conscience with which officers and nationalists of all kinds must prevent the true face of the war from becoming known shows what they have to fear from such publications."[68]

While the debate about the book and its photographs may have been limited in the realm of journalism, *Krieg dem Kriege!* engendered a battle to secure the war's legacy through visual representation and it made the first strong case for photography as a powerful medium of such contests. As mentioned earlier, authors such as Ernst Jünger, Franz Schauwecker, and Hermann Rex responded in kind, asserting the same truth-telling power of photography albeit tied to different "truths." They not only implicitly and explicitly attacked Friedrich and his book, they also sought to fix the dystopic vision of the war embodied in the photographs of violence and death that permeate *Krieg dem Kriege!* Central to that effort was a reinscription of the meaning of death during the war that focused on a range of positive notions, such as sacrifice for the nation or the metaphysical transformation of the frontline soldier. Jünger, for one, chose the same title for his military-affirming book *Das Antlitz des Weltkrieges* as Friedrich gave the portrait

67. Tucholsky, "Waffe gegen den Krieg," 312.
68. Tucholsky, "Waffe gegen den Krieg," 312.

series of mutilated soldiers in *Krieg dem Kriege!* In other picture books, death was simply erased from sight (again) or was partitioned off into neat rows of well-kept war cemeteries that preserved German honor while addressing the unavoidable. The final section of *Krieg dem Kriege!*, showing vandalized war cemeteries and the unequal attention paid in memorializing officers and enlisted men, highlights the centrality of funerary commemoration in disputes surrounding the war's legacy.

Krieg dem Kriege! was not the only pacifist picture book published in Weimar Germany; other notable examples include *Kamerad im Westen: Ein Bericht in 221 Bildern* (Comrade on the Western Front: A report in 221 pictures; 1930) and *Wehrlos hinter der Front: Leiden der Völker im Krieg* (Defenseless behind the front: Suffering of people in war; 1931), both published significantly later by the Frankfurter Societäts-Verlag. But their effect pales in comparison to Ernst Friedrich's radical book, both in terms of the scandal that *Krieg dem Kriege!* aroused and the reverberations it caused in the microcosm of picture books in the Weimar Republic. In the latter sense, *Krieg dem Kriege!* is the crux for understanding how the genre came to be a major factor in the discourse surrounding war memory and its meaning in the present. Other factors, such as a renewed interest in the war among the reading public during the very late 1920s and early 1930s and the general fascination with photography during the Weimar-era "photo-boom," help prepare the fruitful ground on which many later war picture books were planted, but the rhetorical practices and the terms of debate were set almost half a decade earlier by Friedrich. The picture books that followed his were forced to respond, either explicitly or implicitly, to the damning account of the war based in the destruction, deformity, and death so passionately exposed and excoriated in *Krieg dem Kriege!*

CHAPTER THREE

National Rejuvenation and Expunging Defeat

Walter Bloem's *Deutschland: Ein Buch der Größe und der Hoffnung in Bildern, 1914–1924*

One of the first patriotic picture books not only to connect Germany's war experience to the postwar situation but also to "fix" the gruesome vision of war presented in Ernst Friedrich's *Krieg dem Kriege!* was *Deutschland: Ein Buch der Größe und der Hoffnung in Bildern, 1914–1924* (Germany: A book of greatness and hope in pictures; hereafter *Deutschland*). The volume was published in 1924, the same year as Friedrich's book, by Otto Stollberg & Co. (Berlin) in cooperation with the Reichsarchiv. The volume's editor remains unnamed, but the book is often credited to Walter Bloem (1868–1951), who wrote its introduction. It is plausible Bloem also served as the volume's editor, as he had experience and interest in the picture-book genre. He produced two volumes of photographs that celebrated Germany's scenic wonders, both with clear nationalist overtones: *An heimischen Ufern* (On native shores; 1912) and *Unvergängliches Deutschland* (Immortal Germany; 1933). Although the editorial decisions in *Deutschland* concerning the photographs (selection, ordering, writing of captions, and the like) cannot be definitively ascribed to Bloem, his introduction to the volume is key in understanding the overall framework through which the photographs are meant to be viewed.

For Bloem, Germany's greatness was not reduced by its material defeat, and pride for the nation flourishes in a hopeful future characterized by technological and economic might. The volume's hurrah-patriotism expunges all those signs of suffering during the war that saturate Friedrich's *Krieg dem Kriege!* and instead pictures the war as a grand drama in which the German spirit prevailed across and against the entire globe. Coupled with this patriotic vision of war is a misleading account of comfort and wealth in the years between 1918 and 1924 that elides another negative consequence of the war: the significant economic misery in the first half decade after the war and before the introduction of the Dawes Plan to stabilize Germany's economy. When one considers Bloem's own war experience as a member of the privileged officer class, the volume also takes on tones of self-rationalization for the actions of Germany's military during the war. In sum, the titular assertion of *Größe* (greatness) from 1914 to 1924—achieved by erasing all negative implications of war and falsely exaggerating a handful of positive aspects—is meant to preserve the honor of the military and the nation. In light of significant challenges to the war's positive legacy in the immediate postwar years, whether from specific publications like *Krieg dem Kriege!* or more general conditions of economic and societal instability, the volume strives to foster self-preserving, affirmative memories through an attempt to reinvigorate the Volk with feelings of pride that were so characteristic of the fever pitch of August 1914. Bloem's introduction, titled "Zehn Jahre Geschichte!" (Ten years of history!), uses the 1924 publication date to explicitly frame the volume's tenth-year anniversary commemoration in the optimistic spirit of mobilization rather than the pessimistic outlook of defeat.

Attention to Bloem's biography illuminates aspects of how his war experience and feelings of nationalism shaped the interpretation evinced in his introduction and then carried throughout *Deutschland.* Walter Bloem was a high-ranking military officer with a long record of service before and during the First World War. A lifelong writer, he became one of the most widely read and financially successful war novelists and dramatists during and after the war. In 1916 Bloem was promoted to the General Staff and tasked with founding and then expanding the influential military press office,[1] which controlled the shape of opinion on the war through the popular soldier-centered "trench papers."[2] The kaiser, who had read many of his prewar militaristic and nationalist works, even invited Bloem to personally accompany him on inspection tours during the summer of 1916.[3] Because his patriotic literary works found a broad audience in the war enthusiasm of 1914, Bloem greeted the Weimar Republic as a millionaire.[4] In the postwar years, he positioned himself beyond the sphere of party politics but fashioned himself as an "unconditional nationalist" and understood himself foremost as a *Frontkämpfer* (frontline warrior) who carried on the war's legacy.[5] Bloem interpreted the publication of Remarque's *Im Westen nichts*

1. Stauffer, *Walter Bloem*, 49.
2. Lipp, *Meinungslenkung im Krieg*, 48.
3. Stauffer, *Walter Bloem*, 49.
4. Stauffer, *Walter Bloem*, 53.
5. Stauffer, *Walter Bloem*, 66, 53.

Neues (1929) as a disgrace toward the legacy of the frontline soldiers and took the work seriously as a personal insult; he wrote the novel *Frontsoldaten* (Frontline soldiers; 1930) as an explicit rebuke of Remarque.[6] In a polemical 1932 open letter responding to Heinrich Mann's explanation of the World Committee Against War and Fascism, Bloem connected a vehement defense of the literary works of "pro-war" authors with an affirmation of the broad nationalist movement of the late Weimar period:

> All of us [authors] are far from trying, I repeat, to "sugarcoat" the war. We know it too well for what it is. But whoever dares to mock and insult our most sacred and powerful memories or the proudest and most unshakable faith of the "militarist" and the "nationalist," they will have to deal with us.
>
> Today we are believers in heroism, champions of the idea of the fatherland, no longer a lost bunch in the midst of an "intellectuality" that drags our ideals into the mud. The Volk is waking up and gathers around us.[7]

Although initially espousing philosemitic and anti-Nazi views during the early and middle Weimar years, such as in his book *Brüderlichkeit* (Brotherhood; 1922), Bloem drifted closer and closer to the National Socialist camp, spurred in part by the left's attack on the war's legacy.[8] By 1933, he was greeting the Third Reich with "unbridled joy and boundless gratitude," as he wrote.[9] He joined 87 other authors in signing the 1933 "Gelöbnis treuester Gefolgschaft" (Proclamation of utmost loyalty) to Hitler and on several occasions received personal preferential treatment from Joseph Goebbels, although his literary and political influence never reached the same zenith as during the era before, during, and immediately after the First World War.[10]

Following the reasoning of Bloem's contemporary Carl von Ossietzky, a pacifist and Nobel Laureate in 1935 for his work exposing Germany illegal's rearmament and extrajudicial *Femegerichte* murders by the so-called Black Reichswehr during the Weimar Republic, the biographer

6. Stauffer, *Walter Bloem*, 68.
7. Quoted in Stauffer, *Walter Bloem*, 72.
8. Stauffer, *Walter Bloem*, 58, 68. Other reasons for Bloem's shift to the radical right include his family's dire financial situation after the 1929 stock market crash, exclusion among his leftist journalism colleagues in Berlin, and a gradual abandonment of his earlier philosemitism after it found little resonance with his reading public (Stauffer, *Walter Bloem*, 65–66).
9. Quoted in Stauffer, *Walter Bloem*, 75.
10. Stauffer, *Walter Bloem*, 80–85.

Peter Stauffer labels Bloem a political opportunist.[11] The sea change that occurred between an apolitical work by Bloem like *Der Weltbrand* (The world on fire; 1922), which called for a postwar national reconciliation and explicitly included the proletariat and Jews, and the Nazi apologetics of *Unvergängliches Deutschland* (Immortal Germany; 1933), is just one piece of evidence for the obvious radicalization of Bloem that turned him from a "well-intentioned defender of humanity" to an "ill-intentioned defender of inhumanity," as Stauffer criticizes.[12]

Bloem's support for National Socialism, whether as a political opportunist or a dyed-in-the-wool nationalist, is outside the scope of his 1924 introduction to *Deutschland*, but it does serve to highlight the volume's relatively subtle political nature. At the time of its publication, Bloem would have been concerned primarily with defending the war's legacy, a personal crusade he shared with the volume's central supporter, the Reichsarchiv. According to his diary, in the immediate postwar years Bloem claims to have been far more upset by the lack of thanks shown to the returning troops and the disdain directed at the officer class to which he belonged than any change in Germany's political reality; the physical injuries he sustained during the war were a burden far more easily managed than postwar criticisms of the military.[13] Accordingly, in his introduction to *Deutschland*, there is no overt engagement in any of the party politicking that runs through other nationalist picture books of *Deutschland*'s ilk and defines his later work during the Third Reich.

Nevertheless, Bloem's war service, his firsthand witnessing of the November Revolution, and his front-row view in Berlin of major political moments of the Weimar Republic make him a significant literary witness to the mentalities of nationalist circles before, during, and after the war.[14] He writes with the authority of such a witness in *Deutschland*'s introduction when describing the turbulent decade from the war's beginning in 1914 to the present-day of 1924. Although he perceives the First World War as a sort of penance for Germany's "frenzy of ego" in the late 1800s[15]—a complicated issue for an author like him who actively contributed to it—he uses patriotic rhetoric to champion pride after the humiliating and debilitating war defeat and even refers to the years 1914–24 as Germany's "proudest decade of

11. Stauffer, *Walter Bloem*, 78–79.
12. Stauffer, *Walter Bloem*, 83.
13. Stauffer, *Walter Bloem*, 53–54.
14. Stauffer, *Walter Bloem*, 5.
15. Bloem, "Zehn Jahre Geschichte," 6.

life." It was "Germany against the world!" but—in a phrase repeated multiple times throughout the introduction—"we did not fall apart."[16] The military may have been beaten back by the Entente's overbalanced material power, yet the Volk is not only entitled to but also obliged to maintain the highest feelings of pride.[17]

Bloem's patriotic vision of the war is not limited to commemoration of the past but also serves nationalist goals in the present. His introduction states explicitly the nation-building aim of the book: "It is addressed to everyone, but also to every member of the Volk. Out of all the events to which this work is dedicated, no lesson speaks to us more clearly and more shockingly than this: the people of our day and age are not allowed to lead an isolated life."[18] Bloem's historical reduction of the war to the phrase "Germany against the world!" legitimizes his call for a new *Gemeinschaft* (fellowship) to reawaken the nation. He discounts a humanitarian vision of mankind and the international cooperation of Europe and instead envisions a different *Gemeinschaft* that will justify the war's legacy: "the Volk, whose language we speak, whose nature shaped and directed ours, whose prosperity is the root of our assured happiness, whose misery and downfall would mean the destruction of our mental and physical existence."[19] Just as Ernst Friedrich likely saw the entanglement of military power and economics in the early 1920s as an omen for possible future war, Bloem also understood Germany's postwar situation as an existential threat, although his response is much different. While Friedrich worked to stem future conflict through international cooperation and reconciliation, Bloem beat the drums of nationalism by reinvigorating patriotism and advancing military-affirmative views of the war. In this light, *Deutschland* is largely focused on presenting the strength of the German spirit in war and the economic and technological support it would need for a future war. Of course, in 1924 Bloem could not have foreseen the Second World War, but the sense of crisis that pervaded the early Weimar era, to say nothing of postwar revanchist movements, likely influenced Bloem's sense of urgency in "reawakening" the Volk from its postwar slumber.

The exact effects of defeat are largely elided in Bloem's introduction. Disarmament, the Ruhr occupation, and the fact that other countries

16. Bloem, "Zehn Jahre Geschichte," 5.
17. Bloem, "Zehn Jahre Geschichte," 6.
18. Bloem, "Zehn Jahre Geschichte," 7.
19. Bloem, "Zehn Jahre Geschichte," 7.

oppress Germany, which is only accepted with "a begrudging yes," are some of the few specific targets of his bitterness. Despite Germany's "unprecedentedly unfortunate, tragic, blood- and tear-soaked national history," it retains its noble character.[20] The book's aim is to remind readers of those titular qualities—*Größe* (greatness) and *Hoffnung* (hope)—that draw the Volk together in pride for the nation. Bloem claims that after a brief postwar period of "paralyzing fatigue" and an existence spent "half in dreams," the Germans are beginning to reawaken to their fate:

> A clear sign of such psychological processing and the mastering of our fate is the elementary need of Germans to relive the tremendous experience of this phenomenal decade, captured in words and pictures, to reflect and remember one more time with seriousness and loyalty, with faith and affirmation.[21]

Bloem explicitly connects the newfound feeling of national pride and meaning in the postwar era with a conscious effort to remember and make sense of the war experience, an enterprise to which the present picture book is just one contributor, as he notes. Remembering the two million German war dead—a portion of the book's profits were donated to the newly founded German War Graves Commission—is part and parcel of accepting the *Schicksal* (fate) handed to Germany after the war, a fate that entails defeat but preserves honor. Accepting the facts of the postwar situation while reaffirming German greatness ensures that "Germany lives." Bloem asserts that "we" want to regain the lost belief in greatness, a belief that can be redeemed and bolstered by simply looking back on the honorable war effort. Bloem ascribes a unique power to text and image to foster an affective experience with the past—literally, to live through the past again—in order to change present subjectivities. Recalling the war experience will serve as "guide and comrade . . . through the dark shadowy paths that [Germany] is inevitably destined to walk."[22] The exact characteristics of these "shadowy paths" are left to the imagination of the reader, who would supply the necessary connotation with firsthand knowledge about the physical and existential suffering after 1918.

Aspects representing Germany's titular "greatness" and "hope" are more clearly presented in the book's photographs. Around 80 pages of images are

20. Bloem, "Zehn Jahre Geschichte," 6.
21. Bloem, "Zehn Jahre Geschichte," 6–7.
22. Bloem, "Zehn Jahre Geschichte," 7.

divided into three sections: Germany before, during, and after the war. A strict uniformity in the presentation of photographs persists throughout. Photographs are reproduced either two to a page at a size of 3.75 × 6 in. or occupy the entire page, more often than not turned on their side, at a size of 6 × 8.5 in. A thin black line around each photograph provides a simple frame. These details are significant for the book's reverential style, especially in comparison to other picture books that are more playful with the genre in cropping photographs at nonrectangular angles or overlaying images in collage. The volume's captions employ no irony, sarcasm, or hyperbole; instead, they maintain a simple style that briefly identifies what is pictured. There are only a few instances that deviate from this neutral style, most of which are to praise the military. The "message" of the photographs in the book must therefore be read through attention to what is pictured (and what is not) and to the threads running between images, a result of the selection and ordering of photographs.

The middle section showing Germany during the war covers 60 pages, over three-fourths of the volume's length. It is also the most diverse section in terms of subject matter, as the predominant focus in both the first and last sections is on industrial might. The first section showing prewar Germany provides glimpses of its technological innovation: the Hamburg America Line passenger ship *Imperator* (the largest of its kind at the time) towers over other ships in a smoky harbor; an imposing Zeppelin enters its hangar flanked by a crowd of tiny observers; and two aerial photographs (fig. 18) show the sprawling factory complexes of the Borsigwerke in Berlin-Tegel and the Königs- und Laurahütte in Upper Silesia.[23] These photographs celebrate German industry through the towering presence of its physical products and facilities.

In an image in the prewar section, the vaulted ceilings of the Krupp steel factory in Essen appear as a modern-day cathedral in which the workers are busy casting steel. The ovens around the factory floor's periphery and the chunks of molten metal carried by the workers are the only source of light in the dark scene, and a crowd of workers assembles around a plume of ghostly smoke rising to the rafters in the middle of the expansive hall. The sum of these visual details creates a sense of visual splendor and mystery, as if the viewer is invited to glimpse some sort of modern-day, arcane ritual of man's mastery over machinery. On closer inspection, however, the image reveals itself as a painting, not a photograph. Its realistic style and lack of credit to its

23. *Deutschland*, 15, 18, and 24.

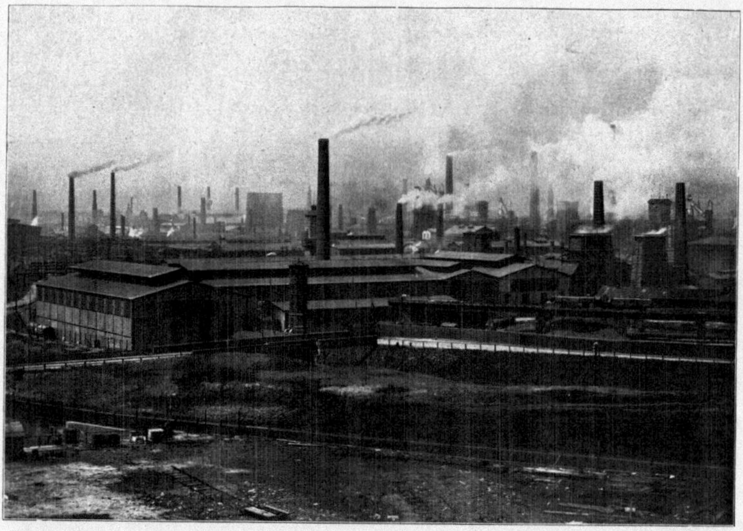

Fig. 18. *Deutschland. Ein Buch der Größe und der Hoffnung in Bildern, 1914–1924* (Germany: A book of greatness and hope in pictures) (Berlin: Otto Stollberg, 1924), page 24.

creator are sufficient enough to fool the undiscerning page-turner. Although captioned "Weapons Forge, Krupp-Essen 1910," the work is originally titled "Tiegelstahlguss im alten Schmelzbau bei Krupp" (Crucible steel casting in the old smelting plant at Krupp). It was painted in 1912 by Otto Bollhagen, a turn-of-the-century artist known for his industrial landscapes who was commissioned by the Krupp company and other firms to create flattering images of their factories.[24] While Bollhagen painted other views of the Krupp weapon works,[25] the painting in the *Deutschland* picture book is not of the weapons forge but is presented as such to suggest how Germany's manufacturing power was engaged for war.

Even photographs that do not primarily showcase industrial strength through physical size attest to German technological superiority and global

24. Grütter et al., *200 Jahre Krupp*, 164.
25. See a sample of his other work in Türk, *Bilder der Arbeit*, 373.

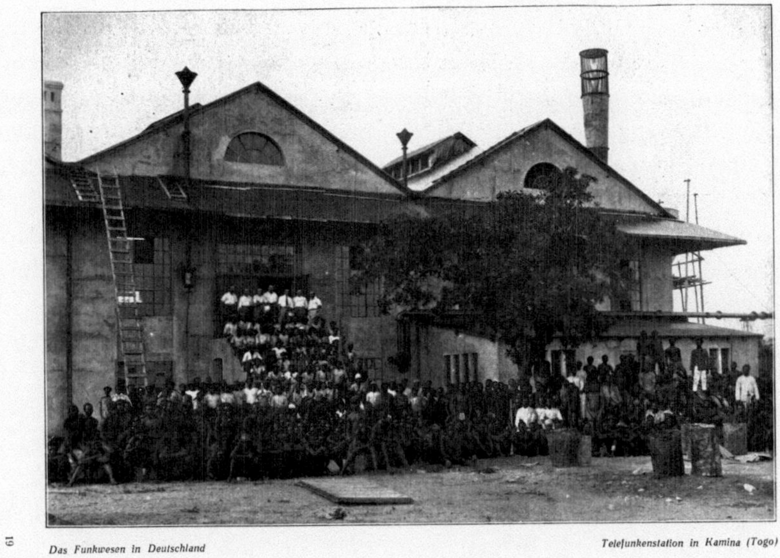

Fig. 19. *Deutschland. Ein Buch der Größe und der Hoffnung in Bildern, 1914–1924* (Berlin: Otto Stollberg, 1924), page 19.

reach before the war. This applies especially to the two-page spreads of photographs captioned "Germany's colonies" and "German shipping." Germany's prewar colonies, which were revoked as a condition of surrender in a massive blow to national pride, are shown in photographs of an exhibition in Windhoek (German South West Africa, now Namibia) that showcased modern wind-powered water pumps and other agricultural machinery and in an image of Qindao (China) that features its modern shipyard and its "18,000 Tons-Dock."[26] A photograph of the "Telefunken Station in Kamina (Togo)" (fig. 19) combines rapidly developing broadcast technology with Germany's imperial ambitions: the photograph is a group portrait of around a hundred Togolese men, the majority of whom are half naked, in front of the Telefunken station steps; at the top of the steps, seven white men in dress shirts and trousers lord over the black "primitives" beneath them. The image recalls

26. *Deutschland*, 16–17.

the pernicious intersection of photography, racism, and wartime propaganda apparent in the treatment of minority POWs and colonial "subjects."[27] German global influence and technological modernization is represented also in photographs of its shipping industry, such as the previously mentioned image of the *Imperator*. The focus of photographs showing "German shipping" is largely on the Hamburg America Line (Hamburg-Amerikanische Packetfahrt-Actien-Gesellschaft or HAPAG), with photographs of the Hamburg harbor and the St. Pauli piers, as well as the HAPAG pier in Hoboken, New Jersey, and the German pier in Manila. "Transport and technology" are embodied by a picture of new maritime locks on the Kaiser Wilhelm Canal (today the Kiel Canal).[28]

Pictures of people figure less prominently than technology in the prewar series, with the exceptions of two snapshots of "The old army" during training exercises and a photograph of "our *Schutztruppen*" (colonial army) in German South West Africa.[29] This focus in subject matter shifts immediately in the next section on Germany during the war, where the first photographs show crowds of people caught up in the war enthusiasm of 1914 and the march of troops into Belgian territory.[30] The initial military success on the Western Front is represented by columns of German troops marching triumphantly into Brussels and Bruges, the destroyed cityscapes of the captured Longwy and Leuven, and a destroyed fort at Diksmuide. Such pictures of German-caused destruction are unironically presented next to those of "The sorrows of East Prussia" that show "The remains of a burned down village," a result of the war in the east with Russia.[31]

The scope of the series widens to include all fronts pictured from land, sea, and even air, as two aerial shots over Egypt and Jerusalem show. (In a mistake that attests to apparent inexperience with understanding the perspective of such aerial shots, the photograph of Jerusalem is reproduced upside down in the book.) The novel photographs taken from airplanes—the aerial picture of Egypt shows the pyramids of Giza, entirely unrelated to the

27. See Riesz, "Afrikanische Kriegsgefangene." János Riesz considers picture books not discussed in this study, including the racist propaganda book *Der Völkerzirkus unserer Feinde* (ca. 1916) by Leo Frobenius. For a consideration of prewar photography and German colonialism, see also Siebrecht, "Seeing the 'Savage' and the Suspension of Time."

28. *Deutschland*, 20–22.

29. *Deutschland*, 12–13.

30. *Deutschland*, 27–30.

31. *Deutschland*, 30–35.

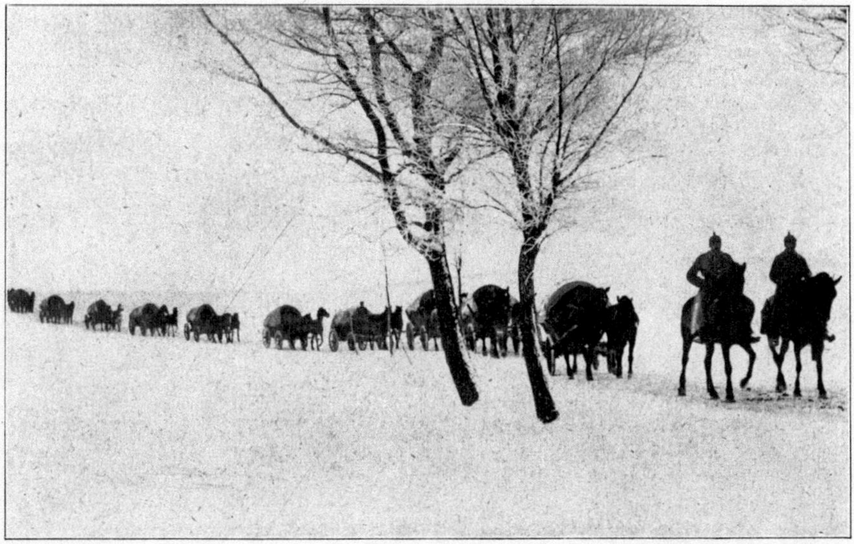

Winterschlacht in Masuren — Munitionskolonne auf dem Marsch

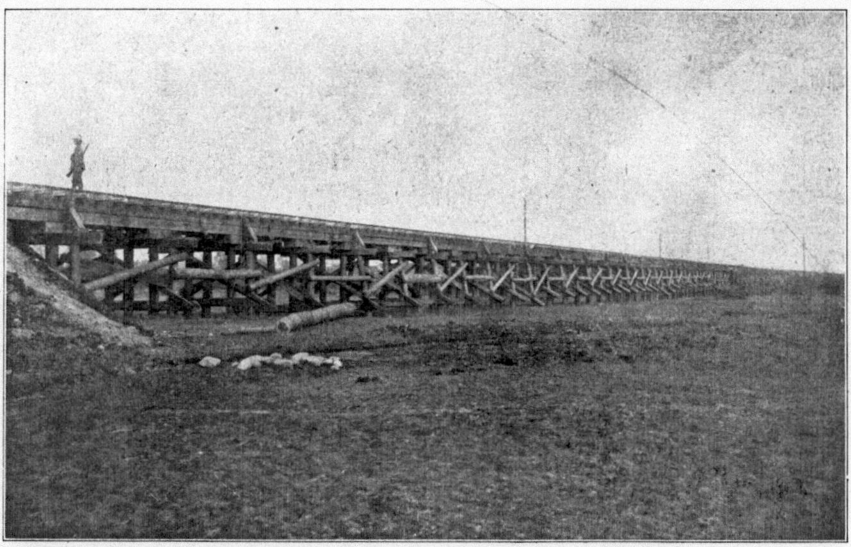

Meisterwerk unserer Pioniere — 840 m lange Eisenbahnbrücke in Polen

Fig. 20. *Deutschland. Ein Buch der Größe und der Hoffnung in Bildern, 1914–1924* (Berlin: Otto Stollberg, 1924), page 42.

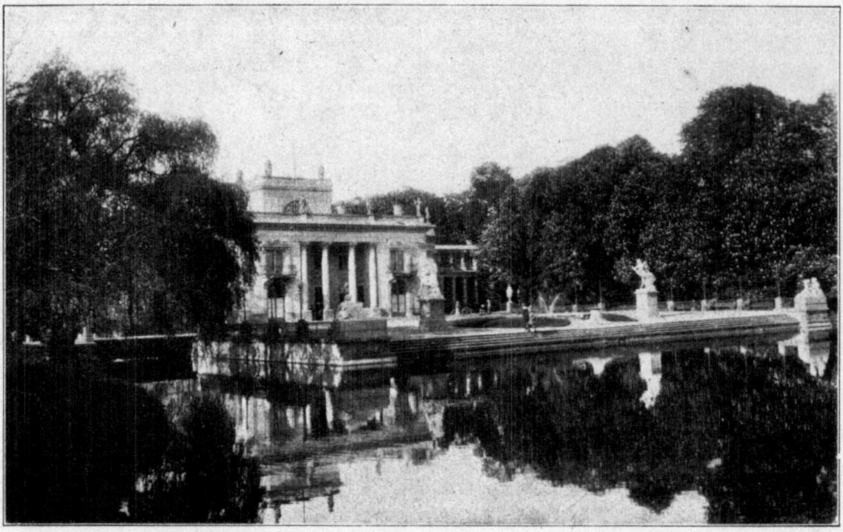

Der Vormarsch in Polen — Warschau in deutschem Besitz

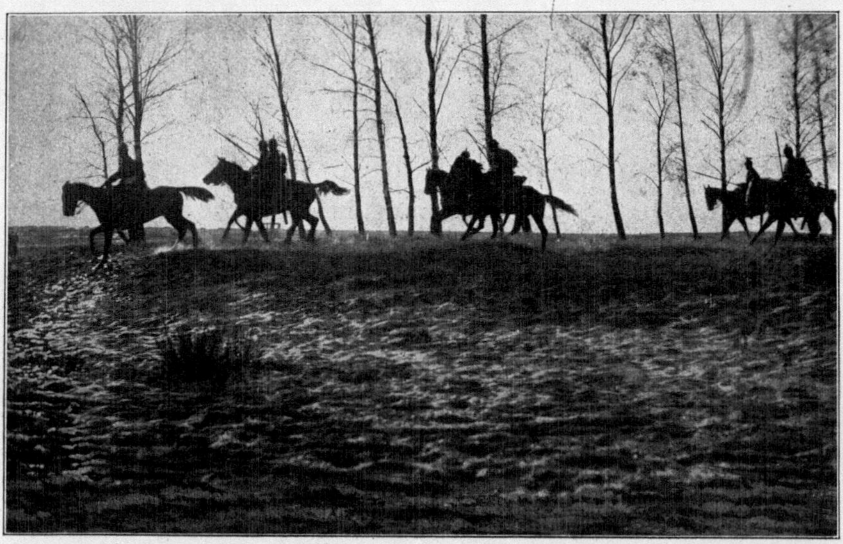

Der Vormarsch in Polen — Kavalleriepatrouille

Fig. 21. *Deutschland. Ein Buch der Größe und der Hoffnung in Bildern, 1914–1924* (Berlin: Otto Stollberg, 1924), page 43.

war—typify the selection criteria used to choose which photographs would represent the war. The series' photographs jump arbitrarily from one locale to another, albeit in rough chronological fashion, to present a visually exciting war account. Although there are relatively few photographs of combat, a sense of adventure is established through the wide geographical scope. The result is a narrative of German troops successfully traversing the world and conquering most everything in their path.

The trench warfare so characteristic of the public's understanding of the First World War today, and which was also central to the contemporary narratives of other nationalist war picture books, such as those edited by Franz Schauwecker, is outweighed by a sense of movement and progress in *Deutschland.* The military's initial, quick success conquering territory in Belgium and western France, which is presented in some of the first photographs in the series, is parlayed into a sense of progress throughout the section. Although photographs of the trenches on the Western Front are present, they are few in number and are immediately offset by photographs connoting motion and attesting to apparent war conquest, like those of the advance into Poland (see figs. 20 and 21). The book's visual representation of the war, even in its end stages, centers on the success of war exploits around the world through its focus on German troops (and cavalry, ships, and airplanes) in a wide range of geographical locations, the repetitive use of action words like *Vormarsch* (advance), *Anmarsch* (approach), *Einzug* (marching in), and *Einnahme* (capture) in the captions, and the trope of mastery over nature with technical expertise.

The connection between Germany's technological power and its global reach, which the first section on the prewar era establishes, is continued in the photographs representing the war effort. It is reflected in pictures of Germany's advanced naval forces, with pictures of "torpedo boats" stationed in the Libau (Liepaja, Latvia) harbor and the "Heldengeschwader" fleet of armored cruisers under Maximilian von Spee,[32] the leader of the East Asian Squadron that traversed the Pacific in 1914–15. Although not labeled as such, the image of Spee's squadron shows the fleet leaving Valparaiso, Chile, shortly after the Battle of Coronel,[33] the first German victory over the British Royal Navy since the Napoleonic Wars.[34] A dynamic photograph of "U-Boot 35 vor Perasto" (fig. 22) shows a sailor standing atop the deck of a

32. *Deutschland*, 37.

33. "NH 59638."

34. Sondhaus, *The Great War at Sea*, 79.

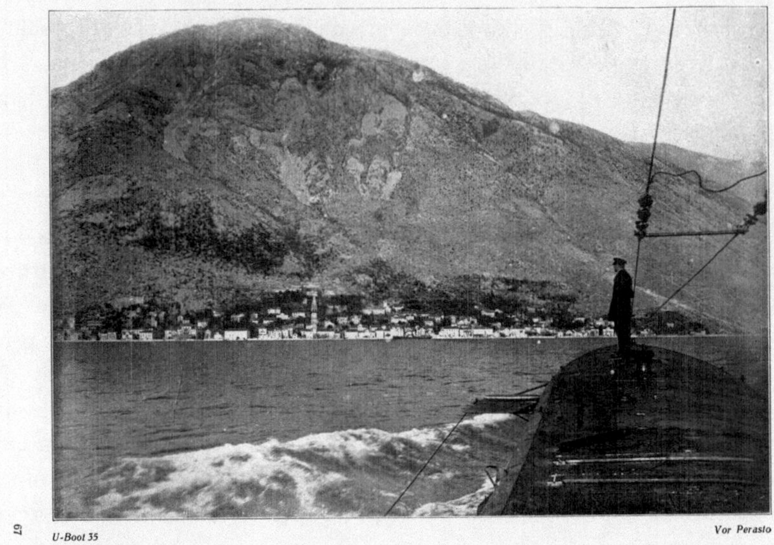

Fig. 22. *Deutschland. Ein Buch der Größe und der Hoffnung in Bildern, 1914–1924* (Berlin: Otto Stollberg, 1924), page 67.

submarine as it approaches the idyllic town of Perast in Montenegro's scenic Bay of Kotor region. The sailor in the foreground looms over the small town in the distance, a harbinger of German mastery at sea over the provincial Entente-aligned kingdom. Photographs of the commerce-raiding submarine SM *U-9*, the blockade-breaking Handels-U-Boot *Deutschland*, and the occupation of the Estonian island of Saaremaa (German: Ösel) by the navy round out the trope.[35] A photograph of the SMS *Emden*, wrecked following a 1914 skirmish with the British in the Cocos Islands, is the only suggestion of German vulnerability, although due to its exceptional war service prior to its beaching, the *Emden* was one of only two ships (along with SM *U-9*) that were awarded the Iron Cross and retained a high level of public recognition and honor in defeat.

In the same way the volume emphasizes how German ships apparently conquered the high seas, it repeats how civil engineering on land enabled the

35. *Deutschland*, 58, 63. 65.

advance of German troops, again drawing attention to the war effort's positive aspects. This is the case for a photograph of an 804m-long railway bridge constructed by German forces, part of a two-page spread of photographs on the *Vormarsch* into Poland (fig. 20). The caption labels the engineering feat a "masterpiece of our pioneers."[36] Another photograph of the reconstruction of destroyed streets in the wasteland of the Western Front in Bapaume, France, is not especially dynamic in terms of visual composition but contributes to the implicit claim of German technology overcoming circumstance made throughout the series. The same assessment applies to a rather mundane image of a wooden bridge under construction over the Argeş River outside Bucharest. The photograph below it shows the work's logical conclusion and symbolic importance: German troops muster for a ceremonial guard mounting in occupied Bucharest.[37]

Although the technologically advanced warships and submarines can be understood as a type of superiority through weaponry, German might is represented in *Deutschland* more saliently in the geographical spread of military forces across the globe. One picture of English flamethrowers and another of a destroyed English tank are the only indications of the role that new weaponry played in the war, but the technology is cast as being the sole property of the enemy.[38] This fits with the popular revisionist claim that Germany remained *im Felde unbesiegt* (undefeated in the field) and was beaten only by the sheer *Überwucht* (overbalance)—as the volume's introduction calls it—of the Entente's resources. Instead of drawing attention to the reasons for defeat, which must include to some extent material disadvantages, the volume preserves German honor by shifting its subject matter focus.

The capture of major European cities is one motif throughout the war series that attests to success during the war while avoiding a necessary reckoning with defeat on the Western Front. Like those photographs of the capture of Brussels, Bruges, and Bucharest already mentioned, the volume includes photographs that show German forces in major cities like Warsaw, Brest, Kiev, Kharkiv, and Helsinki. The photograph of "Warsaw in German possession" (fig. 21) points to the symbolic victories the book emphasizes. Unlike other photographs, such as that of Bucharest, for instance, which shows troops lining up for review on a city square, the image of Warsaw contains no obvious visual connection to the military, and there is no indi-

36. *Deutschland*, 42.

37. *Deutschland*, 54.

38. *Deutschland*, 59, 61.

cation, besides its inclusion in this series, that the photograph has anything to do with the war or was even taken during the German occupation. The image shows only a rather idyllic view of the Łazienki Palace (built in 1689), its façade framed by luscious trees and reflected in the pond to its north. This cultural treasure of the Polish baroque, which lies at the heart of the major park of the same name in central Warsaw, serves as a visual stand-in for the larger enterprise of German war success. The conquered palace does not represent any sort of tactical victory—the palace was not an important strategic position—but is pictured to stress a symbolic victory. Adding to the list of smaller locales like Perast and Saaremaa mentioned previously, the book also includes photographs of Liège, Przemyśl, Prilep, Ternopil, Bapaume, and Peronne, cities around Europe that fell to German occupation. Such a focus on the worldwide engagement of Germany's military not only accentuates the more easily pictured victories (which are symbolically if not tactically important) but echoes the introductory claim of "Germany against the world!,"[39] a claim also found in other nationalist picture books, such as *Eine ganze Welt gegen uns* (The whole world against us; 1934) by Wilhelm Reetz with Werner Beumelburg.

Many of the strands that run through the series on the war, including mastery over nature, the global impact of Germany's military, a sense of war as adventure, and the German spirit's triumph, are combined in a telling pair of images. Positioned on the opposite page from two images of defensive forts in Przemysl (Poland) and Brest (Belarus) that German forces reduced to rubble are two photographs of German soldiers at the peaks of mountains in the Waldkarpathen, a northern section of the eastern Carpathian mountain range that lies mostly in Ukraine (fig. 23). The bottom photograph shows two smiling soldiers perched atop a pillar of rock that extends upwards from the mountain top. Considering the steep cliff and rough terrain they navigated to reach the position high above the surrounding landscape, theirs is an apparent feat of daring. Their relaxed poses and smiling faces, however, suggest a natural talent for overcoming such obstacles and an inclination for adventure, even in the face of considerable danger. The photograph's capacity to document historically significant information about the war is limited. But that is not the image's purpose, nor, as should be clear, the purpose of the volume generally. The photograph is part and parcel of the volume's subjective war portrayal that carefully curates its contents for an ideological bent. Far more significant than the fact that two soldiers climbed to the top of a

39. Bloem, "Zehn Jahre Geschichte," 5.

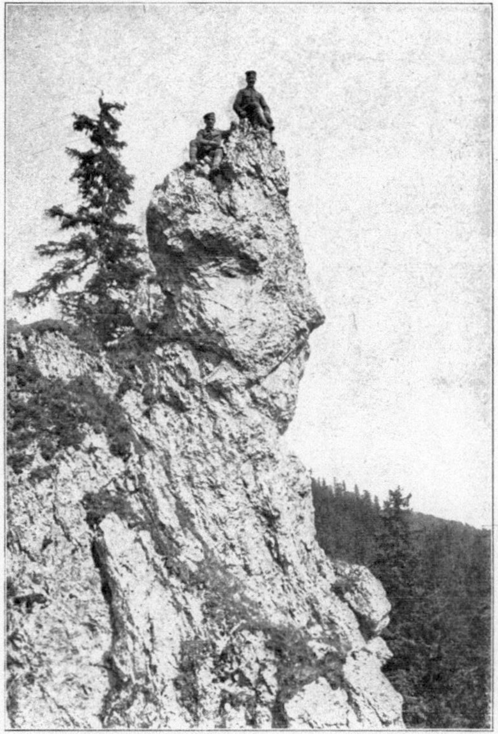

In den Waldkarpathen

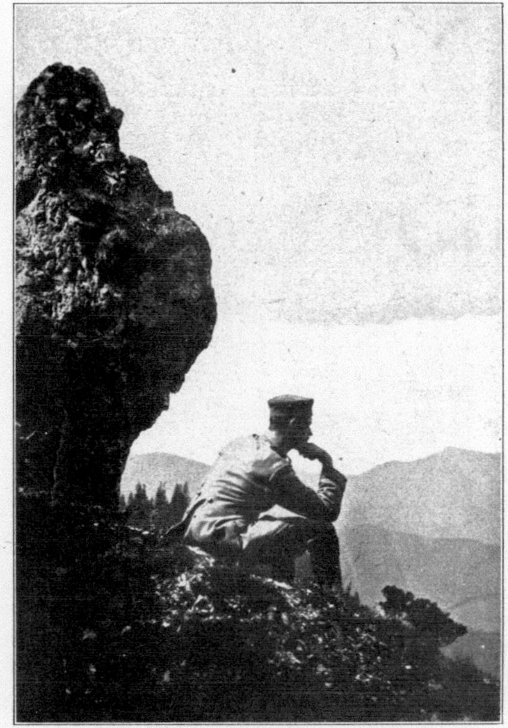

In den Waldkarpathen

Fig. 23. *Deutschland. Ein Buch der Größe und der Hoffnung in Bildern, 1914–1924* (Berlin: Otto Stollberg, 1924), page 44–45.

rocky outcrop is the act's symbolic nature. It serves as a metaphorical representation of the spiritual triumph that lies at the heart of many patriotic-nationalist war accounts.

The other photograph on the page can be understood in the same vein, but it recalls even more layered connotations about German nationalism. The image seems to have been taken at the same locale as the first or at a similar one in the Carpathians. The camera catches a German soldier from behind, who overlooks the mountainous landscape from a seated position. His arm is resting on his knee and his hand is under his chin, a pose that is not unlike Auguste Rodin's famous sculpture of *The Thinker*, with the exception that the soldier does not stare down pensively at the ground before him, but looks forward confidently to survey his surroundings. The soldier represents many of the same spiritual qualities as his two rock-climbing counterparts, but the spirit he embodies is less adventurous than it is reflective. The photograph can be better elucidated with reference to a second work of art, the Romantic painting *Wanderer über dem Nebelmeer* (Wanderer above the sea of fog; 1818) by Caspar David Friedrich. The obvious visual similarities that the two works share—for example, the rocky terrain, the hazy mountainscape, the figures viewed from behind, the vertical orientation—are not the only reason a comparison between the photograph and Friedrich's painting is apt. By sharing in visual likeness, the photograph activates the political resonances that are fundamental to Friedrich's oeuvre and shaped its reception as nationalist (in a broad sense) in the prewar Wilhelmine era.

Although the enigmatic nature of his paintings has made him one of the most debated nineteenth-century German artists, Friedrich and his work must be considered from his political and ideological worldview.[40] Not just a Romantic painter, Friedrich actively incorporated politics into his compositions through symbols and allegory, revealing a position that was vehemently opposed to the occupation of Germany by France under Napoleon and that strongly supported the German Campaign of 1813 that drove out the French. In this sense, Friedrich must be understood as "a patriotic-democratic and, at the same time, Nordic-Protestant painter . . . , for whom the national revolutionary mood between 1806 and 1815 was the central intellectual, religious and political experience of his life, and who constantly reflected on it in his paintings."[41] His work found broad resonance during the wars of

40. Hermand, *Politische Denkbilder*, 15, 19.
41. Hermand, *Politische Denkbilder*, 32.

liberation for its affirmative portrayal of a "national-democratic longing for a German unified state."[42]

Friedrich's political viewpoint made his paintings undesirable after the Congress of Vienna (1815), which shifted the political atmosphere in Germany as the major conservative powers of Europe opposed any national-revolutionary movements and "restored" the continent to the monarchical rule of the pre–French Revolution era. Although Friedrich died poor and bitter in 1840, his work was rediscovered in the early 1900s and was quickly co-opted by nationalist reactionaries during the Wilhelmine period. While art historians debated the significance of Friedrich's often foggy and cloudy scenes in paving the way for impressionism, nationalist circles championed his work for its underlying patriotic, political message, while eliding parts of Friedrich's worldview that were humanistic and democratic.[43] A bull market for his paintings arose especially in the year 1913, the hundred-year anniversary of the German Campaign, as nationalist voices pushed Friedrich's work in the service of prewar sensationalist imperial propaganda against the French.[44]

The history of Friedrich's reception in the Wilhelmine era makes it likely that viewers of the photograph of the soldier on the mountain in the *Deutschland* picture book would have understood the visual similarities it shares with Friedrich's *Wanderer* and be receptive to the transposition of patriotic sentiments from the German Campaign of 1813 to the World War. For example, the nationalist *Altdeutsche Tracht* (old German dress) of Friedrich's wanderer in 1818, one clear indication of the painter's national-democratic political standpoint,[45] is replaced by the uniform of a First World War soldier, which retained a different nationalist connotation in 1924, when pro-republican veterans' groups like the Reichsbanner were hesitant to don their uniforms for fear of appearing militaristic. Even the sense of uncertainty that Friedrich personally faced after 1815 in Germany, and which is reflected in the foggy expanse that stretches out before his *Wanderer*, can be translated to the postwar era. The editors of *Deutschland* likely saw a reflection of their own political situation in Friedrich's *Wanderer*, which combined intense national pride with uncertainty about Germany's future, for Fried-

42. Hermand, *Politische Denkbilder*, 16.
43. Hermand, *Politische Denkbilder*, 17, 35.
44. Hermand, *Politische Denkbilder*, 17.
45. Hermand, *Politische Denkbilder*, 30.

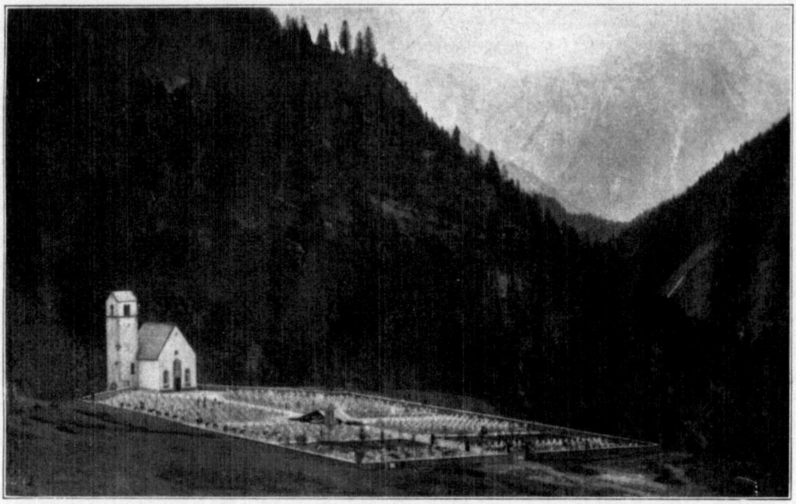

Militärkirchhof von Pian di Salasei (Provinz Trento) mit 900 Gräbern

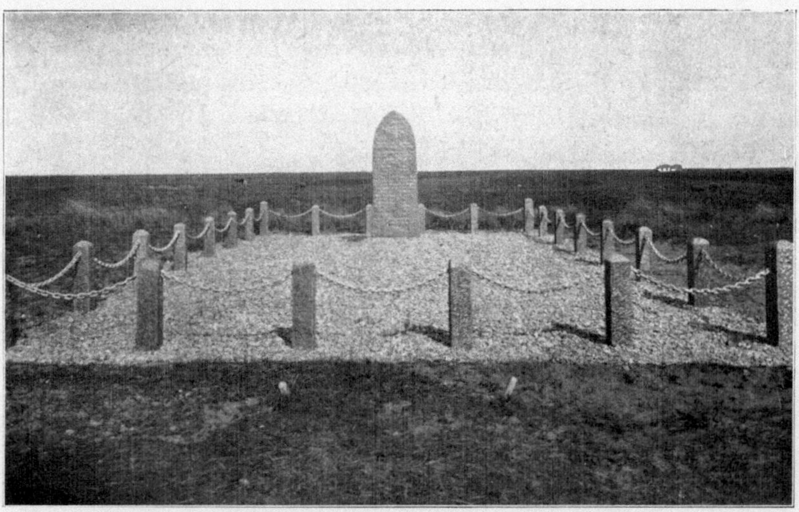

Ruhestätte der Helden aus der Skagerrak-Schlacht bei Skagen

Fig. 24. *Deutschland. Ein Buch der Größe und der Hoffnung in Bildern, 1914–1924* (Berlin: Otto Stollberg, 1924), page 57.

rich during the so-called Concert of Europe, and for the editors following the turbulence of the immediate postwar years in the Weimar Republic. The *Rückenfigur* motif, showing a figure from behind, that runs through Friedrich's oeuvre, is mirrored in the photograph, so that viewers can associate themselves with the figure and imagine the shared (and mastered) space beyond the frame of the image. The photograph of the reflective soldier in the Carpathians was an obvious choice to tie Germany's effort during the First World War to these layers of meaning.

As stated before, the pair of photographs showing German soldiers at the top of mountains in the Carpathians, although not a representation of significant historical events during the war, has clear political and aesthetic resonances indicative of mentalities of postwar nationalism. The same must be said for the way that *Deutschland* handles the unavoidable matter of death during the war. While the volume includes examples of vast physical destruction through photographs such as those of devastated city scenes or locales near the Western Front in the districts of Ypres, Bapaume, or Peronne, its presentation of dead soldiers is typical for patriotic picture books of its sort. Death is recognized openly by *Deutschland*, and is indeed a critical impulse for admonishing readers to remember the war, but the metonymy of war graves masks the horrors of war; photographs of dead or injured soldiers are nowhere to be found. Three of the four photographs presenting cemeteries in the war series (none are shown in the postwar series) give an orderly, dignified sense of dying during the war. A small military cemetery, the Sacrario Militare di Pian di Salesei, is carefully built into the idyllic mountainous countryside of the Italian Dolomites. The photograph (fig. 24) is labeled simply "The military cemetery at Pian di Salasei (Provinz Trento) with 900 graves." Although initially administered under Austro-Hungarian authority, the cemetery is actually the final resting place for far more Entente-aligned Italian soldiers.[46] Despite the factual absence of any clear tie to the German war effort and German pride, its neat rows of well-maintained graves and the sublime scenery of its location, accentuated by the camera's high vantage point, contribute to a whitewashed idea of death that avoids any information that might tarnish a positive image of war honor.

The photograph that accompanies that of the Italian cemetery on the same page is also of a war graves site. One simple headstone stands at the head of a small square area covered in gravel and marked off by short stone pillars connected to each other with metal chains. Like the Italian cemetery,

46. "Sacrario Militare di Pian di Salesei."

the grave site is orderly and dignified, and the photograph is framed so that the site is the only discernible man-made intrusion in the wide expanse of flat Jutland countryside. The surrounding landscape's vastness heightens the spiritual overtones of the pictured cemetery, and the caption connects the dead to acts of heroism worthy of eternal devotion: the photograph is labeled "Resting place of the heroes from the Battle of Jutland near Skagen." Not only is the caption one of the few examples in the volume where text adds meaning to an image that goes beyond mere identification, its effect is also not limited to the one photograph, but is applied to the photograph of the Italian military graveyard above it. That first photograph has a simple identifying caption that nevertheless withholds key information about who exactly is buried there and leaves the meaning of the photograph's inclusion in the volume open to interpretation. The caption of the latter photograph, which is marked as a German cemetery through its praise of the "heroes" of the Battle of Jutland, therefore extends its connotation to the photograph of the Italian cemetery, so that those readers who were not intimately familiar with the history of one small Italian mountainside cemetery would mistake it to be the scenic final resting place of German war heroes. The error is enticed through the juxtaposition of photographs and the less-than-forthright use of captions, but it is also undergirded by the volume's fundamental focus on Germany's war effort across the globe; a later photograph showing the orderly "graves of German pilots near Nazareth" reinforces the assumption that Germans found honorable burials all over the world.[47]

The last photograph of war graves (fig. 25) is largely incongruous with the ones that precede it. Although it shares the same impulse "to remember," as the caption states, the image of "Warrior graves at the Western Front" draws in the violent reality of trench warfare more so than any other image in the book. The photograph shows several makeshift graves, low mounds of gravel marked by simple wooden crosses, at the bottom of an unnatural crater amid the ruined landscape of the Western Front. Rubble and man-made debris litter the scene, and one solitary soldier stands in the middle distance, perhaps the caretaker of the area or someone just passing through. The photograph lends gravity to one of the volume's central impulses: the importance of commemorating fallen soldiers. Although its depiction of devastation contrasts with the neat and orderly picture of the war that the volume cultivates, it is not matched with a particular name or other identifying information and therefore can only signify a general sense of death. Like all

47. *Deutschland*, 80.

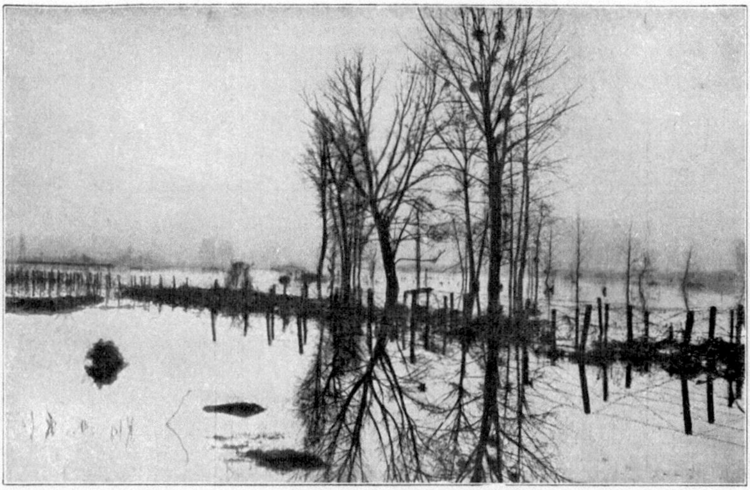

Im Rückzugsgelände — *Das Ueberschwemmungsgebiet der Aisne*

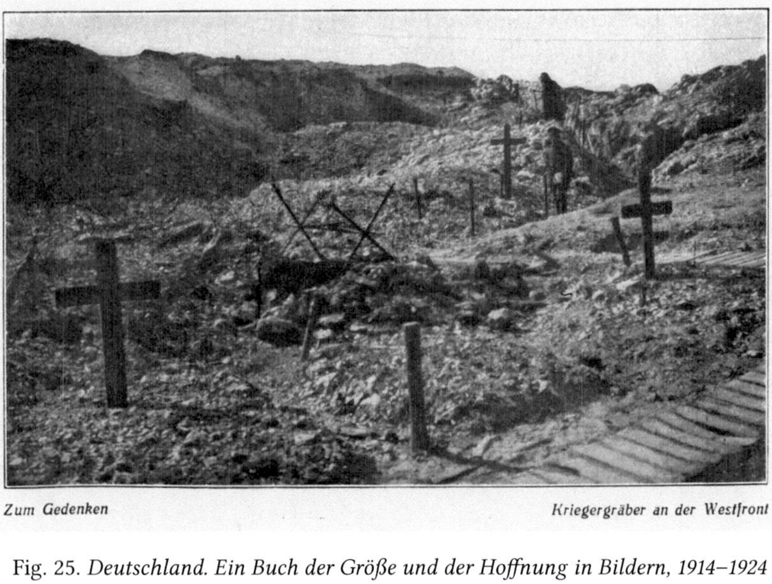

Zum Gedenken — *Kriegergräber an der Westfront*

Fig. 25. *Deutschland. Ein Buch der Größe und der Hoffnung in Bildern, 1914–1924* (Berlin: Otto Stollberg, 1924), page 77.

the pictures of war graves in the volume, it recalls the common practice of sending photographs of grave markers to family members of fallen soldiers. Such a practice, as the editors of *Das Bild: Monatschrift für photographische Bildkunst* (Monthly magazine for photographic visual art) claimed in July 1918, served as an "amelioration of pain," and grave photographs were seen as "a valuable testament and souvenir" for "families whose member died a heroic death."[48] Recontextualized in the *Deutschland* volume, the practice of showing grave photographs is still intended to evince the soldiers' "heroic death"; however, it has been twisted for reasons beyond familial remembrance, as the headstones' signifier has been extended to the entire German "family": the nation.

In comparison to the image of improvised graves on the Western Front, the few other photographs that show trenches do not impart the same sense of real danger or unglamorous violence enacted on German bodies. This can be ascribed to several circumstances of the photographs' creation. First, the majority of trench views were taken from an improbable camera position that would be entirely unsafe for the photographer had the photograph not been staged after the fact or taken during training exercises, a common "faking" practice among both amateur and official photographers.[49] Such is the case for "In the Vosges mountains / German trenches,"[50] "Trench warfare in the West / Improvements to barbed wire barricades,"[51] or "The fighting in the West / Storm troopers go through barbed wire barricades,"[52] in which the photographer catches other soldiers ducking down to avoid the enemy's rifle scope, while standing openly himself in a vulnerable position above the scene to take the photograph. Other examples, such as "Defense / Abandoned Russian trenches" and "Bapaume-Arras / Stormed English line" combine the same camera perspective with the explicit indication that the photograph was made long after the referenced action posed any real danger.[53] Two other images, captioned "Battles in France 1916 / Trench positions in winter," are taken from a more inconspicuous perspective close to the ground, but they only show the still surface area of a wide swath of landscape intersected by trenches, effectively masking all the less palatable details of trench warfare.[54]

48. "Grabphotographien," 49.
49. Arendes, "Wirklichkeitsbilder," 37.
50. *Deutschland*, 30.
51. *Deutschland*, 68.
52. *Deutschland*, 73.
53. *Deutschland*, 35, 70.
54. *Deutschland*, 49.

Just one photograph in the entire volume shows a form of action that cannot be immediately dismissed as having been staged or taken from a safe temporal distance. "Between Reims and Laon / An advancing division under fire" (see fig. 26) shows several soldiers advancing up an incline through a tangle of barbed wire that is unlike the orderly set-up used for training pictured elsewhere in the volume.[55] The camera's perspective, anchored on the ground and looking upward, and an unfocused object blocking a large portion of the photograph's foreground suggest an improvised snapshot taken during actual combat. (Although German soldiers were prohibited from using their personal cameras during combat, written reports and the body of photographic evidence reveal that officers did not enforce the rule uniformly.[56]) The photograph imparts a heightened sense of authenticity because of its close proximity to "real" combat and its obvious "shot-from-the-hip" visual style. But this type of documentary authenticity only applies to the volume's claim that one can (and should) reexperience the past, and it is largely incongruent with the volume's overall intended message. The combat photograph, like that of the improvised trench graves, invites reflection on the harsher realities of death during the war, although the volume as a whole works to elide the horrors of that death in the service of an affirmative national patriotism. This "correction" is especially obvious when the book's subject matter is compared to that of Ernst Friedrich's *Krieg dem Kriege!*, which attests to the amount of gruesome visual material that did arise from the war.

The two photographs of trench warfare introduce a significant source of friction in remembering and celebrating the war that inheres in most patriotic picture books of this sort: the impulse to remember the war triumphantly always runs up against the horrors of the war experience. In the case of *Deutschland: Ein Buch der Größe und der Hoffnung*, the way around this roadblock is to ignore the more shocking details. Bloem's introduction invites its readers to recall and relive the past "to reflect and remember one more time with seriousness and loyalty, with faith and affirmation,"[57] but the photographic selection makes clear such an endeavor is intended to be largely one of "faith and affirmation." Although it mentions the number of German soldiers who were killed in an appeal to remember the war, Bloem's

55. *Deutschland*, 52. Compare the photograph captioned "Das Ringen im Westen / Sturmabteilung geht durch den Drahtverhau," *Deutschland*, 73.

56. Dewitz, "German Snapshots," 154.

57. Bloem, "Zehn Jahre Geschichte," 7.

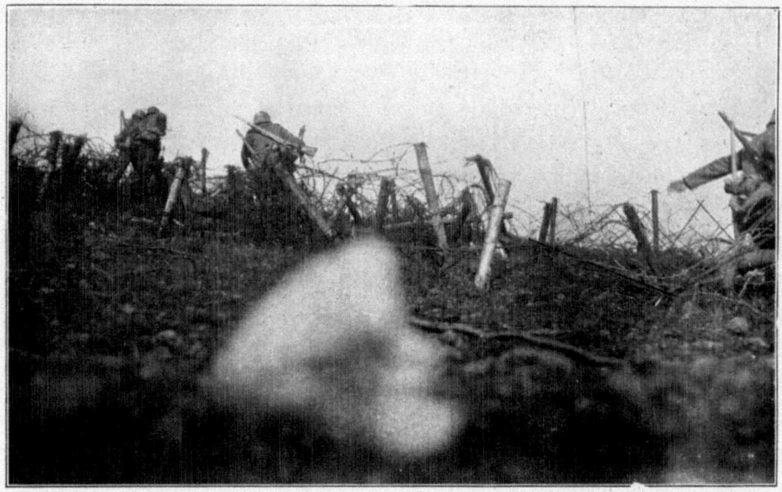

Zwischen Reims und Laon — Im Sturm vorgehende Abteilung

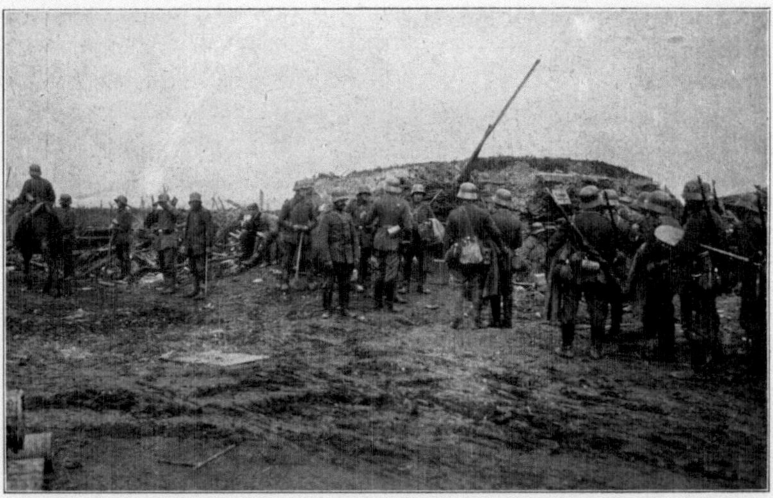

Zwischen Reims und Laon — Im Kampfgelände

Fig. 26. *Deutschland. Ein Buch der Größe und der Hoffnung in Bildern, 1914–1924* (Berlin: Otto Stollberg, 1924), page 52.

introduction does not dwell on the grim details of death. For instance, the closest Bloem comes to addressing the devastation of war is when he speaks of "the bled-out body of our young Reich."[58] The category of mourning remains a superficial act and is useful only as long as its political persuasiveness does not swing too far in the opposite direction of revealing the war's cruel aspects. Bloem's repeated claim that "we did not fall apart"—"we" referring to all of Germany as much as the *Frontkämpfer* (frontline warriors) among whom he counted himself—punctuates the introduction's patriotism and contributes to the whitewashing of the more disturbing facts of war. He uses the phrase to champion the apparent spiritual victory of Germany not buckling under difficult circumstances, but its meaning clearly does not jibe with the physical loss of life, nor the economic and social turmoil at home following the war's end, obvious and numerous cases of "falling apart." The phrase's use in the introduction is therefore made ironic by the most clearly visible suggestions of death that slip past the careful eye of the editor(s) in the two photographs of trench combat and improvised war graves. The uniqueness of these images' grittiness among all others is punctuated by the rather mundane image placed below the combat photograph, which shows a group of soldiers standing around rather aimlessly and unconcerned "In the battlefield" (see fig. 26).

The meaning of the repeated phrase "we did not fall apart," used in the introduction to extol the triumphs of the German spirit during the war, is extended to the present of the book's publication (1924) and into the future: "and we will not fall apart," Bloem asserts.[59] In this way, the postwar situation is tied up with the outcomes of the war, and any future stress on the German spirit will require the type of admirable resolve shown during the war. Indeed, Germany's return to its titular *Größe* was achieved effortlessly, if one is to believe the selection of photographs that appear in the book's last section, "Germany after the war." In the same manner that the previous section fosters an affirmative interpretation of the war that—overlooking a few inconsistencies—focuses on triumphs and minimizes tragedies, the postwar series completely ignores the negative aspects of the years following the armistice to present a picture of Germany's might. Although Bloem states in the introduction that it was not just the war alone that caused (and continues to cause) consternation, the specific details are not laid out for the reader, and his language remains on the level of patriotic proselytizing. He

58. Bloem, "Zehn Jahre Geschichte," 6.
59. Bloem, "Zehn Jahre Geschichte," 6.

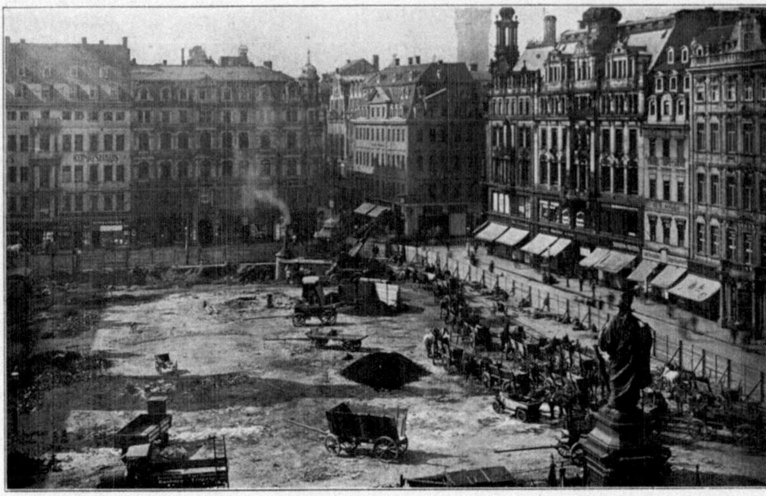

Die Leipziger Messe *Errichtung eines Untergrundmeßhauses 1924*

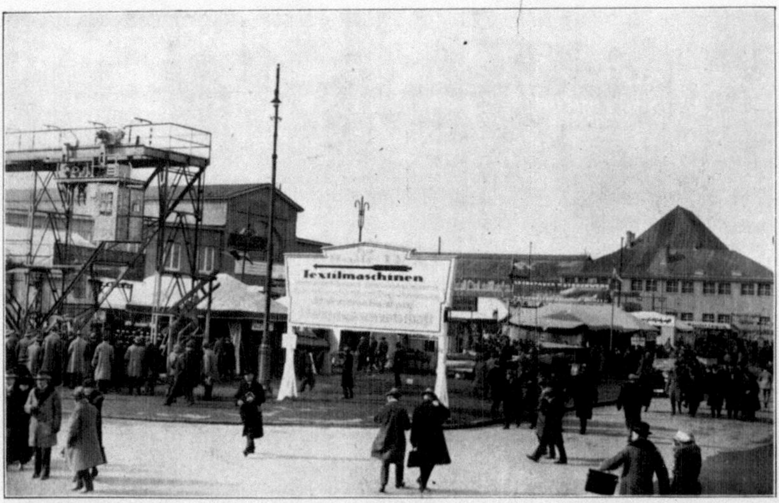

Die Leipziger Messe *Technische Messe 1923*

Fig. 27. *Deutschland. Ein Buch der Größe und der Hoffnung in Bildern, 1914–1924* (Berlin: Otto Stollberg, 1924), page 93.

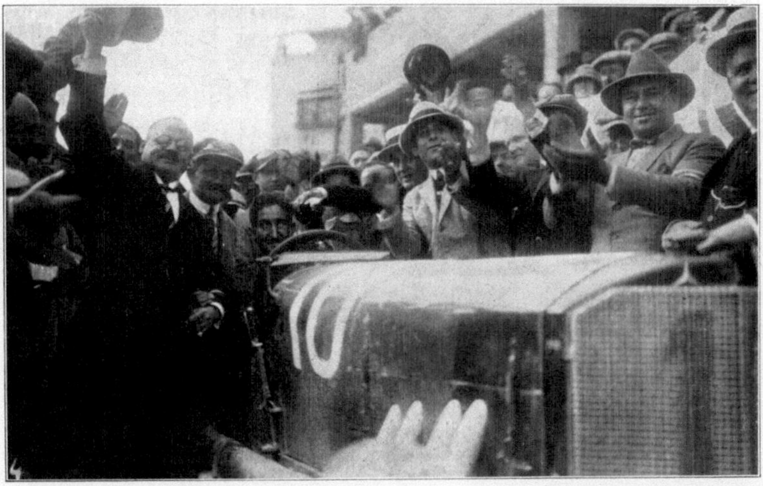

Die deutsche Automobilindustrie — *Sieg in Targa Florio 1924*

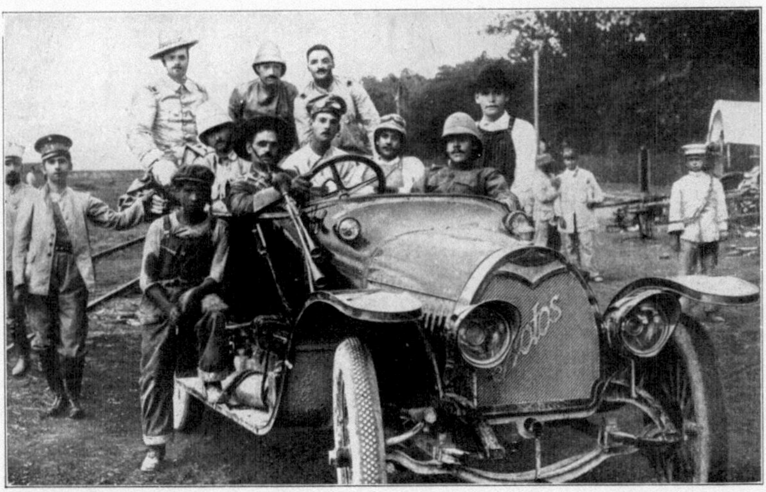

Die deutsche Automobilindustrie — *Ein deutscher Wagen in Mexiko 1921*

Fig. 28. *Deutschland. Ein Buch der Größe und der Hoffnung in Bildern, 1914–1924* (Berlin: Otto Stollberg, 1924), page 92.

begins the introduction with the lament, "What a ten years it has been! What a history! As long as people have walked upright across our planet, they have never seen, suffered, or done such things as we have done, the witnesses and fighters of this unimaginably eventful decade."[60] These melodramatic opening sentences cue the reader into expecting an overt critique of the postwar situation alongside a consideration of the war, that is to say, an examination of the full decade between 1914 and 1924, not just the years between 1914 and 1918. Perhaps Bloem simply does not need to remind his readers of the postwar economic and political turmoil that was fresh in their minds in 1924, but there are no sustained sociopolitical critiques one might expect from a national-conservative writer addressing this time period. As stated earlier, the volume contains only a few indirect references to negative aspects of the postwar situation that were a disappointment across the political spectrum, including the Ruhr occupation starting in 1923.

The thirteen pages of photographs in the postwar section only reinforce the unexpected lack of political critique by avoiding images of all major postwar events, foremost among them the November Revolution. The volume does not engage with the typical postwar sources of national-conservative ire, such as the Treaty of Versailles, the "stab-in-the-back" myth, the Spartacists, the Weimar Republic, liberalism, communism, or party politics of any kind. Instead, the section focuses on showing off industrial and military might, returning to the exact same patriotic message and visual material as the first series of photographs showing Germany before the war. As in the earlier section, photographs are selected to provide evidence of nautical prowess ("The new imperial navy / Wilhelmshaven 1924," "The HAPAG harbor in Hamburg," and "'Columbus,' the largest ship of Germany's new trade fleet"),[61] technological advancement ("Radio technology in Germany," "The German airplane as means of transport," and "The first German turbine locomotives"),[62] and economic strength ("The Leipzig Trade Fair / Construction of an underground exhibition hall 1924" and "The Leipzig Trade Fair / Technology Fair 1923"; fig. 27). Even the global spread of the military that is so salient in the first two sections finds expression in two photographs of "The German automobile industry" that show the winners of car races in Targa Florio, Italy (1924), and Mexico (1923) sitting behind the wheel of German-manufactured vehicles (fig. 28). Photographs of the global auto-

60. Bloem, "Zehn Jahre Geschichte," 5.
61. *Deutschland*, 83, 94–95.
62. *Deutschland*, 88–90.

mobile industry act as useful replacements for the photographs of actual colonies in the prewar section, as they communicate the imperial aspirations that lingered after Germany was stripped of its oversea territories under the Treaty of Versailles.

The selected photographs of industrial and technological might are meant as celebrations of a reborn Germany, but the militaristic connotation is carried over from the wartime series. The featured technologies—radio, trains, airplanes, cars, and ships—appear in the postwar series on the surface as products of Germany's reorganized industrial sector that now focuses on the improvement of civilian life. Two images from 1924 show the tangible results of such a transformation: the first shows diesel motors being built in the former Imperial Shipyards of Kiel, and the second shows locomotives being built in the former Krupp cannon factories in Essen.[63] Another page shows the before and after of the HAPAG Harbor in Hamburg: "After the overseas merchant ships were handed over, 1919" and experiencing a "New life, 1924."[64] Four photographs in the postwar series of youth sports and the Reichswehr, which highlight the mass participation in those groups, as well as the aforementioned photograph of "The new imperial navy," anchor the entire series' connotation in the militaristic.[65] The volume ignores the reality of a drastically reduced military, both in terms of servicemen and weaponry, and all the feelings of hurt pride that accompanied that provision of the Treaty of Versailles to present a picture of an ostensibly active military and the nation's potential to quickly transition back to wartime production. The volume thus ends with not only a final visual affirmation of Germany's *Größe* and sense of *Hoffnung* for its own citizens but also a veiled threat to Germany's enemies. The patriotic words of Bloem's introduction echo here in the book's final pages. In response to the fact "that foreign power exercises sovereignty on our homeland"—a reference to the Ruhr occupation—Bloem warns that "we" must reawaken from national tragedy so that "the superiority" of enemies does not trample Germany again. "Germany lives. . . . And because we want it, so it will be."[66]

63. *Deutschland*, 86–87. The latter image of the Krupp factory is the second example of a realistic painting being included in the volume, likely to heighten the romanticism of the pictured content. Its provenance could not be determined.

64. *Deutschland*, 94.

65. *Deutschland*, 83–85.

66. Bloem, "Zehn Jahre Geschichte," 7.

CHAPTER FOUR

War History as "National Task"

Commemorative Myth-Making in Publications from the Reichsarchiv and George Soldan

Deutschland: Ein Buch der Größe und der Hoffnung in Bildern, 1914–1924 affirms Germany's fighting spirit and connects the war experience to the postwar situation. One of its central implications—that the postwar era was taxing and unfair to the German spirit—is explicit in Walter Bloem's introduction and was a belief that transcended political ideologies to be shared by wide swaths of society. His intention to celebrate the war effort as a way to bring light to dark times, however, was a mostly new notion in 1924. Up until then, the majority of the German public had been ready to evaluate the war's legacy critically and to reject war as an instrument of politics.[1] Pacifist movements representative of those feelings, such as Nie Wieder Krieg (Never Again War), had lost much of their steam by 1924, when a "short period of insight" that saw the widespread publication and successful reception of critical, republican war memories ended.[2] Historian Benjamin Ziemann blames the breakdown of criticism of the war after 1924 on the outpouring of jingoistic emotions unleashed when French and Belgian troops occupied the Ruhr in January 1923, the uneasy coalition among the diverse political parties of the left on which many of the critical commemorative initiatives rested, and the geographically limited audience of major republican newspapers, which were based in Germany's large cities.[3] The Ruhr occupation

1. Ziemann, *Contested Commemorations*, 56.

2. Ziemann, *Contested Commemorations*, 56. Ziemann borrows the term "short period of insight" from Franz Carl Endres, a former German officer who served during the war and afterwards wrote a series of books and articles on the legacy of the war, including a critique of the "stab-in-the-back" myth. He noted in 1924 that preparations already seemed underway for a persistent glorification of the war.

3. Ziemann, *Contested Commemorations*, 58–59.

was certainly a driving factor in the picture book *Deutschland*; it is one of the few postwar issues to be referenced with any explicitness in that volume.

Beyond *Deutschland*, other patriotic and nationalist efforts to commemorate the war and fix its meaning began in earnest around the same time as the Ruhr occupation. Foremost among the many accounts that cemented what Ziemann calls the "hegemony of the right-wing camp in the field of literary representations of the war" were novels written by former military personnel, such as Werner Beumelburg and Edwin Erich Dwinger.[4] Their writings not only found success in the mass-market book trade but were also legitimized through cooperation with important government institutions concerned with military history, chief among them the Reichsarchiv, which was founded in October 1919 following the suggestion of high-ranking military leaders. Although officially detached from the military, the state organization continued to employ a large number of former officers and had as its first president the former Major General Hermann Ritter Mertz von Quirnheim.[5] It undertook some of the archival and historiographical tasks that had once fallen under the scope of the German General Staff after that group was dismantled as a condition of the Treaty of Versailles. Alongside typical archival functions, the Reichsarchiv conducted research for a planned official history of the military effort from 1914 to 1918, and it produced popular war narratives in cooperation with established novelists and amateur soldier-writers alike.

The Reichsarchiv also played a prominent role in the organization and dissemination of photographs from the war. The collections of the wartime Bild- und Filmamt (BUFA; Picture and film bureau), which coordinated and produced Germany's wartime visual propaganda from 1917 to 1919,[6] were held by the Reichsarchiv after BUFA's dissolution. The collections were mined for later picture books, such as *Der Weltkrieg im Bild* (The World War in pictures; 1926; introduction by George Soldan), which explicitly names BUFA-created images as its source. Photographic book series produced by the Reichsarchiv, such as "Schlachten des Weltkrieges" (Battles of the World War) and "Erinner-

4. Ziemann, *Contested Commemorations*, 246. Despite the huge success of Remarque's *Im Westen nichts Neues* and the war-critical, or at least war-ambivalent, novels by the likes of Ludwig Renn, the circulation of war books by right-wing authors portraying positive messages of war outnumbered the negative ones.

5. Pöhlmann, *Kriegsgeschichte*, 19, 82. Hermann Mertz von Quirnheim should not be confused here with his son Albrecht, one of the main conspirators in the July 20, 1944, plot to assassinate Hitler.

6. German Federal Archives, "Der Krieg im Bewegtbild—das Bild- und Filmamt."

ungsblätter deutscher Regimenter" (Commemoration papers of German regiments), sought to bring *volkstümlich* (popular; of and for the Volk) histories of the war to the masses.[7] Leaders of the Reichsarchiv debated the terms through which they would historicize the war and the role that photography should have in supporting their vision. This chapter traces those debates, first in the organization's internal deliberations on historiography, and then in the photographic projects mentioned above, both efforts headed by Reichsarchiv section head George Soldan. By combining popular history writing with photography and propaganda, the Reichsarchiv made a strong impact in the memory contests surrounding the war, fixing a conservative, military-affirming view of the war into the public eye. The reverential portraits of the officer class that often covered the first pages in picture books from the Reichsarchiv (see, for example, fig. 29) are just the first hint of how the organization worked to reassert the military's greatness in light of postwar defeat.

Although the stated purpose of the Reichsarchiv to collect and compose military history was for practical use in training future officers, the boundary between specialist historical writing and patriotic propaganda was blurred in the publications of the Reichsarchiv and its various subsections.[8] Historian Markus Pöhlmann concurs that the continuity of former military personnel in the Reichsarchiv, especially from among privileged members of the officer classes, meant that the institution was civilian in name only. Reichsarchiv employees largely retained the worldview of the Wilhelmine military elite and evinced a strong antirepublican spirit. The simple recommendation to move the archive from politically volatile Berlin to tranquil Potsdam, residence of the Prussian kings and the German kaiser until 1918, was indicative of the Reichsarchiv leadership's self-understanding. The decision by the Interior Ministry in the early 1920s to counter the obvious antirepublican tendencies in the Reichsarchiv by hiring more civilian historians was perceived as a serious affront to the military's monopoly on war history. The former military personnel of the Reichsarchiv worked together to successfully marginalize their civilian colleagues to ensure that military-affirming war accounts remained standard.[9]

7. Mass accessibility continues in the digital age (with different end purposes). The complete "Schlachten" series has been digitized and is available to researchers through the Digital State Library of Upper Austria, and some volumes of the "Erinnerungsblätter" have been scanned by the Hamburg State and University Library Carl von Ossietzky.

8. Ziemann, *Contested Commemorations*, 221.

9. Pöhlmann, *Kriegsgeschichte*, 158.

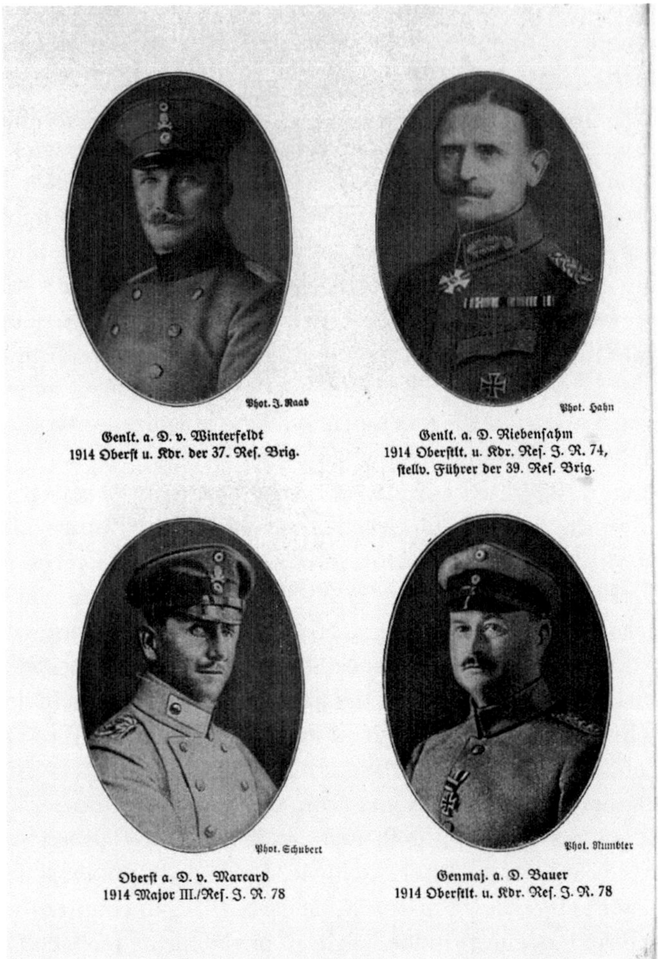

Fig. 29. Kurt Heydemann, *Die Schlacht bei St. Quentin 1914, I. Teil: Der rechte Flügel der 2. deutschen Armee am 29. und 30. August* (The battle of Saint-Quentin 1914, Part 1: The right wing of the Second German Army on August 29–30; volume 7a of "Battles of the World War") (Oldenburg/Berlin: Stalling, 1925), plate 2.

In the months following the war's end and those preceding the Reichsarchiv's founding in late fall 1919, however, there was a brief period when General Staff officers responsible for war history were surprisingly ready to evaluate the war in a critical light and question their role in writing its history.[10] According to top brass like Colonel Reinhold von Sydow, who headed the German General Staff's War History Department I ("Major Operations"), the prewar impulse to preserve the military's prestige by any means was no longer an adequate way of dealing with five years of bloody war and civil war. Von Sydow suggested new historiographical approaches that shifted the focus of war writing to the psychology of individuals in an effort to provide more nuanced critiques of the war open to the reader's interpretation.[11] Mertz von Quirnheim, until 1919 chief quartermaster for war history in the General Staff and then Reichsarchiv president until 1931, even wrote that "the horrors of war must be put into perspective."[12] Faced in May 1919 with a draft of the peace treaty that dismantled the German General Staff and its war historical archive, Mertz von Quirnheim advocated the founding of a civilian archival institute so that the task of writing the war's history maintained a more objective position.[13] These and other accounts from officers reveal an initial postwar willingness to critically examine Germany's war effort in the official military history being prepared under the aegis of the General Staff and then under the Reichsarchiv.

A shift in mentality among General Staff historians toward less critical history writing is evident after May 1919, when the brief period of reflection among top war historian officers ended. Hans von Seeckt, the last chief of the German General Staff and then chief of staff for the Reichswehr in the first years of the republic, summarized recommendations from the department heads of the various war history subsections in a memorandum dated July 12, 1919, about the necessity of a new Reichsarchiv. Like his subordinates in the War History Department, he was concerned with practical questions about the institutional continuity of the military's large archival collections from the war. But unlike Mertz von Quirnheim's focus on preserving a factual account, which might or might not invite criticism of the military, Seeckt advocated a more openly propagandistic approach to war history. Perhaps this was an outgrowth of wartime propaganda practices that focused on pro-

10. Pöhlmann, *Kriegsgeschichte*, 62.
11. Pöhlmann, *Kriegsgeschichte*, 63.
12. Quoted in Pöhlmann, *Kriegsgeschichte*, 65.
13. Quoted in Hollmann, "Die Gründung des Reichsarchivs," 33.

moting the military's "certain social order," which to fight a total war needed the support of a home front that rejected that very social order.[14] In his July 1919 memorandum, which was sent to Chancellor Gustav Bauer's cabinet, Seeckt claimed that the primary goal of any historical account should be to reawaken the faith of the "spiritually, mentally, and physically broken Volk" through "reviving the memory of the great deeds performed during the World War."[15] Furthermore, the state should have priority access to and critical purview over the thousands of war records, as private authors work for their own material interests.[16] In Seeckt's eyes, only the state could properly employ the military archive's vast holdings to counter the "campaign of lies from enemy propaganda" that is "already poisoning the German character and German name."[17] One way he saw the Reichsarchiv functioning in this manner was through the sustained production of official texts on the war that satisfied "the desire [of the public] to read, to refresh and supplement their memory."[18] Such a feat would not be imaginable with just *one* representation but would require a volkstümlich representation of the war.[19]

The primary influence on the propagandistic tone of Seeckt's memorandum is a 41-page document prepared on May 22, 1919, by George Soldan, a lower-ranking captain in the War History Department IV (Archives).[20] Titled "Die deutsche Geschichtsschreibung des Weltkrieges: Eine nationale Aufgabe" (The German historiography of the World War: A national task), Soldan's manuscript was intended for private publication outside the General Staff's scope but was circulated within his department and then passed to Mertz von Quirnheim by Soldan's superior; Seeckt even lifted lines from Soldan's manuscript for his own text. It became an official position statement on the impending reorganization of the General Staff's war history unit, one that shifted the conversation surrounding questions of a new Reichsarchiv to a more politically overt register.[21] The text apparently impressed Mertz von

14. Deist, "Censorship and Propaganda," 207.

15. Quoted in Hollmann, "Die Gründung des Reichsarchivs," 47. Seeckt's "Denkschrift über die Zukunft der Archive und kriegsgeschichtlichen Abteilungen des Großen Generalstabes" (Bundesarchiv, BArch R 43 I/866, Bl. 2–17) is reproduced in its entirety as an addendum to Hollmann's article.

16. Quoted in Hollmann, "Die Gründung des Reichsarchivs," 47.

17. Quoted in Hollmann, "Die Gründung des Reichsarchivs," 49.

18. This line, among others, is lifted directly from George Soldan's position statement analyzed below. It appears on page 16, fol. 65 of the Soldan text.

19. Quoted in Hollmann, "Die Gründung des Reichsarchivs," 49.

20. Pöhlmann, *Kriegsgeschichte*, 72.

21. Pöhlmann, *Kriegsgeschichte*, 66.

Quirnheim, as he made Soldan head of a new department for volkstümliche historiography within the General Staff's war history department,[22] a position that was almost identical to the one he then held until 1929 in the Reichsarchiv. Soldan, whose conception of historiography evinced racial, nationalist, and populist *völkisch* ideals, stood in contrast to his superiors at the time, whose prevailing mentalities were aligned more closely with old monarchist worldviews.[23] Pöhlmann stresses that Soldan's text represents the end of the brief period of relatively open critique of the war among the military's highest historians, at the same time that it is "programmatic testament to national revolutionary tendencies in the early Reichswehr."[24] In addition, Soldan's text is a programmatic statement for the methods—textual and visual—employed by his influential section on volkstümliche publications, which produced, among other things, the two illustrated book series "Schlachten des Weltkrieges" and "Erinnerungsblätter deutscher Regimenter."

Central to Soldan's memorandum is the idea that popular history writing is a continuation of the war effort by other means. It has the power to consolidate and sustain nationalist feeling during and after a war if it can appeal to the Volk in the broadest sense. According to Soldan, history writing has three national missions: (1) to raise up a broken people and restore their faith in themselves; (2) to allow a German national feeling to grow that illuminates a path forward through dark times; and (3) to use the educational value of history to lead a people who think and feel apolitically to maturity.[25] Successful "populäre Geschichtsschreibung" (popular historiography) would address the needs of variously educated audiences by balancing general overview, critical assessment, and pure entertainment.[26] Although a "popular" presentation style would not be suited for the planned official and discipline-specific history being written by the German General Staff (and then completed by the Reichsarchiv), "popular" accounts can also not be left to the discretion of private authors, who could not properly complete the intended educational mission of the state.[27] That mission, as Soldan explains, has less to do with informing people of individual events from the war and more to do with evaluating and fixing the meaning of the overall war for the

22. Pöhlmann, *Kriegsgeschichte*, 68.
23. Pöhlmann, *Kriegsgeschichte*, 68.
24. Pöhlmann, *Kriegsgeschichte*, 68.
25. Soldan, "Die deutsche Geschichtsschreibung des Weltkrieges," fol. 64.
26. Soldan, "Die deutsche Geschichtsschreibung des Weltkrieges," fol. 65–69.
27. Soldan, "Die deutsche Geschichtsschreibung des Weltkrieges," fol. 71.

future.[28] His concept of "populäre Geschichtsschreibung" thereby exemplifies an instrumentalization of war memory to educate the public in line with predetermined messaging. The endeavor is measured as a success or failure to the extent that it is able to appeal to the Volk's emotional heart and influence their simultaneous understanding of past and present. Soldan's efforts to reach a broad audience also served the goal of securing the primacy of official government organizations, like the General Staff and then the Reichsarchiv, in the postwar contests of memory.[29]

Although Soldan does not provide an exact list of what content can best serve the three broad "national tasks" of history writing, examples of what shape a positive, nationalist account of the war might take are mentioned in passing throughout his memorandum. The most prevalent and clearly specified aspect is praise of the military's "glorious tradition," which should be portrayed "with wistful warmth."[30] This is the main strategy of the picture book *Deutschland: Ein Buch der Größe und der Hoffnung in Bildern, 1914–1924*, which was produced in collaboration with the Reichsarchiv. As analyzed in the previous chapter, *Deutschland* elided the war's tragic qualities and focused on a celebration of Germany's worldwide reach, its technological superiority, and a sense of adventure during the war. Walter Bloem's introduction to the book shares with Soldan's memorandum the metaphor of light (remembering the war effort) breaking through dark and shadowy times (the postwar present). Affirmations of the military do not at first glance appear political, especially in comparison to the radical messages of picture books like Ernst Friedrich's *Krieg dem Kriege!* But the strategy espoused by Soldan and evinced in *Deutschland*, for example, intentionally uses more subtle methods to influence positive feelings about patriotism and the nation. It may not concern itself with the partisan rhetoric of the current political situation, but praise for the war effort, even after resounding defeat, gave new life to the nationalist and chauvinistic mentalities of Germany's old military elite. In Ziemann's assessment, the Reichsarchiv's publication efforts that eventually put into practice the theory behind Soldan's 1919 manuscript, including the two volkstümlich-conceived illustrated book series produced by Soldan's department, contained "hardly any outright glorification of war."[31] "But that was part of their success," Ziemann claims, "and a deliberate attempt to dif-

28. Soldan, "Die deutsche Geschichtsschreibung des Weltkrieges," fol. 72.
29. Pöhlmann, *Kriegsgeschichte*, 196.
30. Soldan, "Die deutsche Geschichtsschreibung des Weltkrieges," fol. 69.
31. Ziemann, *Contested Commemorations*, 223.

fuse any remaining bitterness about the war experience."[32] The popular picture book *Deutschland* stretches the limits of such a categorization, however, as its celebration of the war effort is inextricably tied to nationalist rhetoric about the Volk in the postwar era, a mode of interpreting the war that is at its most extreme in the ultraconservative picture books of Franz Schauwecker, in which the metaphysical experience of war creates a new breed of man who will carry the banner of nationalism (as will be explored in chapter 5).

In another obvious sense, Soldan's conception of war-historical writing—spearheaded as it was by many former General Staff officers—is cast in light of adversarial mentalities that persisted even after the war ended and military historians like himself were rehoused in the civilian Reichsarchiv. He repeatedly stresses the competitive nature of war memory, in which the work of war historians must reckon with the accounts of Germany's enemies (*feindliche Staaten*[33]). Historians must keep tabs on the shape of war narratives and stand ready to intervene should any misrepresentation deserve criticism and correction. For this reason, history writing must stand in close cooperation with broader networks of the publishing world, which can disseminate the aforementioned volkstümlich representations of war that are useful for influencing opinion. "The German interpretation of the war must prevail," Soldan asserts.[34]

It is clear from the Reichsarchiv's publication output that the organization broadly recognized the usefulness of photography in appealing to popular audiences and crafting suitable interpretations of the war. They understood that photographic illustration could be useful—following Soldan's ideas—for balancing the competing needs of detail and overview, analysis and entertainment. And although it was left unsaid, photographic illustration was also employed to obscure the political as apolitical under claims of photographic authenticity. Soldan makes limited mention of photography in his 1919 memorandum, although the few references are illuminating to understand how he and his colleagues in the section for volkstümliche publications valued the medium.

Soldan praises Franz Kugler's 1840 illustrated history of Friedrich the Great, which contained woodcuts by Adolph Menzel, as an example of how historiography can be *populär* and *volkstümlich*. In Soldan's view, such illustrations were an important aspect of a book's form if the author wanted to

32. Ziemann, *Contested Commemorations*, 223.

33. Soldan, "Die deutsche Geschichtsschreibung des Weltkrieges," fol. 78.

34. Soldan, "Die deutsche Geschichtsschreibung des Weltkrieges," fol. 66.

speak to the "Volkssinn" (spirit of the people) and attract interest among readers.[35] In contrast to book packaging that is "too cold and too sober," if a picture was included on the cover of a book—for example, a representative scene from a battle described in the text—the book would better catch the buyer's eye.[36] With a title that "promises something in and of itself and entices you to buy it," such a volkstümlich-conceived book would be hard for any buyer to pass up, he claims, even for someone who was crippled during the portrayed battle![37] Soldan also praises the exemplary use of pictures and picture albums in the official account of the Russo-Japanese War produced by the Japanese General Staff. In writing their historiography of the war, the Japanese General Staff smartly supported popular, richly illustrated works by officers and published their own collection of pictures in "tasteful" albums.[38] Soldan's early praise for picture books acquires special significance in this book for the way it presages many of the methods used in Soldan's own later involvement with picture books. He introduced the first volume of *Der Weltkrieg im Bild* (The World War in pictures), published in two lengthy volumes around 1926, and authored *Zeitgeschichte in Wort und Bild* (Contemporary history in words and pictures), a similarly monumental visual account of the postwar era published in three thick volumes from 1930 to 1934.

Before turning to Soldan's own picture books, the role of photography in the two series published by his department for volkstümliche publications at the Reichsarchiv should be considered. Neither the "Schlachten des Weltkrieges" (Battles of the World War; 36 volumes, 1925–31) nor the "Erinnerungsblätter deutscher Regimenter" (Commemoration papers of German regiments; over 250 volumes from 1920 to 1928) are primarily focused on photographic representations of the war, but they employ photography as an aid in fulfilling some of the strategies laid out in Soldan's 1919 essay on *populär* and *volkstümlich* history writing. These include the straightforward tasks of making the volumes more attractive to a broad reading audience and showing the military in a positive light. The latter was the overall approach of the two series, as they sought to foster—in contrast to the professional and sober language of official histories—the recovery of personal experiences by focusing attention on the actions of individuals within a larger framework.[39] The result of such personal engagement with war memory was intended

35. Soldan, "Die deutsche Geschichtsschreibung des Weltkrieges," fol. 72.
36. Soldan, "Die deutsche Geschichtsschreibung des Weltkrieges," fol. 73.
37. Soldan, "Die deutsche Geschichtsschreibung des Weltkrieges," fol. 73.
38. Soldan, "Die deutsche Geschichtsschreibung des Weltkrieges," fol. 57.
39. Pöhlmann, *Kriegsgeschichte*, 195–96.

as "positive meaning-making and glorification," as Pöhlmann calls it,[40] and was certainly aided by the use of photography to illustrate exciting details of the war (seen in the "Schlachten" series) and to elicit reverential pride in one's military service (seen in the "Erinnerungsblätter"). Although they did not explicitly thematize photography or deploy it in a critical manner, these two Reichsarchiv projects used photography to reawaken and capitalize on interest in the war. Their lack of meta-reflection on the meaning of photography in picturing and remembering the war enables a seemingly naturalistic presentation common among other popular postwar pictorial representations. In this mode, photographs are employed as mere aids of illustration, complementing the text in ways that do not attempt to create their own meaning, for example, through techniques of sequencing and collage or combinations of text and image. But the reduction of photography to illustration does not always follow intended routes and appears only on the surface as "realistic" or apolitical. Selective editing ensures that photographs amplify underlying messages, and even individual photographs can generate connotations that the text cannot contain. As seen in the following examples from the two volkstümliche book series produced under Soldan's leadership, the propagandistic overtones of the Reichsarchiv's conservative, military-affirming war historiography remain largely absent in the actual text but are nevertheless sustained by the photographs.

The first series created under Soldan's direction in Reichsarchiv Department G, the section on volkstümliche historiography, was the "Erinnerungsblätter deutscher Regimenter." Produced in close collaboration between the Reichsarchiv and representatives of military regiments, the "Erinnerungsblätter" served as chronological histories of individual regiments during the war and as a book of memory for their members. While the volumes were initiated by outside authors or regimental associations, the Reichsarchiv not only provided assistance in locating the appropriate archival records for the undertaking but also played an active role in the resulting manuscripts' formulation and editing. In some instances, Reichsarchiv employees, many of them former military men themselves, authored the histories of regiments in which they served. Soldan, for example, opened the series with his 1920 treatment of the 184th Infantry Regiment and offered it to other authors as an example to be followed. External authors were required to submit their manuscripts to the Reichsarchiv for approval and even signed a contract that said they would accept any suggested revisions. Such censorship was

40. Pöhlmann, *Kriegsgeschichte*, 196.

needed to ensure that the "Erinnerungsblätter" were free of any critique of the military and commentary on domestic or foreign politics.[41]

At the same time that the "Erinnerungsblätter" did not put into practice the more propagandistic conception of military history envisioned in Soldan's 1919 memorandum,[42] its role in the postwar era in fostering pride and nostalgia for the military, a type of opinion-shaping in and of itself, should not be underestimated. Following the Versailles Treaty, many regiments were disbanded as part of the military's radical downsizing, erasing many of the institutionalized bonds of comradeship among military men. The "Erinnerungsblätter" served to fill these gaps where the new, smaller Reichswehr could not maintain the breadth of military tradition.[43] The preservation of tradition was not limited to mere organizational continuity after Versailles but worked also to influence popular attitudes about the military and the war; as seen above, Soldan asserted in 1919 that military traditions must be portrayed "with wistful warmth."[44] Such positive accounts were achieved partially by the Reichsarchiv's ban on critique of the military and partially through the reverential praise of servicemen, especially the dead. Although the main bodies of text in the "Erinnerungsblätter" were devoted to the rather methodical recounting of a regiment's activities during the war based on official daily records, their introductions, afterwords, and photographic illustrations are laden with the type of pathos meant to reawaken reverence for the war effort despite the great tragedy of it all. What George Mosse called the "cult of the fallen soldier" is on full display in the "Erinnerungsblätter" as devotion to the dead serves to "overcome the sense of loss many veterans felt for their fallen comrades and help fashion a new solidarity."[45]

A closer look at just three of the hundreds of volumes confirms the central role that photographs played in the series' titular project of commemoration. *Das 4. Garde-Regiment zu Fuß* (1924), *Geschichte des Garde-Füsilier-Regiments* (1926), and *Kaiser-Franz-Garde-Grenadier-Regiment Nr. 2* (1929), although all histories of important Prussian *Garderegimente*, are representative of the uniformity across the series in content and form. Along with the aforementioned chronology of events, many photographs (in these examples 50–200, depending on overall book length) are spaced regularly throughout

41. Pöhlmann, *Kriegsgeschichte*, 198–99.
42. Pöhlmann, *Kriegsgeschichte*, 199.
43. Pöhlmann, *Kriegsgeschichte*, 198.
44. Soldan, "Die deutsche Geschichtsschreibung des Weltkrieges," fol. 69.
45. Mosse, *Fallen Soldiers*, 78.

the text. The photographs are tailored specifically to the regiment, being either general photographs from the war that cannot be tied directly to the regiment but show places the regiment stayed, or specific photographs of the regiments themselves, often with captions that identify pictured members. Official portraits of regimental leaders and those of the higher officer classes are common, especially near the beginning of the books (see fig. 29). Just like the textual history of a regiment's day-to-day deployment, these photographs served veterans as cues to remember their time during the war and think of their comrades. Each book also contains four to five map inserts that provide a general overview of the arena where the regiment served and more specific views of battles pertinent to the regiment's history. These diagrams helped soldiers to situate their memory in physical space, literally mapping their memory to geography.

The maps and photographs not only served as a guide for soldiers to recall and secure their own memory but also functioned as an explanatory aid when talking with others, such as family members. In the same way a veteran could take out the map inserts to trace and point out to others his position in the war's grand scheme, photographs stimulated the process of remembering for soldiers. They condensed memory into a handful of iconographic visual representations that were meaningful to themselves and also useful for relaying memories to others in a way that was more immediate than through the main text's long and detailed textual chronologies. In this way, photographic illustrations extended the books' possible appeal beyond the *Erinnerung* within the regimental circle, contrary to Soldan's assertion that they would be of little entertainment or educational value.[46] The series' authors are cognizant of the volumes' communicative function and often express the hope that future generations will be interested in what the series attests to. For example, the foreword to *Geschichte des Garde-Füsilier-Regiments* ends with the confirmation that the regiment no longer exists, but its "glory is immortal." Its author continues: "May our children and grandchildren also be inspired by that glorious spirit of the past. Let God ordain it!"[47]

Coupled with the laudatory declarations of honor directed at the fallen, the high prevalence of photographs showing regimental cemeteries, memorial plaques, and individual graves indicates the central memorial function of photographs in the series. Pictures of the fallen, represented through the

46. Quoted in Pöhlmann, *Kriegsgeschichte*, 200.
47. Schulenburg-Wolfsburg, *Geschichte des Garde-Füsilier-Regiments*, 8.

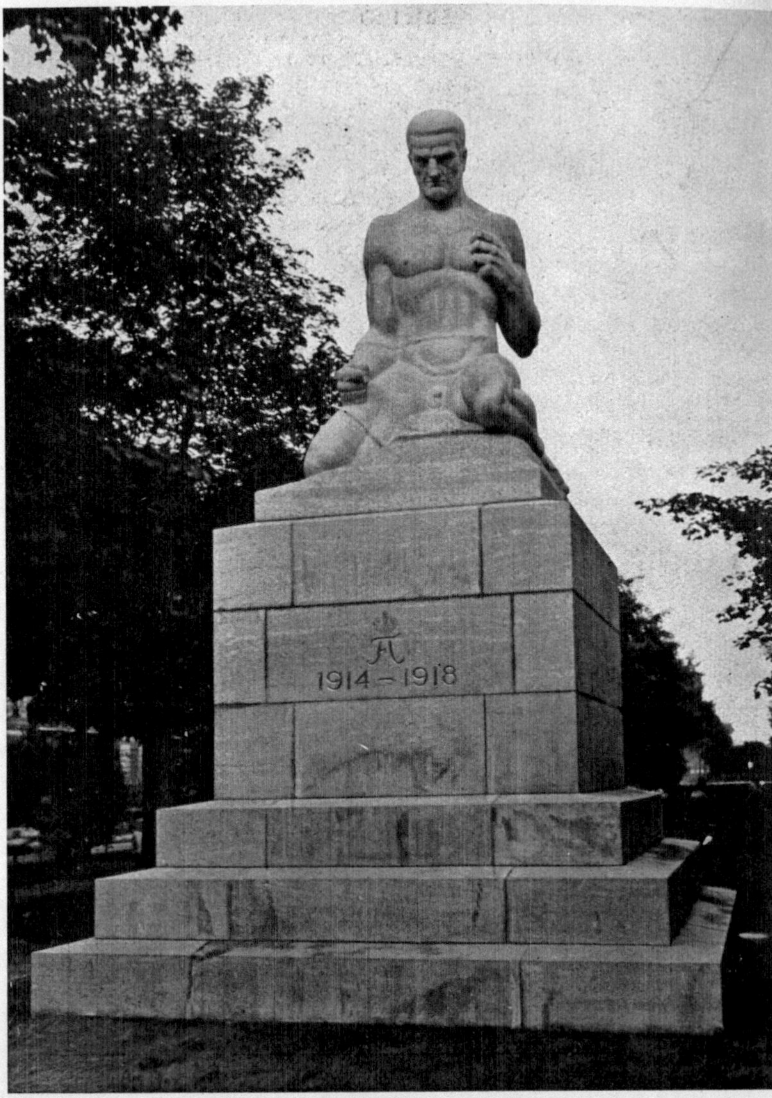

Das Denkmal des Franz-Regts. bei der Kaserne
Invictis — Victi — Victuri!

Fig. 30. Heinrich von Rieben, *Kaiser-Franz-Garde-Grenadier-Regiment Nr. 2* (Volume 279 of the "Commemoration papers of German regiments") (Oldenburg/Berlin: Stalling, 1929), plate 25.

visual metonym of their graves, served living veterans or relatives of fallen soldiers as a conduit for remembering the dead. Supplementing the ceremonies that commemorated the war and the popular pilgrimages made to war cemeteries on the Western Front,[48] the "Erinnerungsblätter" became accessible, personal, and emotionally charged totems of war memory. Mosse explains that physical objects and public places, such as war monuments and cemeteries, recouped the dead's symbolic meaning and elevated their deaths to that of a sacrifice for the nation. Following his assertion that the resting places of the dead became "shrines of national worship" and transformed the fallen soldiers into "symbols which people could see and touch and which made their cult come alive,"[49] the pervasive attention to the dead in the "Erinnerungsblätter" cannot be construed as apolitical. The "cult of the fallen soldier" was ultimately dominated by forces on the right, who used the myth of the war experience to help "transcend the horror of war" and "support the utopia which nationalism sought to project as an alternative to the reality of postwar Germany."[50] Although the Reichsarchiv actively sought to downplay the connection between the war experience portrayed in the "Erinnerungsblätter" and postwar politics, the link inheres in subtle ways. In the afterword to *Das 4. Garde-Regiment zu Fuß*, Wilhelm Reinhard, regimental commander, explicitly ties the task of remembering the dead to national rebuilding, while evincing the revisionist history of the war as a war of German defense: "Deep in the hearts of the German people lies the attachment to those magnificent regiments that marched to France in the sun-drenched days of August 1914 and protected Germany's borders for 4½ years. The longing for them brings a resurrection. May the violets grow again after the storm and winter!"[51] Such arguments may not be found in all volumes of the series, but the photographs of cemeteries and similar tributes are always present, triggering the type of mentalities that contributed to the "cult of the fallen soldier." One telling example from *Kaiser Franz-Garde-Grenadier-Regiment Nr. 2* is the photograph (fig. 30) of a large monument for the regiment, a tall, multi-tiered marble plinth adorned with the statue of a kneeling man whose gaze is directed downwards. The picture precedes the "Ehrentafel," a list of the regi-

48. For a discussion of how the staging of war cemeteries and postwar tourist trips to the Western Front reinforced frames of interpreting the war as a war of defense and contributed to a masking of the harsh reality of defeat that was tied to patterns of wartime propaganda, see Brandt, "Bilder von der Zerstörung," especially 444–49.

49. Mosse, *Fallen Soldiers*, 80.

50. Mosse, *Fallen Soldiers*, 106.

51. Reinhard, *Das 4. Garde-Regiment zu Fuß*, 402.

ment's fallen officers, and is captioned "Invictus—Victi—Victuri!"—a phrase that reaffirms the connection between the war dead and a future victorious tribe, the German nation implied in the "cult of the fallen soldier."[52]

Photographs played a similar role in the second series produced under George Soldan's leadership at the Reichsarchiv, the "Schlachten des Weltkrieges." It was focused on recounting the course of individual battles from the war as a supplement to the general history being prepared by the Reichsarchiv. A central idea of the 1919 memorandum on popular historiography was that the less-educated classes of the Volk were fixated on the details of battles, and to provide such individual accounts to readers allowed them to engage on an emotional level with the war. The "Schlachten des Weltkrieges" series translated this into practice through its content as well as its form: famous battles, portrayed in an accessible writing style by established authors, were of more universal interest than the often mundane regimental histories of the "Erinnerungsblätter," and thinner volumes with a uniform layout that could be sold cheaply were better sellers than the Reichsarchiv's monumental official history.[53] Reichsarchiv president Mertz von Quirnheim claims in the introduction to the second edition of *Douaumont* (1925) by Werner Beumelburg, the first volume in the series, that "the effort to help save the individual deeds of German men from oblivion and to erect a monument to the heroes of the war for their struggle and sacrifice has found universal approval and support."[54]

With a heavy emphasis on text, the 36 volumes in the series, published in five years between 1925 and 1930, do not primarily count as picture books. Nine volumes in the series, including the last three, do not contain a single photograph, and the average number of photographs per volume can be estimated around 20 to 30. However, like the "Erinnerungsblätter," the majority of volumes incorporated photographs—and, as analyzed below, drawn illustrations—to complement the text, and these extend the series' symbolic and ideological purpose. A look through all 36 volumes reveals the predominance of only a few categories of photographs: wide landscapes showing the terrain of battlefields and surrounding areas, including trenches and other points of interest, such as castles, churches, and villages; views of destruction, including before and after shots of ruined forts, villages, and natural landscapes;

52. Rieben, *Kaiser Franz-Garde-Grenadier-Regiment Nr. 2.* The Latin translates as "the unconquered—the (having been) conquered—the going to conquer."

53. Pöhlmann, *Kriegsgeschichte,* 197–99.

54. Mertz von Quirnheim, "Vorwort des Reichsarchivs," 5.

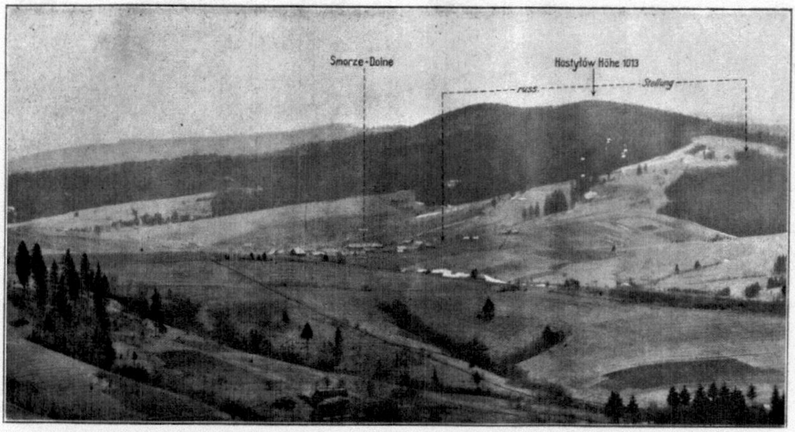

Angriffsgelände der Garde-Füsiliere südlich Smorze am 31.1.1915 (von der Misiowka-Höhe südwestlich Krasne gesehen).

Fig. 31. Friedrich von Friedeburg, *Karpathen- und Dnester-Schlacht 1915* (Battle of the Carpathian Mountains and the Dniester 1915; volume 2 of "Battles of the World War") (Oldenburg/Berlin: Stalling, 1925), plate 3.

official portraits of generals, field marshals, and other commanding officers; group shots of foreign prisoners of war, never German; and commemorative images of German cemeteries, funerary monuments, and war graves. Each of these broad categories has a role in the basic illustration of the text, but also carries, in varying proportion, secondary connotations that increase the symbolic meaning of the depicted battles to include, even in the cases of harsh defeat, repeated affirmations of the war experience and its heroes.

The first category of landscapes is used primarily as a visual guide to orient readers into the space of the represented conflict that is treated with a high level of detail in the text. The category is useful for establishing the visual "facts" of what a specific battle was like and often incorporates panoramas of battle terrain that have been marked with identifying information. An example in the second volume in the series, *Karpathen- und Dnester-Schlacht 1915* (Battle of the Carpathian Mountains and the Dniester; 1925), shows German positions on a specific day of fighting in the Carpathian Mountains (fig. 31). Other typical photographs in this category show the infrastructure of war, including trenches, forts, and the transport network used to support the front. At times, however, the photographs stray from technical knowledge about the battle at hand and support a broader tourist's view of the world. This is especially the case for volumes 4 and 16, titled

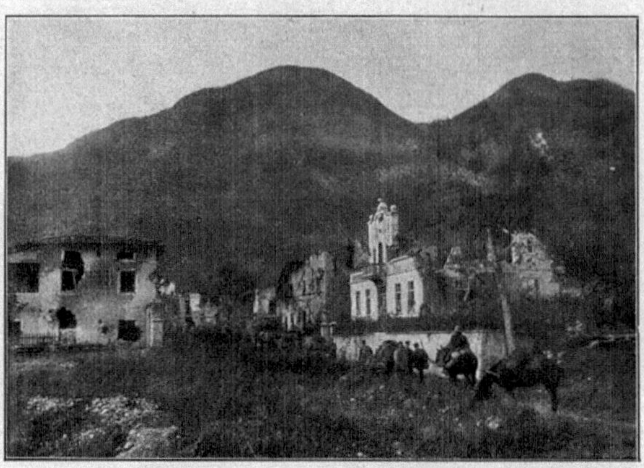

Woltschach.

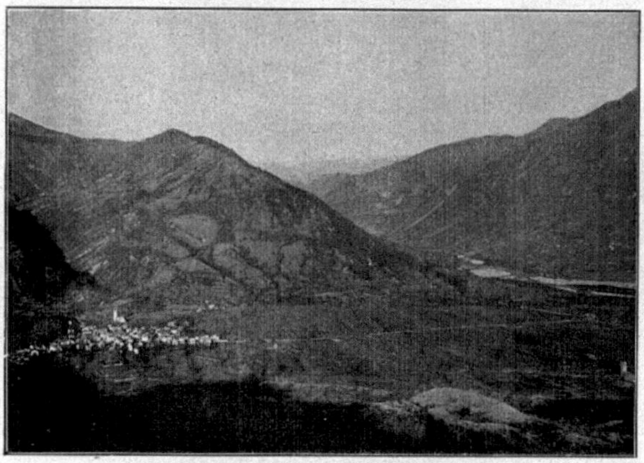

Woltschach (von Sv. Maria aus).

Fig. 32. Konrad Krafft von Dellmensingen, *Der Durchbruch am Isonzo, Teil I: Die Schlacht von Tolmein und Flitsch* (Breakthrough on the Isonzo, Part 2: The battle of Tolmein and Flitsch; volume 12a of "Battles of the World War") (Oldenburg/Berlin: Stalling, 1926), plate 6.

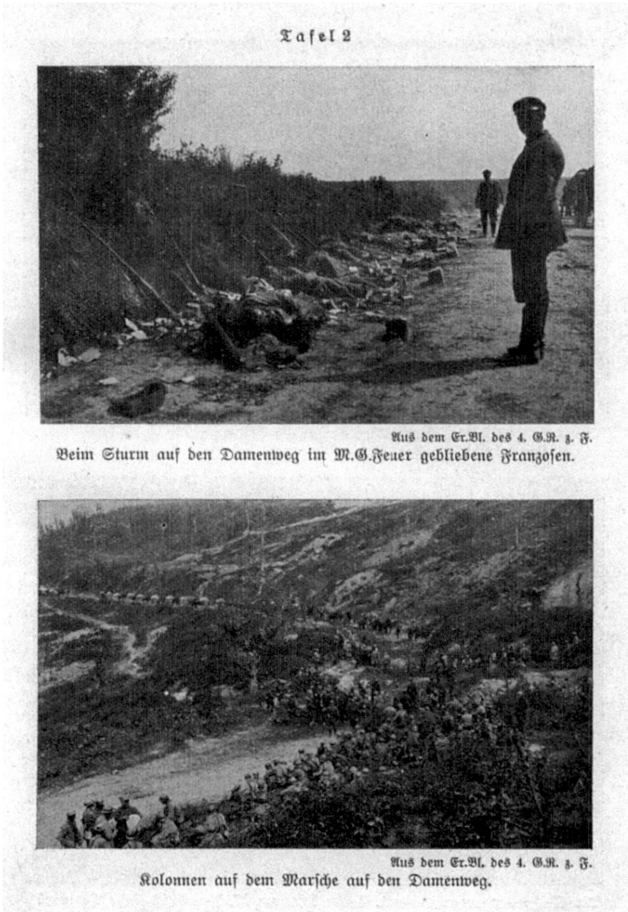

Fig. 33. Thilo von Bose, *Deutsche Siege 1918* (German victories 1918; volume 32 of "Battles of the World War") (Oldenburg/Berlin: Stalling, 1929), plate 2.

Jildirim: Deutsche Streiter auf heiligem Boden (German fighters in the Holy Land) and *Der Kampf um die Dardanellen 1915* (The fight for the Dardanelles). In those volumes, which count among the series' most richly illustrated, the visual depiction of the war becomes exoticized, for example, in photographs of a water seller in Aleppo,[55] or Turkish oxen and camel convoys.[56]

55. Steuber, *Jildirim: Deutsche Streiter auf heiligem Boden*, insert before page 49.
56. Mühlmann, *Der Kampf um die Dardanellen 1915*, plate 4.

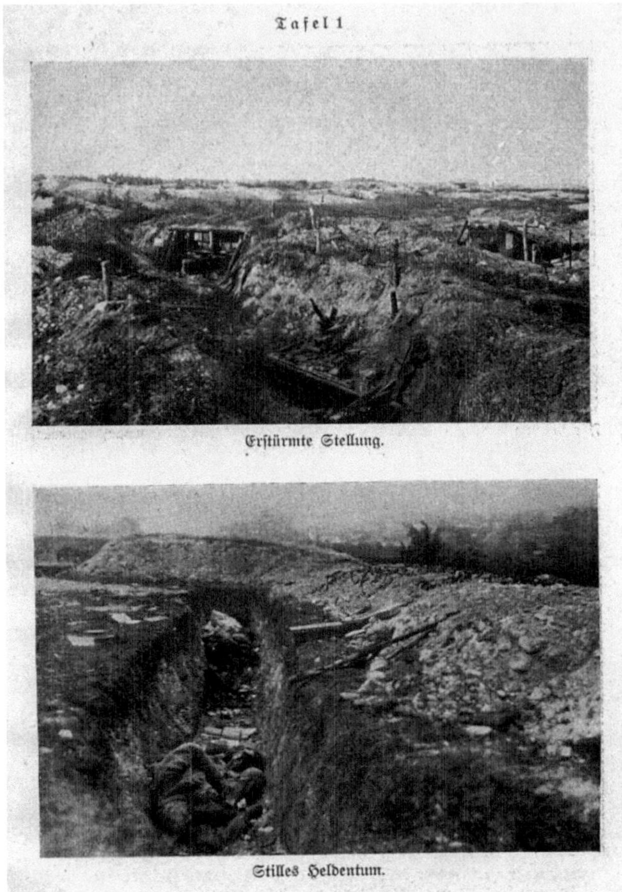

Fig. 34. Thilo von Bose, *Wachsende Schwierigkeiten 1918* (Mounting difficulties; volume 33 of "Battles of the World War") (Oldenburg/Berlin: Stalling, 1930), plate 1.

The series' voyeurism, however, is at its peak in the many views of the war's destruction. Before-and-after shots, like the aerial images of Fort Vaux in volume 14, *Die Tragödie von Verdun 1916, Teil II* (The tragedy of Verdun 1916, part two), give a spatially and metaphorically distanced glimpse into destruction.[57] Views of destroyed villages, such as those in northern Italy in volume 12, *Der Durchbruch am Isonzo* (Breakthrough on the Isonzo) (fig. 32),

57. Schwenke, *Die Tragödie von Verdun 1916*, plate 1.

or of nature turned into wasteland, such as the forests of Argonne in volume 18, *Argonnen*,[58] give a similarly detached impression of conflict. The same cannot be said for photographs of dead soldiers and civilians. Although they are rare in the overall series, the pictures have the highest potential to evoke an emotional response that would stray from largely positive messaging about the war. While the series freely acknowledges the horrors of war in its text, and it seems that the photographs of death complement this objective historical representation, it is significant that this category contains photographs showing only enemy dead. Pöhlmann maintains that Soldan did not want to repress the horrors of war in the volkstümliche series so much as he wanted to create an encounter with the war that fostered "positive meaning-making and glorification."[59] Accordingly, photographs of the war dead in the "Schlachten" series do not hide death or destruction from view, but they are framed in a German-positive interpretation by being labeled the effect of German military might. Three examples fix this connection: the caption of a picture of dead horses and French soldiers lying next to cannons states explicitly that they were killed by the 28th Field Artillery Regiment;[60] a photograph of "Frenchmen who remained in machine gun fire during the storming of the Chemin des Dames" displays a German soldier looking over a line of dead Frenchmen, and the image below that shows a column of German soldiers marching onwards, apparently triumphant when considered in relation to the photograph above (fig. 33); finally, a snapshot of a trench position captured by the Germans is coupled with a photograph of a dead French soldier lying on his side in the trenches—although it is labeled "silent heroism," he is marked a victim of the might implied by the above "assault" (fig. 34).[61] These photographs of war violence would be at home in a work like Ernst Friedrich's *Krieg dem Kriege!*, but they have been channeled differently and thereby been given a different significance. With no photographic representation of dead German soldiers in the entire series, "Schlachten des Weltkrieges" reinforces chauvinistic war attitudes of Germany conquering its enemies at the same time that it creates space for a different, more heroic, and more dignified representation of death in the photographs of German cemeteries and memorials.

In the same way that photographs of the dead turn Germany's enemies

58. Schmidt, *Argonnen*, plate 5.

59. Pöhlmann, *Kriegsgeschichte*, 196.

60. Bose, *Das Marnedrama 1914, Teil III*, plate 2.

61. The photograph is separately labeled "fallen Frenchman" in the German Federal Archives collection (Bild 102–00170A, Westfront, Gefallener Franzose).

into the faceless product of its war machine, photographs from two further categories reinforce chauvinistic attitudes that may otherwise be absent from the text. The first is composed of portraits of leading battle commanders, and the second of photographs of POWs. Most of the volumes contain at least one portrait of a commanding officer; some volumes, such as volume 7, *Die Schlacht bei St. Quentin 1914* (The Battle of Saint-Quentin), incorporate over twenty such photographs (see fig. 29). These portraits give a face to the most important commanders during various battles, a critical aspect of war historiography in the eyes of Soldan, who called it "the human side of the decisive personalities" in his 1919 memorandum on writing popular war history.[62] Beyond a simple visual representation of the leaders that controlled the course of battles described in the text, the portraits mark the men as Germany's most honorable heroes, reinforce reverence for their authority, and hold them up as role models for a postwar era. Such a positive representation of the officer class and those above was an important goal for the former military elite, including leaders at the Reichsarchiv and the individually approved authors who penned the "Schlachten" volumes, many former officers themselves, often with noble titles. Raising the prestige of commanders through such reverential portraits could play a part in counteracting influential republican war accounts that focused on indicting the corruption of the *Etappe*, the physical and metaphorical space between the front lines of common soldiers and the military's Wilhelmine officer corps, the term being used as a derisive metonym for the latter group. Republican war memory used the *Etappensumpf* (the *Etappe* swamp) idea to highlight the economic disparity between the military's classes, to paint a picture of staff officers' incompetence and cowardice, and to assert the primacy of republican war accounts in the postwar memory contests. All three tasks shared in the end goal of legitimizing socialism and democracy in the new republic, contrary to the nationalism and authoritarianism that existed in many shades among the former military elite and more extreme right-wing circles.[63]

Photographs of POWs reinforce the message of German military might over its enemies in the same manner as the photographs of exclusively non-German victims of war. Of the 27 volumes in the "Schlachten" series that contain photographs, eight also contain photographs of foreign POWs.

62. Soldan, "Die deutsche Geschichtsschreibung des Weltkrieges," fol. 56. In this use of "Persönlichkeiten," Soldan means the leading commanders of a war, not the average soldier, as he makes a parenthetical reference to Aleksey Kuropatkin, Russian imperial minister of war, when discussing the historiography of the Russo-Japanese War.

63. Ziemann, *Contested Commemorations*, 48.

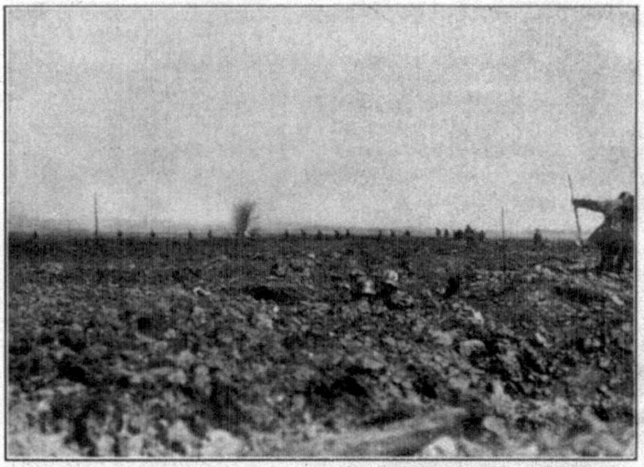

Deutsche Infanterie greift an.

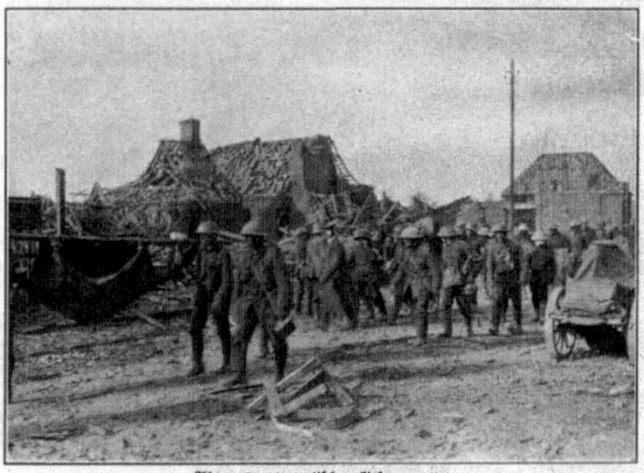

Abtransport englischer Gefangener.

Fig. 35. Franz Berhmann, *Die Osterschlacht bei Arras 1917, I. Teil: Zwischen Lens und Scarpe* (The Easter battle near Arras 1917: Between Lens and the Scarpe; volume 28 of "Battles of the World War") (Oldenburg/Berlin: Stalling, 1929), plate 3.

Although not the largest category of photographs in the series, it is one that appears frequently enough to draw attention, especially since its ability to illustrate any historical fact is far outweighed by its obvious patriotic employment. Take for instance a pair of images (fig. 35) from volume 28, *Die Osterschlacht bei Arras 1917: Zwischen Lens und Scarpe* (The Easter battle near Arras 1917: Between Lens and the Scarpe). At the top of the page an image captioned "German infantry attack" shows German troops advancing across a flat, trench landscape, pictured from a far distance. (Whether the image shows an actual battle or a training exercise is unclear.) Below it is a photograph showing English POWs, pictured in very close proximity. The juxtaposition of the two photographs creates an implicit connection between them, although they are not explicitly linked to the same events by any supporting textual information. The pair attests to the apparent fact of victory in the top photograph's action by proudly displaying the bounty of said action, the English prisoners of war in the bottom image. What explanatory worth either picture alone has in a series that is devoted to an accessible yet technical account of military tactics is open to debate. However, the connotation created between the photographs as a pair goes beyond objective information to generate the type of military-affirming, patriotic message that was expected under Reichsarchiv historiographical theory and practice.

In summarizing the role "Schlachten des Weltkrieges" had in shaping war memory, Pöhlmann dismisses the idea that the series partook in revisionist discourses surrounding the state of politics and governance after defeat and the Treaty of Versailles. He calls the texts "unspectacular tactical war historiographies,"[64] and he understands the series' pleas to remember the war dead, often found in the volumes' introductions and dedications and cast as a call of reinvigoration for a future national greatness, as largely posturing.[65] The series does not trade in the techno-futuristic and nihilistic myth of the *Frontkämpfer* (frontline warrior), born from the industrial war of attrition at Verdun and the Somme, for example, that would pervade later, more extreme nationalist accounts (including Franz Schauwecker's picture book *So war der Krieg!*). In contrast, the "Schlachten" series adheres to an earlier strand of war interpretation: the contemplative, quasi-religious myth of the heroic victimhood of fallen soldiers, like those from the disaster at the Battle of Langemarck, whose deaths early in the war were used to transform physi-

64. Pöhlmann, *Kriegsgeschichte*, 216.
65. Pöhlmann, *Kriegsgeschichte*, 214.

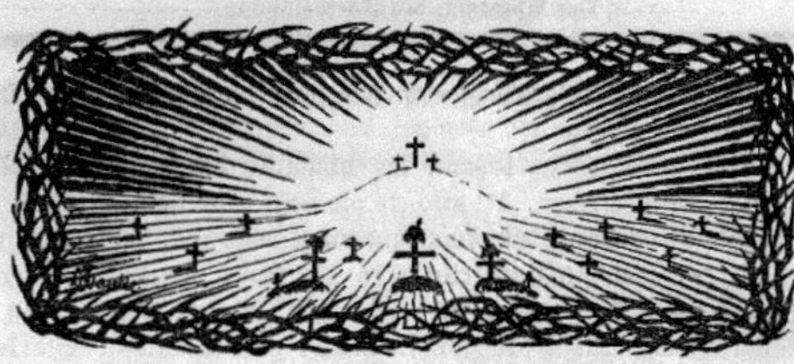

VII.

Allerseelen.

2. November 1916.

Einen ganzen Tag lang war das Fort leer*). Zwischen dem Abgang der Deutschen und dem Einzug der Franzosen gehörte Fort Vaux den Toten. Dieser Tag, das Schicksal hatte es so gefügt, war der Tag „Allerseelen".

„Ein Tag im Jahre ist den Toten frei!" (H. v. Gilm.)

In den Gängen und Kasematten, in den Gräben vereinen sich die Geister der Gefallenen. Sie ordnen sich nach Regimentern: Die vom R.J.R.6, R.J.R. 19 und R.J.R. 37, die in Frost und Schnee beim Sturm dahinsanken; die von R.J.R. 98, J.R. 155, Füs.R. 37, Res.Jäg. 5, die am Hange des Berges zu Winters Ausgang die Wacht hielten; die von R.J.R. 7 und J.R. 60, die an seinem Fuße im kalten April endeten; die lange Reihe der Toten der 50. J.D., die die Nr. 39, 53 und 158 trugen, die von J.R. 126, 143, 132, 172, die von bayr. R.J.R. 15, die im nassen Frühjahr, in des Sommers Hitze und in kühlen Herbstnächten hier litten und starben; die von J.R. 105 und 192, von 245 und Ers. 23, noch umbraust von den letzten Stürmen auf dem Vaux-Berg; und alle diese mit ihren treuen Kameraden, den Pionieren. Die da um die Trümmer schwebten und wogten, waren unsere Brüder, waren Söhne aller deutschen Gaue: Ostpreußen, Schlesier, Posener, Brandenburger, von der Wasser-

*) Nach H. Bordeaux betrat die erste französische Patrouille das Fort am 3.11. in der ersten Morgenstunde.

Fig. 36. Alexander Schwenke, *Die Tragödie von Verdun 1916, Teil II, Das Ringen um Fort Vaux* (The tragedy of Verdun 1916, part two, the struggle for Fort Vaux; volume 14 of "Battles of the World War") (Oldenburg/Berlin: Stalling, 1928), page 222.

cal defeat into a symbolic moral victory.[66] However, because the series was written and produced by former military staff—many carrying names from the Wilhelmine nobility—with a near monopoly on the military files held by the Reichsarchiv, the publications were, in the assessment of historian Alan Kramer, "not surprisingly tendentious and generally uncritical of the army" and exhibit a certain amount of "distortions and suppression of evidence."[67]

While text in the "Schlachten" series remains removed in most ways from contentious postwar debates about the conflict's legacy, including the "stab in the back" and the founding of the Weimar Republic, Pöhlmann notes correctly that the illustrations in the series sustained the influential nationalist "cult of the fallen soldier" that was monopolized by right-wing commemoration practices.[68] Of special note are the many pen-and-ink drawings made by a handful of artists in a plain graphic style that adorn the beginnings and ends of chapters. They feature predominantly the work of Albert Reich, a war painter whose glorification and romanticization of the war experience matched neatly with the right-wing ideology that would later lead him to become an eager National Socialist and even the co-designer of the first-edition book jacket for *Mein Kampf*.[69] One telling example of Reich's work in blending military and religious symbols is the illustration of an Iron Cross extending into a cross of Christ, intersected by two bayonets and surrounded by a palm laurel wreath.[70] The religious overtones Mosse characterizes in the "cult of the fallen soldier"[71] are thereby embodied in the compact visual symbols of drawn illustrations in the "Schlachten" series. The war effort is made meaningful with reference to principles of Christian religious tradition, including the analogy of youthful sacrifice in war to the Passion and resurrection of Christ.[72] Visual signs of such rebirth can be found in an illustration showing cemetery crosses silhouetted by a radiant rising sun, an image that is repeated in multiple variations across the series. In another transparent example (fig. 36) from volume 14, *Die Tragödie von Verdun 1916: Das Ringen um Fort Vaux* (The tragedy of Verdun 1916: The struggle for Fort Vaux), three graves of soldiers, marked by crosses with helmets atop, are paralleled by three crosses on a distant hill, recalling those at Christ's crucifixion. Radiant light beams emanate from the hill, drawing the soldiers' graves

66. Pölhmann, *Kriegsgeschichte*, 214–15. See also Hüppauf, "Schlachtenmythen."
67. Kramer, "The First World War," 388.
68. Pöhlmann, *Kriegsgeschichte*, 214.
69. Schweizer, "*Unserer Weltanschauung sichtbaren Ausdruck geben*," 111.
70. Pöhlmann, *Kriegsgeschichte*, 214.
71. See his chapter by the same name in *Fallen Soldiers*, especially 75–80.
72. See Mosse, *Fallen Soldiers*, 74.

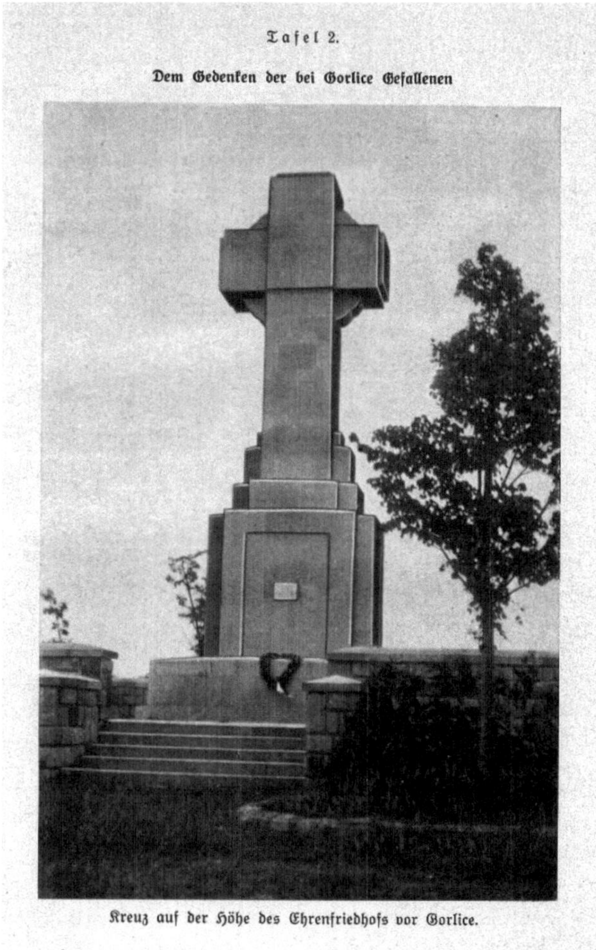

Fig. 37. Oskar Tile von Kalm, *Gorlice* (volume 30 of "Battles of the World War") (Oldenburg/Berlin: Stalling, 1930), plate 2.

toward the Christian crosses and the concomitant promise of resurrection. Such drawn illustrations fit into a broader trend among postwar authors and artists to reemploy earlier visual motifs, like those from illustrated histories of the Franco-Prussian War, in order to stabilize the Great War's meaning in line with reassuring patriotism from the post-unification era.[73]

73. Fox, *Image of the Soldier*, 12.

The "cult of the fallen soldier" is not limited to the idealized visual representation of drawn illustrations and is complemented less abstractly by the final prominent category of photographs in the "Schlachten" series: those of graves and memorials, ranging from the modest "Soldatenfriedhof in der Schlamm-Mulde" (Soldier cemetery in a muddy basin)[74] to the monumental "Kreuz auf der Höhe des Ehrenfriedhofs vor Gorlice" (Cross at the height of the cemetery of honor near Gorlice) (fig. 37). No matter the complexity of their design, however, the memorials all serve the same function of honoring the dead, and the photographs of them extend the reach of their memorial message beyond their fixed physical location. As in the "Erinnerungsblätter," the photographs allow readers to make a repeated and easy virtual pilgrimage to important sites commemorating the sacrifice of Germany's fallen. In inviting the emotional investment of readers, photographs of cemeteries and memorials, more so than any of the previous categories of photographs in the "Schlachten" series, are inconsequential for the technical description of battles in the text. Their purpose goes beyond a historically objective recounting of the war to foster continued admiration and respect for the fallen soldiers in the postwar era. In this regard, the space for emotional identification opened up by the photographs of war memorials actually went hand-in-hand with the text, which "encouraged readers to situate their own war memories in the complex dynamics of the major battles."[75] By extension of their positive, emotionally invested interpretation of death, the photographs of war memorials can be seen to stand in service to the myth of Langemarck, which interpreted the death of Germany's youth as a willing and heroic sacrifice for the nation in order to turn physical defeat into moral victory. Even when contemporary political issues were actively rejected from the Reichsarchiv series, photographs opened up alternative spaces for connoting the "cult of the fallen soldier," a realm of commemoration that was dominated by the political right for purposes that extended the ideological meaning of remembering the war dead. In this way then, the rather factual text of the "Schlachten" series could not fully circumscribe the meaning of the photographs, as Barthes and other theorists might have it.

The two popular publication series coordinated by George Soldan's department on volkstümliche historiography at the Reichsarchiv may not have completely fulfilled the theoretical ideas on war history as propaganda that can be found in his 1919 memorandum and other contemporaneous

74. Beumelburg, *Loretto*, plate 1.

75. Ziemann, *Contested Commemorations*, 224.

statements from the Reichsarchiv's directors, but they engaged photography and other visual media to shape the form of war memory into one that was more affirmative toward the military and perpetuated influential conservative myths about Germany's war dead. The task was not initially an easy one for the Reichsarchiv, which not only struggled with organizational challenges after its founding but also faced a noteworthy opponent in the war-critical and pro-republican memories that found popular resonance in the first five years after the armistice. Soldan wrote to his superior in 1924 about the uphill struggle nationalist circles faced in trying to circulate positive reminiscences about the war. Not only leftist newspapers but those supporting more moderate parties like the Center Party and the German People's Party seemed hesitant to publish anything positive about the war experience.[76] Ziemann claims that "any efforts to utilize war remembrances for 'nationalist publicity work' had in fact only increased the 'reluctance' of left-leaning and moderate newspapers to print them."[77] However, a shift in outlook occurred with the Ruhr occupation, which fostered a national mood that allowed more nationalist, military-friendly mentalities to prevail, not just in the realm of daily politics but also in the contested arena of war commemoration. The Reichsarchiv capitalized on the shift, as popular series like the "Erinnerungsblätter deutscher Regimenter" and "Schlachten des Weltkrieges," among others produced by the Reichsarchiv,[78] were initiated around the same time (the first volume in the "Schlachten" series, for example, was published in 1925). Ziemann concludes that "with their comprehensive coverage of events, the writings of the Reichsarchiv clearly had a hegemonic position in the popular historiography of the war, at least from the 1920s."[79] The reach of the "Schlachten des Weltkrieges," for example, can be measured in concrete numbers: by 1928 there were 40,000 to 50,000 copies of each volume in circulation.[80]

George Soldan, who led the department for volkstümliche publications and championed theories on war historiography as propaganda that became foundational to the memory politics of the influential Reichsarchiv, left the institution in 1929 and took over the editorship of the military newspaper

76. Ziemann, *Contested Commemorations*, 57.

77. Ziemann, *Contested Commemorations*, 57.

78. See Pöhlmann, *Kriegsgeschichte*, especially chapter 5, "Das publizistische Instrumentarium," 162–247.

79. Ziemann, *Contested Commemorations*, 223.

80. Linder, *Princes of the Trenches*, 183.

Deutsche Wehr.[81] His influence in the realm of picturing the war expanded beyond his functions at the Reichsarchiv, which itself continued to play a central role in the depiction of the war as it held the principal collection of photographs used by independent authors and editors in their own picture books and other war publications. In 1925, Soldan wrote the introduction to the first of two volumes in the series *Der Weltkrieg im Bild* (1926), a monumental collection of photographs from Germany's and the Entente powers' official war archives, and he authored and edited the similarly monumental *Zeitgeschichte in Wort und Bild*, a history of the Weimar era that appeared in three thick volumes from 1931 to 1934.

Soldan's lengthy history of the postwar era in *Zeitgeschichte in Wort und Bild* can be seen as the culmination of some of the theories on popular historiography he put to paper a little over a decade earlier. Although he makes only brief mentions of photography in his 1919 memorandum on "Die deutsche Geschichtsschreibung des Weltkrieges," in the introduction to the first volume of *Zeitgeschichte*, Soldan acknowledges the power of photographs: "The work uses for the first time a presentation style, which, in view of the unprecedentedly well-developed photo reporting of our time, should be available to any historiography of the future that aims to be understandable and convincing."[82] The first volume is indeed richly illustrated: photographs take up over half of the space on more than 500 pages, with every right-hand page devoted to larger images (with the exception of the beginning of chapters) and with smaller photographs frequently mixed in with the text of the left-hand pages. At first glance, the book's inner design is far more dynamic than other picture books, including *Der Weltkrieg im Bild.* Photographs are variously sized and arranged on the page, and their cropping is far from uniform; two typical techniques have photographs cropped into circles or background information completely cut from images so that the photograph's focal point, often figures, pop out from the page's white background.[83]

The relative dynamism in the book's design does not necessarily enhance the book's self-proclaimed mission. Soldan writes that he, someone who loves his Volk and his *Vaterland*, created the book "with the firm belief in the greatness of Germany." Its intention is to reveal the tragic nature of recent history, to show how events like the World War, revolution, inflation, and so forth are connected. "But from this knowledge," he continues,

81. Pöhlmann, *Kriegsgeschichte*, 195.
82. Soldan, *Zeitgeschichte in Wort und Bild*, "Zum Geleit," n.p.
83. Soldan, *Zeitgeschichte in Wort und Bild Bd. 1*, 229.

"let that strength arise which rests solely in the unity of the Volk."[84] The political program that this endeavor entails unfolds only in the subsequent chapters, which hint at the most prevalent sources of postwar conservative ire: a weak and revolutionary home front, personified by leftists like Karl Liebknecht and moderate parliamentarians like Philipp Scheidemann of the Social Democratic Party, is blamed for the war effort's collapse, even as the military retained its honor through decisive defeats; the Russian Revolution spawned harmful ideas unfit for Germany and instigated unrest at home; the Kapp Putsch (a failed attempt in 1920 to overthrow the Weimar Republic) was a laudable expression of the people's national will, which had been defamed by criticism of the war effort; and the Treaty of Versailles had disastrous consequences for the shape of postwar governance, the military, and honor.

The exact argumentation of these issues, which touch on only a fraction of the themes present in the book's first of three volumes, cannot be fully reviewed here, but it suffices to say that photography does not seem consciously employed to support the text's conservative, nationalist, or military-affirming program. Instead, photographs are presented with neutral identifying captions, and although the body of Soldan's text, meant as an objective history of recent times, is tinged by his ideology, the photographs' role in the book is most akin to the illustrative role of press photographs. Such a use of photography, of course, is not by nature apolitical, but certain editorial choices confirm photography's relative nonparticipation in Soldan's ideology as the volume's rule. Take, for example, the photographs accompanying a chapter on the Spartacist uprising. Among other photographs showing the street fighting from the perspectives of both the military and the revolutionaries, the chapter includes photographs of funerals for the fallen of each side. Photographs of Karl Liebknecht's and Rosa Luxemburg's funeral processions are presented without difference to those showing government soldiers burying a comrade; none are framed as evidence for a political argument and merely add illustration to the events explained in the text. One juxtaposition on a single page is telling for the unbiased use of photography in *Zeitgeschichte*: a photograph of 80 Spartacists being arrested—perhaps to the delight of pro-government, conservative forces—has its potential political boast counterweighted by a reverent photograph taken at the funeral of Spartacists who died in Dresden.[85] The second photograph displays a large crowd of mourners that is undeniable evidence of

84. Soldan, *Zeitgeschichte in Wort und Bild*, "Zum Geleit."
85. Soldan, *Zeitgeschichte in Wort und Bild Bd. 1*, 261.

the support enjoyed by the Spartacist movement among the public. There are also relatively few instances when text is used to subvert the impartial illustration of the images. One exception to the rule is the quotation marks around the word "Kriegsverbrecher" (war criminals) in the label to a photograph of three English representatives arriving for the Leipzig War Criminal Trials. The caption questions the fairness of the Entente-mandated trials, which drew skepticism from large swaths of the German public. The one example, however, remains rather insignificant in proportion to the book's much larger composition.

Soldan's use of photography in *Zeitgeschichte in Wort und Bild* is not concerned with the war's visual record and its role in shaping the postwar understanding of the war. The book's relatively dynamic design is not employed for political messaging, and photography is used mainly to authenticate the text's more ideological claims. Soldan asserts the legitimacy of his textual arguments through claims of photography's objectivity. The way he describes photography in the introduction assumes the relay of factual information through images. As quoted above, he welcomes photography for its natural ability to lend any historical writing its "understandable" and "convincing" nature. His phrase "unprecedentedly well-developed photo reporting of our time" extols photography as technically perfect and places it in the realm of impartial reporting, marking it as implicitly trustworthy.

Soldan made a similar claim about photography in his introduction to an earlier picture book: volume one of the monumental collection of war photographs *Der Weltkrieg im Bild* (1926), which was compiled from the Reicharchiv's holdings of the former Bild- und Filmamt (BUFA). According to Soldan, the richness of photographic illustration in *Der Weltkrieg im Bild* ensures that "the true war" will be portrayed in "convincing strength."[86] In contrast to the paintings that soldiers used to imagine what war was like when they were called to duty in 1914, even if their creators strove for a true "reproduction of reality," photographs are far more capable of delivering the "facts" of "the living war." He proclaims that words alone cannot represent the full experience of modern *Materialschlacht* (attrition warfare), implicitly assigning photographs primacy in rendering the "real" war for the present. Furthermore, he welcomes the special authenticity of photographs made by BUFA, which represented "our" side and was tasked with capturing the war experience for the edification of future generations. This propagandistic allusion matches the very reason BUFA took over the central collection

86. Soldan, "Zum Geleit."

and censorship of amateur and official photographs alike in 1916: the first war years saw the uninhibited sale of photographs from the front to various publication outlets, a considerable risk to the military's careful management of public perception.[87] Soldan praises the BUFA photographic collection for supplementing the personal collections of amateur photographers, who were not able to capture the essence of battle for the practical reason that "the wilder the battles rage, the more we forgot about our small apparatuses." In this sense, Soldan, at the time still employed at the Reichsarchiv, privileges the "official" archive of photographs over the amateur, and he faults the latter with a gap in its representation of the war: "But if we [soldiers] want to use those [personal] pictures to convey an idea of the enormity of our experience to those who do not know the war personally, then the inadequacy of our collection becomes all too clear to us."[88]

In Soldan's assessment, the BUFA photographs collected in *Der Weltkrieg im Bild* will not only be welcomed for the way they supplement the record of soldiers who missed out on recording their front experience because they were too busy trying to survive it, they will also enact a postwar memorial function that is tied to an implied political agenda. Soldan describes the photographs' meaning in terms that easily recall some of the main components of *soldatischer Nationalismus* (soldierly nationalism) propagated by Franz Schauwecker and others. He espouses conservative ideals of an organic community that arises from the camaraderie of the frontline experience and that should play an active role in securing the "future of the fatherland" from the "distress of the present."[89] To legitimize this claim, he supports the *Frontkämpferlegende*, which heroized a superhuman breed of frontline soldiers, born of the war of attrition in the trenches (e.g., Verdun, Somme). To be counted among such a "pure and nobly developing comradeship" is only possible through a sort of baptism by fire at the front line ("Getöse der Schlacht"). The myth legitimized and elevated the position of former soldiers and conservatives alike in the postwar political debates. By 1933 the Frontkämpferlegende had largely supplanted an earlier interpretation that framed the heroic sacrifice of Germany's youth in the first war years (e.g., the Yser Front, the Battle of Langemarck) as a moral victory born

87. Dewitz, "Schießen oder fotografieren," 53. For the censorship conditions imposed on reporters and the illustrated press during the war, see Keller, "Der Weltkrieg der Bilder."

88. Soldan, "Zum Geleit."

89. Soldan, "Zum Geleit."

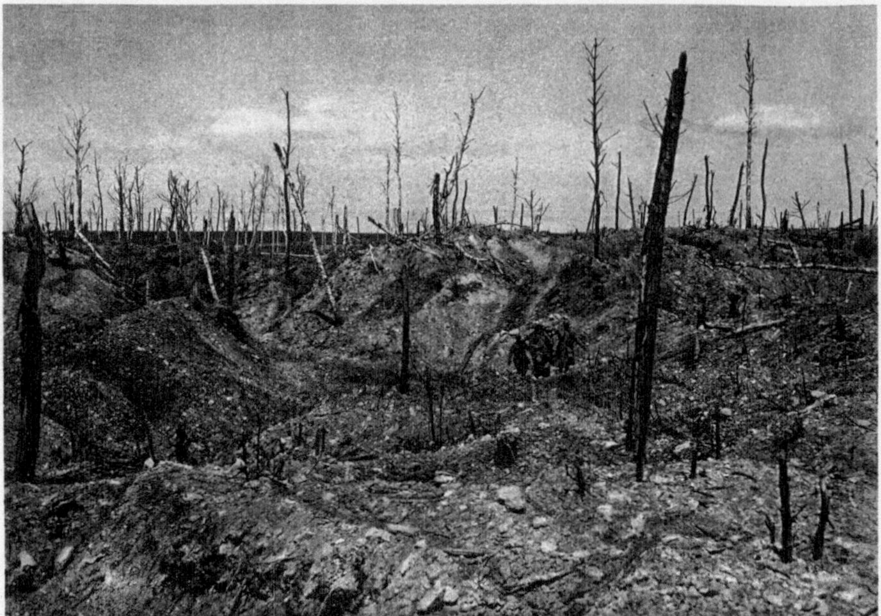

Charakteristisches Kampfgelände am Chemin des Dames.

Fig. 38. *Der Weltkrieg im Bild, Bd. 1: Originalaufnahmen des Kriegs-Bild-und-Filmamtes aus der modernen Materialschlacht* (The World War in pictures, vol. 1: Original images of modern material warfare from the War Picture and Film Bureau) (Berlin/Munich: National-Archiv, 1926), page 157.

of military defeat.[90] In comparison to this earlier myth, the Frontkämpferlegende sought to stake out a specific political position interested in postwar political and societal discourses that stretched beyond simply remembering the sacrifices of soldiers. The shift is clearly evident when comparing the rhetoric of *Der Weltkrieg im Bild* to the earlier picture series produced by Soldan's department for the Reichsarchiv.

The first volume of *Der Weltkrieg im Bild* not only carries a dedication to the *Frontkämpfer*, but its visual focus is also squarely aimed at the front line. It also gives preference to the Western Front, which occupies the book's first 250 pages; "Other theaters of war" are haphazardly lumped together and consigned to the book's last 100 pages. Although it is unclear if Soldan himself played a role in selecting and ordering the images, a measured

90. See Pöhlmann, *Kriegsgeschichte*, 213–14.

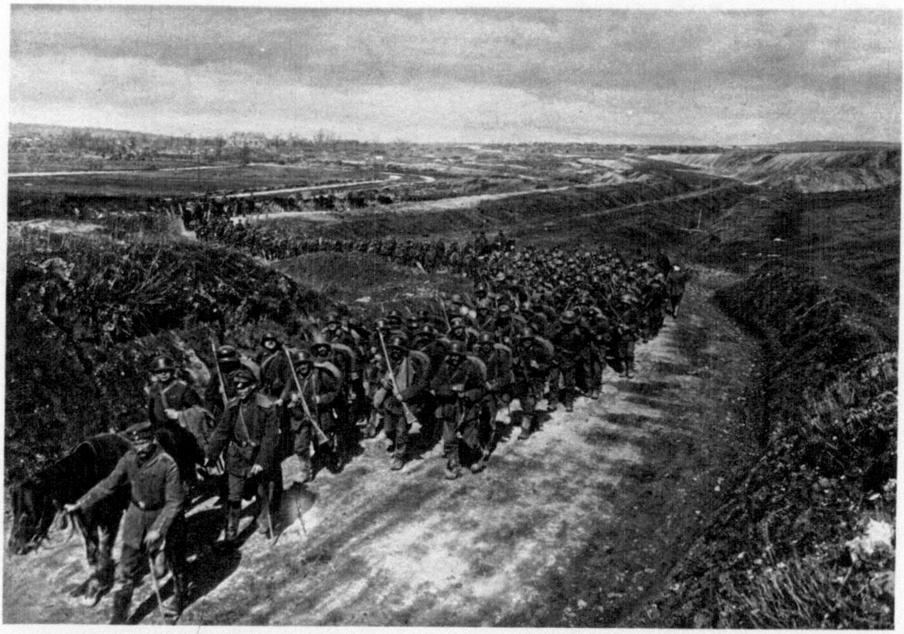

Fig. 39. *Der Weltkrieg im Bild, Bd. 1: Originalaufnahmen des Kriegs-Bild-und-Filmamtes aus der modernen Materialschlacht* (Berlin/Munich: National-Archiv, 1926), page 85.

overview of the 400 or so photographs included in *Der Weltkrieg im Bild* reveals that they bolster the rhetoric of the Frontkämpferlegende. Although there is no formal organization to the book beyond a differentiation between the Western Front and everything else, the first 30 pages of photographs focus on the technologically advanced weapons employed during the late-war *Materialschlacht*: flamethrowers, tanks, and massive artillery guns. Soldan describes the effect of these weapons in the introduction as "that tangled knot of iron, fire, smoke, noise, terror, savagery, and death," visually represented by photographs showing destructive aftermaths. Along with a few images of actual explosions, photographs of bombed-out buildings and "characteristically" pockmarked landscapes prevail throughout (see fig. 38). The book also does not shy away from including grisly photographs of destroyed animal and non-German human bodies, to which a pair of images

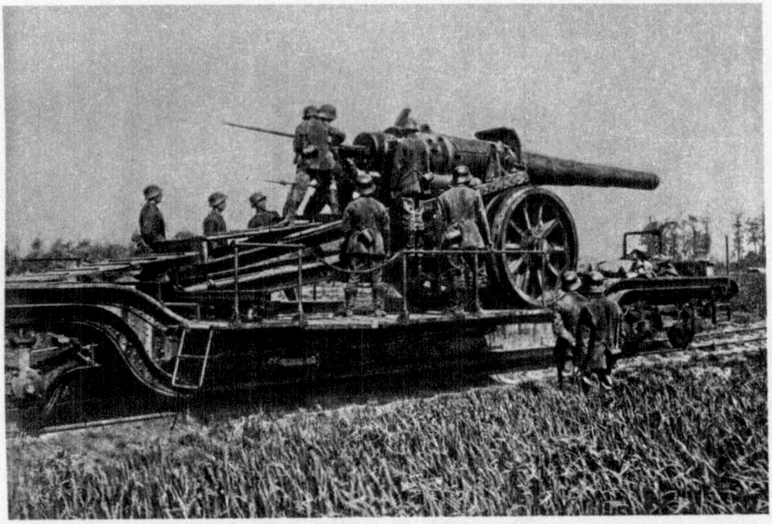

17 cm Schnelladekanone in Radstafette auf Eisenbahnwagen. Einsetzen der Granate.

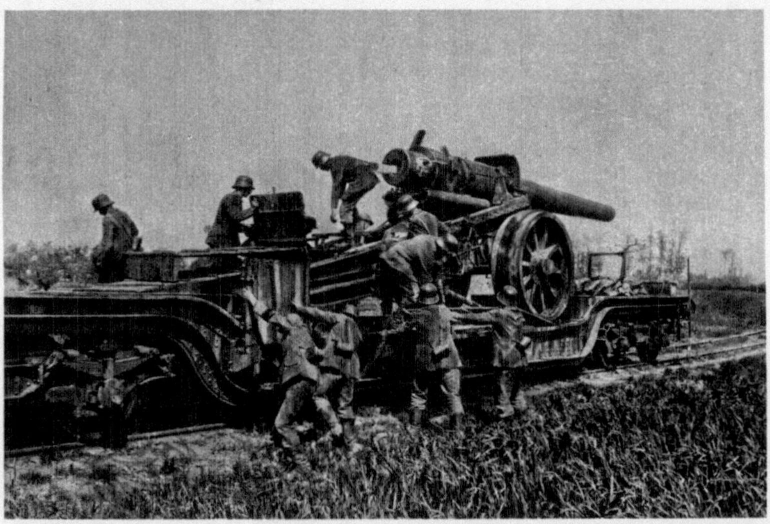

17 cm Schnelladekanone in Radstafette auf Eisenbahnwagen. Fertigmachen zur Abfahrt.

Fig. 40. *Der Weltkrieg im Bild, Bd. 1: Originalaufnahmen des Kriegs-Bild-und-Filmamtes aus der modernen Materialschlacht* (Berlin/Munich: National-Archiv, 1926), page 17.

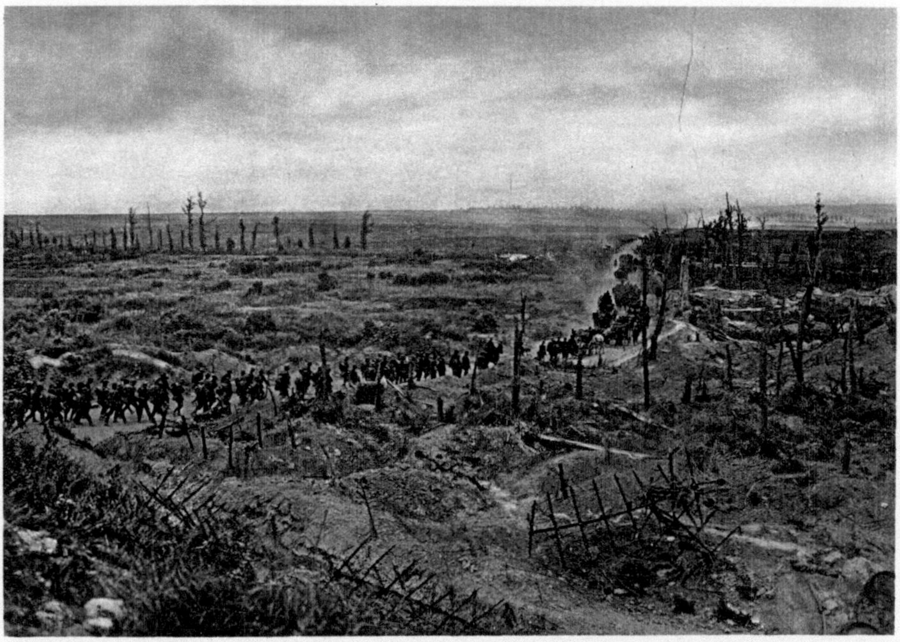

Deutsche Kolonnen passieren die eroberte feindliche Stellung bei Loivre am Brimont.

Fig. 41. *Der Weltkrieg im Bild, Bd. 1: Originalaufnahmen des Kriegs-Bild-und-Filmamtes aus der modernen Materialschlacht* (Berlin/Munich: National-Archiv, 1926), page 222.

from Estaires, France, one coldly labeled "The effect of artillery," can attest.[91] This sort of physical destruction is central to the positive understanding of the war's violence—the metaphysical transformation of soldiers into a new breed of men—that inheres in the Frontkämpferlegende. This is evident when Soldan asserts in the introduction that "powerful and strong-willed figures" arose out of the "roar of battle."

Throughout the volume, a focus on soldiers photographed in groups, marching in columns (fig. 39), or working together to man large artillery guns (fig. 40) emphasizes the ideological concept of the community born from war. Not only are individual soldiers created anew in the fire of battle, they are forged into a group through what Soldan calls "their most difficult

91. *Der Weltkrieg im Bild, Bd. 1*, 109.

yet most uplifting memories of life." The many veterans' organizations that arose after the war testify to the importance of companionship and solidarity among soldiers, but Soldan's introduction—and to some extent the photographs in *Der Weltkrieg im Bild*—assigns a deeper bond between soldiers, one that goes beyond friendship and mutual support to a profoundly felt shared understanding of coming close to death in the storm of the Western Front. Soldan's implicit claim is that such a war experience will inspire love of the fatherland in those who survived. (Organizations like the Reichsbanner proved this conservative sentiment to be limited in reach.) Soldan claims explicitly that the volume will reconnect the fighters through shared in-group memories at the same time that it will tell future generations of "that unique, everlasting German heroism." The photographs seem not only to attempt to visualize the powerful and transformational impressions of war, as noted above, but they also depict how a shared group experience might arise out of it. Take, for example, a photograph of a column of soldiers snaking their way through the wasted landscape of the Western Front (fig. 41). Pictured from a considerable distance, the group appears small and as if swallowed by the ruined landscape of trenches, busted fortifications, and dead trees. Their integration into the landscape is further enhanced by the row of men being visually mirrored by rows of burned trees and the wooden stakes of *chevaux de friese* obstacles. The soldiers stand out only in the foreground because of their darker uniforms, but even those become melded with the landscape as the eye traces the winding column into the darker background. The wasted landscape, its foreboding atmosphere heightened by smoke and fog in the distance toward which the men march, gives an impression that the soldiers are descending into a quite literal hell. The photograph is one of many that work as illustration of the bond forged among soldiers in hardship and peril.

Photographs showing groups of soldiers in true "comradeship" spirit complement—in comparison to some war picture books, and perhaps only second to Schauwecker's *So war der Krieg!*—a relatively high number of images of soldiers "in action" at the front, firing artillery, advancing through trenches, and storming enemy lines. These photographs, such as the one captioned "Infantry advancing in a cratered field" (fig. 42), must count among the relatively few images from the war that captured actual fighting in close proximity. Although they may seem—for lack of a better word—dull to viewers today, who are accustomed to the work of professional, embedded war photojournalists, the photographs stand out among the larger archive of images printed in Weimar-era picture books for their

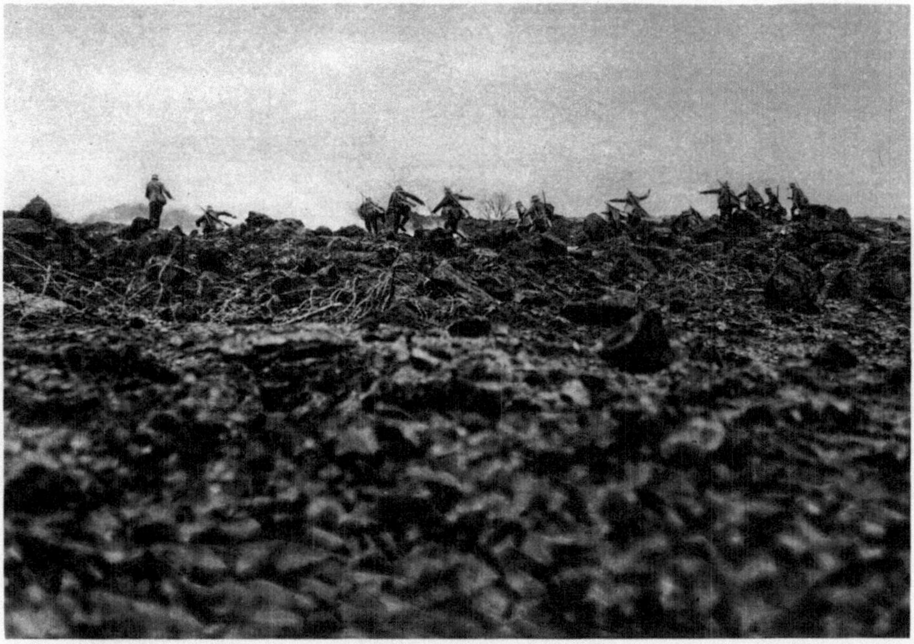

Im Trichterfelde vorstürmende Infanterie.

Fig. 42. *Der Weltkrieg im Bild, Bd. 1: Originalaufnahmen des Kriegs-Bild-und-Filmamtes aus der modernen Materialschlacht* (Berlin/Munich: National-Archiv, 1926), page 35.

"authentic" look at the war's violence. Such photographs were intended to be powerful glimpses into the dangers and heroics that are part and parcel of the Frontkämpferlegende.

Soldan openly admits in the introduction, however, that such a photographic representation does not automatically match an intended worldview. He writes that a danger exists in showing photographs of destruction, as they could invite a skeptical assessment of the war's purpose that runs contrary to his intended vision: one that reaffirms the military's honor and understands the transformational experience of those who served at the front as positive.[92] Beyond removing the war's violence completely from view, a tactic most plainly seen in *Deutschland: Ein Buch der Größe und der Hoffnung in Bildern, 1914–1924*, Soldan needs interpretive strategies to circumvent the

92. Soldan, "Zum Geleit."

possibility that the war's visual record and its unavoidable evidence of large-scale traumatic violence might be understood in a negative light. To a certain extent, *Der Weltkrieg im Bild* already erases some of the more radically violent images, like those graphic portraits in Ernst Friedrich's *Krieg dem Kriege!* that present the mutilated and shattered faces of soldiers. But the volume does not shy away from corpses (if always labeled as non-German) or destroyed cities and landscapes, and it even presents extreme destruction as "typical."[93] Some photographs give an impression of human mastery over the destruction of war, such as an image of a railway construction corps leveling new streets through highly upturned terrain somewhere near the front,[94] or another image showing a group of soldiers attending to an injured horse in the unfavorable surrounds of smoke and rubble from what the caption indicates was a bombed-out dressing station.[95] In any case, Soldan condemns in the introduction any negative reaction to the volume's pictured violence as one that fails to grasp the war experience's foundational meaning: "Weak pacifist circles, clueless to the world and humanity, will certainly be all too willing to exploit this sequence of images for their own ends. Their sense of unreality is contrasted by the history that speaks from this book, which, despite all human resistance, tends to write the most important parts of its development in blood."[96] Soldan repeats a claim about photography in this passage that is characteristic of conservative frameworks for interpreting the war: the ascription of a deep, almost sacral significance to the war experience is fixed squarely to an assumption of the photograph's authenticity. Potential rebuttals to positive interpretations of the war—even when "all the misery of war" is openly acknowledged—can be dismissed outright as detached from the pictured situation's reality, which remains only truly knowable to those on the inside, or, as Soldan calls them, the "initiates" of the front.

The pacifist rebuttal to Soldan's claims is best represented by Gerhart Seger, writing for the preeminent peace journal *Die Friedens-Warte* in July 1927. He lauds the first volume of *Der Weltkrieg im Bild* for its technically superb production but laments the lack of organization, the deferential treatment of Germany vis-à-vis the Entente in its discussion of military capability, death, and defeat, and the twisting of basic historical facts to support a nationalist and affirmative vision of the war. Seger echoes the earlier critique of Kurt Tucholsky in his review of Ernst Friedrich's *Krieg dem Kriege!*:

93. *Der Weltkrieg im Bild, Bd. 1*, 155.
94. *Der Weltkrieg im Bild, Bd. 1*, 124.
95. *Der Weltkrieg im Bild, Bd. 1*, 154.
96. Soldan, "Zum Geleit."

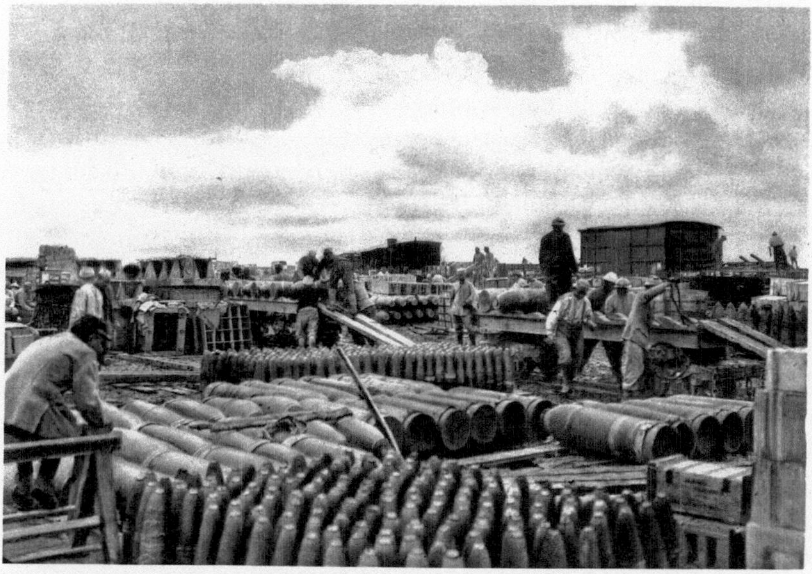

Eines der riesigen und unerschöpflichen Munitionslager, das die französische und englische Artillerie während der Großkämpfe an der Somme im Herbst 1916 mit Geschossen versorgte.

Fig. 43. *Der Weltkrieg im Bild, Bd. 2: Frontaufnahmen aus den Archiven der Entente* (The World War in pictures, vol. 2: Front-line pictures from the archives of the Entente) (Berlin/Munich: National-Archiv, ca. 1928), page 79.

> No one will expect the numerous old officers in the Reichsarchiv, who are busy processing the material handed over by the former army command, to produce pacifist publications about the war, although this office of the republic could provide such a service by shedding light on the true face of the World War. On the other hand, we can demand that the official publications of the Reichsarchiv should not be as antipacifist and scientifically inadequate as the present book.[97]

He recognizes the potential of photography to reveal the "true face of the war" but dismisses the efforts in *Der Weltkrieg im Bild* as "a pitiful effort, . . . all the more pitiful since the superficial accoutrements reveal the rich material that stands at the Reichsarchiv's disposal."[98]

97. Seger, review of *Der Weltkrieg im Bild,* 222.
98. Seger, review of *Der Weltkrieg im Bild,* 222.

The same objections would likely apply to a second volume of *Der Weltkrieg im Bild* (ca. 1928) that contained only photographs taken from the side of the Entente but that was constructed almost identically to the first. With over 400 photographs, the second volume was as richly illustrated as the first, but—despite a chronological progression—similarly lacked any organization by theme. The resulting kaleidoscopic view makes it difficult for the reader-viewer to draw meaningful interpretative threads while engaging with the book. A general overview of the photographs reveals that it is also centered around the same themes as the first volume: the destruction of landscapes and buildings is prevalent, but corpses are absent; the group struggle of the frontline soldiers is emphasized through the many photographs of soldiers together at work and a corresponding absence of individual portraits; and the material superiority of Germany's enemies is on display through photographs of their large artillery guns and "huge and inexhaustible munitions depots," as one caption has it (fig. 43). The last point is central to the introduction written by Walter Beumelburg, a popular war author representing *soldatischer Nationalismus* (see chapter 5), whose work included four volumes in the Reichsarchiv series "Schlachten des Weltkrieges" and the third and last volume of *Der Weltkrieg im Bild.* Titled *Die stählernen Jahre* (1930), it was a monumental version of his war novel *Sperrfeuer um Deutschland* (Artillery barrage around Germany; 1928) that included a dedication by Paul von Hindenburg and infrequent drawn illustrations and even fewer photographs.[99] Beumelburg writes in the introduction to the second volume of *Der Weltkrieg im Bild* that it was impossible for the German soldier to see the enemy at the front, and the present volume should provide a peek "behind the curtain of No Man's Land."[100] In his estimation, the most important revelation that comes from considering the pictures taken on the other side of the front is the Entente's material superiority, which reappears in photographs of trenches, craters, and torn-up forests.[101] Beumelburg praises the ability of photography, among all other forms of depiction, to capture the past in "true-to-nature" detail and keep it alive with "uncanny liveliness." It opens up a new visual horizon to those who served at the front. Taken as a collection, the photographs do provide a strong sense of the type of destructive power that was unleashed upon Germany—or all combatants for

99. See his bibliography entry in Mohler, *Die konservative Revolution*, 442–44.
100. Beumelburg, "Vorwort," 6.
101. Beumelburg, "Vorwort," 6.

that matter—during the war. But Beumelburg reads a special meaning into the photographs that lies far outside photography's documentary capability, despite his problematic over-exaggerations of the medium's "tangible reality." The picture book has in his eyes a "special meaning": the viewer is oppressed by the reality of Germany's material disadvantage, while being uplifted by the fact that it was not enough to defeat "us" on the battlefield: "Thus, like the first, this collection becomes a living, moving, and true monument to the magnitude of what was demanded and borne by German men in four years."[102] In the same way that Soldan frames the first volume of photographs as evidence of an experience inscribed in the frontline soldier and enduring into the present, Beumelburg asserts photography's authenticity as unassailable for his claims about the war's meaning more than a decade after its end. Echoing the popular revisionist slogan of "geschlagen aber unbesiegt" (beaten but not defeated), he affirms the German national spirit despite its material defeat. By connecting the "truthful" nature of photography with the "living" legacy of the war experience, he brings to the fore the war's contemporary meaning, which has a "moving" ripple effect on the present.

The techniques used by the Reichsarchiv and its affiliates, including George Soldan and Werner Beumelburg, are evidence of the effort to transform the war's negative outcomes into something positive through a reworking of photographic archives. The two series produced by the Reichsarchiv's department of volkstümliche publications gave military accounts that presented death in a matter-of-fact manner, embodied in the orderly cemeteries and regimental monuments that preserved German military honor. The two volumes of *Der Weltkrieg im Bild* took the effort to deal with the obvious realities of death and destruction to a further level. They freely acknowledged the aspects of war a picture book like *Deutschland* worked to conceal, even though *Der Weltkrieg im Bild* lacks any reckoning with human destruction, let alone at a level as frank or horrific as Ernst Friedrich's earlier *Krieg dem Kriege!* Death is reinscribed in *Der Weltkrieg im Bild* as a necessary component of the Frontkämpferlegende, one that may bring physical ruin but cannot hamper and even emboldens the German national spirit. These and other mystical claims relied on fixing symbolic meaning to the apparent authenticity and realism of the photographic image.

The uncritical stance toward photography evidenced in Reichsarchiv publications must ultimately be seen as servicing ideological motives.

102. Beumelburg, "Vorwort," 7.

Authors like Bloem, Soldan, and Beumelburg, all war veterans believing in the rightness of their own actions, had individual reasons to justify and make sense of their war service as much as they had career incentives to keep their accounts central to public discourse. Political motivations are also evident, especially in the fashioning of the war experience into a positive national legacy for the present, in which former soldiers will carry the banner for a new Germany. The picture books treated in this chapter largely avoid outright discussion of such politics, although their allusions were nevertheless clear to sympathetic and critical readers alike. The strand of nationalism arising from the war experience that authors like Bloem, Soldan, and Beumelburg implicitly represent in these picture books reaches its fever pitch in the polemical picture books of Franz Schauwecker treated in the following two chapters. There, the transformation of war defeat into a positive experience crystallizes around the concrete political aim of scrapping the Weimar system and ushering in a new style of nationalism, soldier-centered and authoritarian, for a Germany that squandered the legacy of the front.

CHAPTER FIVE

Metaphysical Transformation at the Front

Franz Schauwecker's *So war der Krieg!* and "soldatischer Nationalismus"

The celebration of military tradition and glory found in the photographic publications of the Reichsarchiv glossed over the horrors of the war in service of a positive reaffirmation of the military—a personal concern of the former officers leading the Reichsarchiv—and reflected a general longing for the lost conservative ideals and structures of the Wilhelmine era. The focus in *Der Weltkrieg im Bild* (1926) on soldierly comradeship, heroism, and patriotism is extended in the pictorial works of Franz Schauwecker, who saw in the past not just lost glory to be regained but also something additional to be exploited for political purchase. For Schauwecker, the horrors of the war were not an indictment of the German military, something to be whitewashed or hidden completely, but a formative experience of his generation to be held central in memory, if not celebrated outright. The trenches were the crucible where honor and character were forged, and out of which a new breed of man was cast to assume the mantle of the German nation.

Schauwecker's war picture book *So war der Krieg!* (This is what the war was like; 1927) visualizes these ideas with a photograph titled "Der Gang in das Schicksal" (The march toward fate) (fig. 44). The image shows an unidentified group of four soldiers in the middle ground making their way through a flattened, cratered field that has been churned up by repeated bombardments. Smoke largely obscures the horizon and blends sky with ground into an otherworldly landscape. A smaller group of soldiers farther in the distance scrambles through the destruction, which visually dwarfs all the figures in the photograph, subjecting them to its enveloping might and terror. The caption suggests the soldiers are marching to their fate, but the direction of the soldiers' movement is indiscernible through the photograph alone; the less careful reader will accept the caption without considering that the sol-

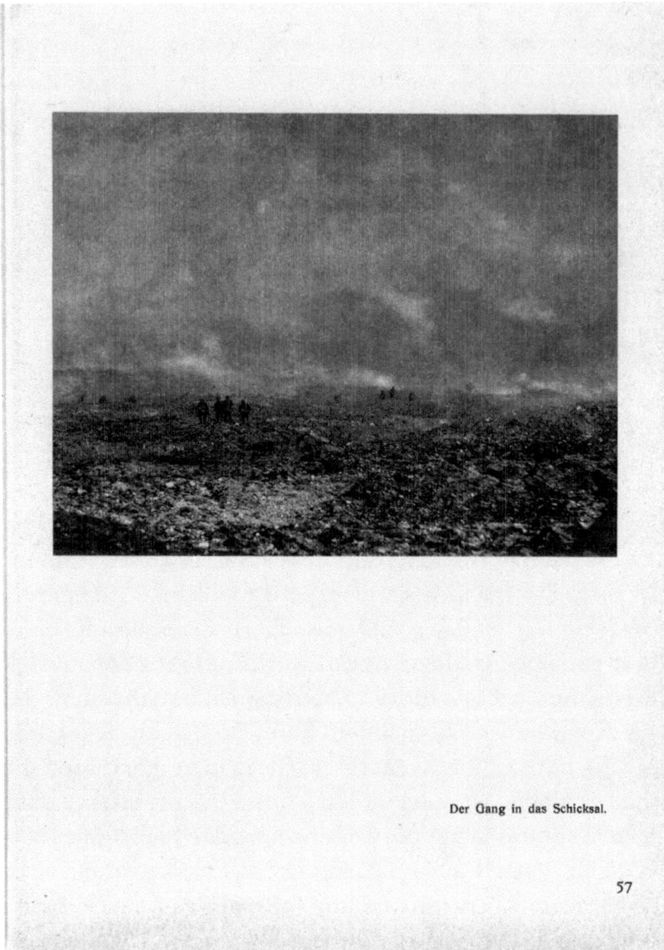

Fig. 44. Franz Schauwecker, *So war der Krieg!* (This is what the war was like) (7th ed., Berlin: Frundsberg-Verlag, 1928), page 57.

diers might actually be running from their fate, with the smoke (an artillery barrage?) in the background. The photograph encapsulates a central tenet of Schauwecker's war interpretation: the seemingly contradictory smallness of the individual soldier swallowed by the endless devastation of war and his heroic grandeur in submitting to the deadly circumstance around him, or, as he asserts: "We must want what fate wants."[1]

1. Schauwecker, *So war der Krieg!*, 7th ed., 56.

While many photographs in *So war der Krieg!* are consigned to a page with from two to upwards of six other images (often unstylishly cropped or even encroaching into each other so that only the most important piece of visual information captured is relayed), "Der Gang in das Schicksal" is given a whole page to itself. The image is not stretched to fill the entire space of the page, but is rather given "breathing room" that other images in the book do not enjoy. The effect is double: (1) the page's white space and the distance between caption and photograph break up the fast visual rhythm of earlier pages, inviting the reader to linger on the one image, while (2) the image is presented with added reverence—as a work of art is framed, hung, and didacticized in a museum gallery—and given memorial significance by the caption's connotation. It is one of the few instances where Schauwecker's use of photography and captions veers from a sort of documentary style, which serves claims of authentic and authoritative representation, to a more open creation of poetic meaning between caption and photograph. "Der Gang in das Schicksal" exemplifies that Schauwecker was not only employing photography's putative realism as a support for ideological arguments, but that he was also interested in directly shaping the war's visual record with critical interpretation. It reveals that Schauwecker understood photography as a powerful tool to shape the public's understanding of the war and recognized the medium's concurrent openness to added layers of meaning with its ability to masquerade successfully—at least for a popular audience—as the real.

So war der Krieg! sought to fix a heroic vision of the war into public view. It did not reveal the visual shocks of war with the bluntness of Ernst Friedrich's *Krieg dem Kriege!*, but it also did not sugarcoat the horror of war as Walter Bloem's *Deutschland* picture book or the publications of the Reichsarchiv did. Schauwecker's picture book *So war der Krieg!* (1927) and its sequel *So ist der Friede* (This is what peace is like; 1928), treated respectively in this chapter and the next, are the most prominent pictorial works of *soldatischer Nationalismus* (soldierly nationalism), a current of the larger German conservative revolution between 1918 and 1933 that idealized the war experience and heroized the frontline soldier as the harbinger of a new, authoritarian nationalism. Before further analyzing how Schauwecker sought to capture and re-create the frontline experience in the text and image of his picture books, the larger background of soldatischer Nationalismus and its literary output should be explained. By contextualizing Schauwecker's picture books within this larger political movement, it should become clear how his interventions into the war's visual record count as foremost sites for interrogating the intersection of photography, memory, and politics in the Weimar Republic.

The self-styled soldatischer Nationalismus that developed in the work of authors like Schauwecker was initially not overtly antirepublican, but as the economic and social situation in the Weimar Republic deteriorated in the late 1920s, the front experience was deployed as a pillar to support a conservative revolution aimed against Germany's nascent democracy.[2] Drawing on long, pre–First World War traditions that viewed war more as a force of nature or a matter of fate than an aberration of human judgment,[3] authors supportive of soldatischer Nationalismus, such as Schauwecker, Ernst Jünger, Werner Beumelburg, Ernst von Salomon, and Edwin Erich Dwinger, all of whom served during the war—or, in the case of Salomon, in the postwar Freikorps—and fashioned themselves as part of a "front generation," idealized not only the recent war experience but the idea of conflict in itself. War was a spiritual source of edification for the individual and the nation.

Although represented by only a small group of authors, the soldatischer Nationalismus movement was highly active in producing literary and journalistic representations of the war that were almost uniformly subsumed by the wider national-conservative movement during the Weimar Republic.[4] Among the most important accounts produced by soldatischer Nationalismus authors were the early works of Ernst Jünger, including the autobiographical novel *In Stahlgewittern* (*Storm of Steel*; 1920), the essay *Der Kampf als inneres Erlebnis* (*War as an Inner Experience*; 1922), and the expansion of episodes from *In Stahlgewittern* in *Das Wäldchen 125* (*Copse 125*; 1925) and *Feuer und Blut* (*Fire and Blood*; 1925).[5] According to Armin Mohler, Franz Schauwecker's *Aufbruch der Nation* (Awakening of the nation; translated as *The Furnace*; 1930), Ernst von Salomon's trilogy of *Die Geächteten* (*The Out-*

2. Krumeich, "Die Präsenz des Krieges im Frieden," 8. Karl Prümm provides greater detail to why soldatischer Nationalismus must be understood as part of a larger, more nebulous "Konservative Revolution" that—after the failed Kapp Putsch in 1920—split with an "older" style of nationalism that sought the restoration of the Wilhelmine monarchy. See his characterization of both terms and their mutual development throughout the 1920s in *Die Literatur des Soldatischen Nationalismus*, 1–77, especially 26–28 on the aftermath of the Kapp Putsch.

3. Wette, "Von Kellogg bis Hitler," 150.

4. Prümm, *Die Literatur des Soldatischen Nationalismus*, 8.

5. Although the main figure of soldatischer Nationalismus in his early work, Ernst Jünger developed his ideas over the course of the Weimar era, eventually veering toward National Bolshevism in his lengthy philosophical essay *Der Arbeiter: Herrschaft und Gewalt* (1932) (see Mohler, *Die konservative Revolution in Deutschland*, 331). The transformation can also be traced in the many articles Jünger contributed to publications—often also edited by him—like the *Standarte* (see Mohler, *Die konservative Revolution in Deutschland*, 294).

laws; 1929), *Die Stadt* (The city; translated as *It Cannot Be Stormed*; 1932), and *Die Kadetten* (The cadets; 1933), along with Edwin Erich Dwinger's trilogy *Die Deutsche Passion* (German passion; 1929–32), comprise "the most impressive testimony of this 'soldatischer Nationalismus.'"[6] As with other currents of the conservative revolution, soldatischer Nationalismus first found its initial spark in countless magazine and newspaper articles, which crystallized into a more distinct ideology in later anthologies like *Krieg und Krieger* (War and warrior; 1930) edited by Jünger.

Literary scholar Karl Prümm characterizes soldatischer Nationalismus as a relatively closed and uniformly structured component of the diverse and at times controversial ideological strains of the conservative revolution.[7] The glorification of war and the front experience did not, however, exist solely to be co-opted by other groups, but was coupled with its own distinct conception of nationalism that had, for example, wishful imperialist dreams that went far beyond those of the Pan-Germans in 1914 and unmistakable political claims to power for the elite of the frontline soldier.[8] Positive aspects of the war experience—such as deeply felt camaraderie, the military's hierarchical structure, and the imposition of a strong leader to whom the unruly masses should submit—inflected the political demands of soldatischer Nationalismus.[9] It seemed every political problem could be solved by referring to the practiced ideals of the soldierly experience and translating them into peacetime.

The shared front experience was indeed enough to bind the proponents of soldatischer Nationalismus together, as the group lacked anything reminiscent of an actual organization. "Members" were often only loosely connected through informal circles of like-minded ideologues that crystallized around leading figures, like Ernst Jünger,[10] or certain publications, such as the *Standarte*, which initially belonged to the influential conservative veterans' group the Stahlhelm.[11] And although the group lacked a political organization and did not neatly correspond to any one political party, the ideas of soldatischer Nationalismus—foremost the war experience's politicization—

6. Mohler, *Die konservative Revolution in Deutschland*, 444.

7. Prümm, *Die Literatur des Soldatischen Nationalismus*, 38.

8. Wette, "Von Kellogg bis Hitler," 164–165. The characterization is problematized by Schauwecker's stance in *So ist der Friede* (see the next chapter here), in which the independence and self-determination of all countries should guarantee an end to imperialistic wars.

9. Prümm, *Die Literatur des Soldatischen Nationalismus*, 42–43.

10. Prümm, *Die Literatur des Soldatischen Nationalismus*, 9.

11. Mohler, *Die konservative Revolution in Deutschland*, 285.

meshed easily with the more overt antidemocratic and antirepublican sensibilities characteristic of conservative groups. They were foremost united by shared mentalities born of the war experience and the belief that those mentalities should be preserved in some way after the war.[12]

In the realm of war commemoration and remembrance, works by authors of soldatischer Nationalismus aimed to erase the individual suffering and destruction from war accounts and preserve "only the Living, the Great, the Procreative," as one proponent, Wilhelm von Schramm, proclaimed in the Jünger-edited volume *Krieg und Krieger*.[13] In this sense, political, social, or economic analyses remained outside the purview of soldatischer Nationalismus, which instead favored "intuitive seeing and feeling . . . transfiguration removed from reality"[14] One obvious exception, though, was the constant suggestion that the Entente had won the war only because of their superior mass of resources and the assertion that the army had been betrayed by civilian politicians at home (the so-called stab-in-the-back myth). The German army, especially its frontline soldiers, had remained "im Felde unbesiegt" (undefeated in the field) and retained their honor and spirit. The war was largely understood as an anthropological phenomenon—a human predisposition for war that evoked the philosophy of Friedrich Nietzsche[15]—and a matter of fate (*Schicksal*). The verbal imagery of natural disasters, for example, pervades accounts of soldatischer Nationalismus, enlarging the war's scope to gigantic proportions that, despite a lack of moral or rational explanation, offered a metaphysical and formational experience to the "Soldier." The war experience could therefore be fashioned into an emotionally effective ideology.[16] This approach—which will become more obvious in the analysis to come of Schauwecker's picture books—was central to the irrationalism of the right's depiction and instrumentalization of war memory.

Irrationalism was indeed prized by proponents of the conservative revolution in their approach to politics, leading to a black-and-white thinking

12. Wette, "Von Kellogg bis Hitler," 160.

13. Schramm, "Schöpferische Kritik des Krieges," 35.

14. Wette, "Von Kellogg bis Hitler," 162.

15. Prümm describes the appropriation of Nietzsche by proponents of a conservative revolution: "Nietzsche habe die zunehmende Nihilisierung des 'Lebens' als Verherrlichung des Schwachen und Unkriegerischen erkannt und ihr ein 'verzücktes Jasagen zum Gesamtcharakter des Lebens' entgegengestellt. Er gehe davon aus, daß dieses 'Leben' notwendigerweise ein gewalttätiges und kriegerisches sein müsse und bejahe den Krieg als Lebensprinzip" (Prümm, *Die Literatur des Soldatischen Nationalismus*, 36).

16. Prümm, *Die Literatur des Soldatischen Nationalismus*, 9.

that negated any position not their own. Schauwecker wrote in the nationalist journal *Der Vormarsch:* "Politics is not a matter of arbitrariness. . . . It unfolds in its historical course according to the inner laws of blood, spirit, and cultural conditions in which it was initiated."[17] Rational thinking and analysis were harangued as elements of a corrupt intellectual caste, who spoiled the national community's "blood" by forcing rules and mechanisms onto what otherwise would be an organic system of unfettered freedom and self-realization. This irrationalism followed clearly from the so-called *Lebensphilosophie* (philosophy of life) that developed in the late nineteenth century in the philosophical writings of the Frenchman Henri Bergson and the German Wilhelm Dilthey, who were inspired by the critique of rationalism to seek new modes of knowledge in the human realms of intuition and instinct.[18] Although it was initially a concern of academic philosophy, conservative thinkers, such as Oswald Spengler, borrowed such antirational elements from earlier metaphysicians and developed and sharpened them in the first decades of the twentieth century. In the ideas of soldatischer Nationalismus, the antirationalism of *Lebensphilosophie* morphed into an understanding of the postwar era in which politics was deprived of practical relevance and placed in metaphysical contexts as a "transformation of the spirit." Concrete political action was therefore understood as the result of a process that could not be grasped rationally.[19]

These beliefs were merged to support the aforementioned rejection of any political organization among the proponents of soldatischer Nationalismus, which clearly set it apart from other Weimar-era political movements or groups. In Ernst Jünger's words: "Nationalism is not an organization; every attempt to organize it is doomed to failure from the outset. It is a conspiracy of a secret and dangerous kind."[20] In contrast to concrete goals and political programs, emphasis was placed on the permanent nature of tried-and-true "personalities" whose moral character outlasted changing political motives.[21] For soldatischer Nationalismus authors, the frontline soldier represented the truest of all "personalities," and, in the words of one Stahlhelm propagandist, "Germany must be governed by its frontline fighters!"[22] The front experience became a measure to gauge the legitimacy of all war expe-

17. Schauwecker, "Südland," 8.
18. Pflug, "Lebensphilosophie," 140.
19. Prümm, *Die Literatur des Soldatischen Nationalismus*, 33.
20. Jünger, "Der unsichtbare Kern," 329.
21. Prümm, *Die Literatur des Soldatischen Nationalismus*, 33.
22. Kleinau, *Stahlhelm und Staat*, 34.

riences and subsequently the rightfulness of claims to power after the war. Historian Kurt Sontheimer describes the exclusionary tactics employed to police the movement, which saw only certain attitudes, such as a fighting spirit, willingness to sacrifice one's life, unselfishness, and nationalism, as genuine. Those who did not experience the transformational experience at the front were not ready to transform the postwar world as it so desperately needed; those who did not feel the bond of the trenches could not feel the bond of a prototypical *Volksgemeinschaft* (national community).[23]

A marked increase in the reading public's interest in soldatischer Nationalismus works and a flood of publications on the war in general coincided with the economic crisis of 1929.[24] Prior to that juncture, during the republic's stabilization phase starting around 1924, war accounts—especially politicized ones that addressed issues like the question of war guilt—did not occupy as central a position in public discourse as they did in the war's immediate aftermath. Despite their marginal position during that time, soldatischer Nationalismus authors continued their activity with a missionary zeal, writing in newspapers friendly to their cause like *Arminius* and *Der Vormarsch*.[25] The newfound public resonance of 1929 meant that many previously ignored works were rediscovered and new works could find wide interest across class divides.[26] The political dimension of fictional war novels in the late Weimar era by nationalist authors like Werner Beumelburg and Franz Schauwecker is clear. They were not written to work through traumatic war memory nor intended to provide a purely factual account of the war; rather, as Sontheimer characterizes it, this politically biased literature put the present credo of nationalism into the mouths of comrades in the trenches of the past.[27]

A boom in novels with military themes (from around 200 in 1926 to more than 400 in 1930) came with a concomitant decline in pacifist works. Despite the success of Remarque's novel *Im Westen nichts Neues* (1929) and Arnold Zweig's *Der Streit um den Sergeanten Grischa* (*The Case of Sergeant*

23. Sontheimer, *Antidemokratisches Denken*, 124–25.

24. Wette, "Von Kellogg bis Hitler," 169.

25. Wette, "Von Kellogg bis Hitler," 161.

26. Prümm, *Die Literatur des Soldatischen Nationalismus*, 64. Soldatischer Nationalismus writings in the stabilization phase of Weimar Germany had an expressed aristocratic nature, which attempted to separate the movement from the lower-class masses by articulating a qualitatively higher political program that ensured the prestige of the *Bildungsbürgertum* (educated middle class).

27. Sontheimer, *Antidemokratisches Denken*, 136.

Grischa; 1927), which itself enjoyed increased sales after the publication of Remarque's war tale, the renewed interest in the war—or the exploits of the postwar Freikorps, to which many soldatischer Nationalismus authors belonged[28]—signaled a discernible shift in the political mood of the late 1920s and early 1930s, what historian Wolfram Wette calls a "remilitarization of public opinion."[29] Pacifist works challenged the right's presumed authoritative version of the war story, and perhaps served more to vitalize the production of further heroizing accounts than they changed the public's attitude about war in any measurable way.

The same shifts in public war memory can be traced in the rise of nationalist picture books about the war in the later years of the 1920s. Spurred in part by Ernst Friedrich's damning *Krieg dem Kriege!* (1924), picture-book editors crafted positive interpretations of the war with text and image to correct previous pacifist accounts and sway present-day political opinion. These two efforts are most closely united in the two picture books of Franz Schauwecker, both published by the Stahlhelm-affiliated Frundsberg-Verlag. *So war der Krieg!* and *So ist der Friede* best typify the ideological extremes of soldatischer Nationalismus while utilizing many of the same representational strategies as other contemporary picture books, such as *Der Weltkrieg im Bild*. Schauwecker's picture books intervene in the war's visual representation by curating a specifically soldier-oriented version of the conflict that asserts an unassailable authenticity. The books combine commemoration with a loosely defined political agenda shared by wide swaths of Weimar national-conservatives, including replacing Germany's fledgling democracy, disregarding the Treaty of Versailles, and preparing for a coming war. In this sense, his picture books of the soldatischer Nationalismus are a prime case study for understanding how war memory—as constructed in its postwar visual depiction—was very much historically conditioned, culturally determined, and politically charged.

Franz Schauwecker wrote from a first-person perspective in his picture book *So war der Krieg!*, reflecting the military experience typical of authors of the soldatischer Nationalismus as well as the voice of authority they assumed from their war service. Disappointed by university study, Schauwecker had met the war with a new sense of purpose in life; although his family did not come from a military background, he enthusiastically enlisted

28. Prümm, *Die Literatur des Soldatischen Nationalismus*, 19.
29. Wette, "Von Kellogg bis Hitler," 170.

as a volunteer in November 1914.[30] Excepting time needed for recovery from two separate incidents in which he sustained serious gunshot wounds to a leg and to a hand, he served the war's entire duration, first as an infantryman on the Eastern Front and later as a lieutenant on the Western Front. Looking back on his discharge in December 1918, after which he struggled to find employment and suffered feelings of despondency, Schauwecker wrote: "What followed was a period of loneliness and resignation that lasted for years and was difficult to bear. . . . It was devoted to clarifying and organizing the inklings and feelings that had been awakened by the experience of the Great War."[31] After another abandoned attempt at university study, he established himself as an independent author, an endeavor that was likely motivated by the need for gainful employment as much as for a psychological and intellectual outlet for processing the war.

Schauwecker leaned heavily on his own war experience to write a score of war stories during the Weimar Republic, including edited versions of his personal diaries published under the titles *In Todesrachen* (In the jaws of death; 1919) and *Das Frontbuch* (Book of the front; 1927), the latter praised by Erich Ludendorff and Erich Maria Remarque alike for its authentic war testimony.[32] He achieved a moderate level of fame with his war novel *Aufbruch der Nation* (1929), and for his frequent contributions to various newspapers, including the *Stahlhelm* and its more radical pullout *Standarte*, which Schauwecker produced with Wilhelm Kleinau. His war stories attest to the strong impact that the front experience had not only on his personal life but also on his political worldview. Although his earlier works are concerned more with entertaining the reader through the adventure of war, his later fictional work and commentary takes on strong political aspirations, as he transformed his war experience from something personal into something rife with symbolic and ideological meaning for the German nation at-large. He sought to shape the meaning of the war's legacy in open attacks on the Weimar "system" and championed national-conservative ideas of the nation, such as the claim to leadership for the battle-tested former soldiers who knew the meaning of sacrifice.[33] An article appearing in 1926 in the *Standarte* that praised the murderers of Walter Rathenau and Matthias Erzberger as "nationalist martyrs" earned the outlet a three-month ban. Important collaborators, includ-

30. Bengsch, "Franz Schauwecker," 177.
31. Quoted in Bengsch, "Franz Schauwecker," 180.
32. Bengsch, "Franz Schauwecker," 180.
33. Bengsch, "Franz Schauwecker," 182–83.

ing Ernst Jünger, quit their work on the paper as a result of the article, and Schauwecker was prosecuted in court, although he was acquitted for the spurious reason that there was no definitive proof he knew of the article's content before its publication.[34] Schauwecker left the *Standarte* in 1927, but continued publishing in national-conservative papers, such as *Widerstand*, *Das Reich*, and *Der Vormarsch*. His novel *Aufbruch der Nation* (1929), which told the coming-of-age story of a soldier in the First World War as a spiritual and political awakening to nationalism, sold with moderate success and reviewers often contrasted it with Remarque's *Im Westen nichts Neues* from the same year.[35] Elements of soldatischer Nationalismus in the novel blended with motifs that later characterized National Socialism, and Schauwecker did enjoy a successful career beyond the Weimar Republic, writing more about the war as well as the need for a new national defense under the Nazi regime. Although never a formal member of the Nazi Party (the National Socialist German Workers' Party, or NSDAP), he was among the 88 authors who publicly proclaimed loyalty to Adolf Hitler in 1933 and was lauded as the first "national poet who seeks leadership in the competition of nations" in a glowing biography published by the Frundsberg-Verlag in the same year.[36] He was similarly hailed by the press as the "poet of the heroic life" seven years later on his fiftieth birthday in 1940,[37] but accordingly fell into obscurity after 1945.

Among Schauwecker's publication successes in the Weimar Republic are the picture books he produced in the late 1920s, *So war der Krieg!* and *So ist der Friede*. Both books are evidence of the more politically minded author, who sought to fashion the front experience as the starting point of a new nationalism that honored the legacy of the dead by reshaping a corrupt Weimar society to fit the bold yet vague vision of a nation ruled by its "front generation." *So war der Krieg!* imparts this idea by focusing on the experience of the frontline soldier, who is metaphysically transformed for the better by surviving the tribulations of the trenches. The picture book is divided into thematic sections covering elements of the front experience, from "Grenade explosions, artillery barrage, and gas" and "Shock troops, attack, and defense," to "Material destruction" and "Injury and death." As such, the book addresses only "the war as such. Staging grounds, parade inspection, and

34. Bengsch, "Franz Schauwecker," 184–85.
35. Bengsch, "Franz Schauwecker," 192–93.
36. Claasen, *Franz Schauwecker*, 70.
37. Bengsch, "Franz Schauwecker," 195–98.

recruit depot, training field and garrison are eliminated. The only decisive factor is the war as landscape and material and the German man as combat soldier."[38] A section on civilian populations was removed in an updated version for the seventh print edition in 1929; its pictures of displaced civilians fleeing their homes and a sympathetic vignette of a French child mourning her dead mother ("One did not see this often, but one saw it enough. Enough to know, to feel: what if the war were in our country—!"[39]) could not be fixed to the stated goal of re-creating just the "frontline combat experience."[40]

That this section was included in the first place is curious, since it is so incongruent to the book's central notion of soldierly experience: one of incredible auditory and visual stimulation through which the frontline soldier's primal instincts are awoken and the soldier is made to feel as if he stood "under a higher power."[41] Schauwecker evokes the frontline experience: "The channels of awareness have somehow been elevated to a higher level, our abilities raised into a different realm, into a new power." Soldiers molt into "higher beings in a very special sense, whose origin is this tormented earth, forerunners, pioneers of a new German man."[42] He clearly restricts this "war as inner experience" (to quote the title of Ernst Jünger's 1922 essay) to the front soldier; that other groups of people like displaced civilians or those safe on the home front could have experienced a similar transformational suffering during the war diverges sharply from the political purchase he wishes to assert for the frontline soldier as the sole inheritor of meaning derived from the war experience. Schauwecker writes of a "homeland incapable of resistance, sick and rebellious, from which nothing could be hoped"; the terrible contrast between the front experience and the home front gives a "judging, warning, and, last but not least, a comforting image" that is "indelibly burned into memory" and "stands now like a symbol before [the frontline soldier]."[43]

That the front experience should translate into a political agenda is self-evident for Schauwecker in *So war der Krieg!*, and the claim is made explicitly. The landscape of No Man's Land was for Schauwecker "the seedbeds of nationalism,"[44] and the soldiers who fell there embodied "the devotion

38. Schauwecker, *So war der Krieg!*, 3.
39. Schauwecker, *So war der Krieg!*, 108.
40. Schauwecker, *So war der Krieg!*, 3.
41. Schauwecker, *So war der Krieg!*, 43.
42. Schauwecker, *So war der Krieg!*, 43–44.
43. Schauwecker, *So war der Krieg!*, 115–16.
44. Schauwecker, *So war der Krieg!*, 5.

of the lesser self for the preservation of the higher, the nation."[45] Despite the war loss, the military was "beaten but undefeated,"[46] and the reasons for the war loss are ultimately inconsequential to Schauwecker, who skirts around rational explanation or a critical engagement with defeat by reducing the outcomes to a matter of a resistless fate that did not favor Germany, despite it having "the best army in the world."[47] Such irrationality—one broad characteristic of soldatischer Nationalismus—allows him to understate the enormous price Germany paid for its war loss and still find meaning in the conflict.

Schauwecker's interpretation of the war's legacy extends the type of patriotic nationalism found in the Reichsarchiv-affiliated publications, which primarily sought to preserve the positive ideals of the old Wilhelmine military elite, into a distinct ideology for a new era. Foremost among his positive interpretations is the spiritual birth of a *new* nationalism in war, spearheaded by a *new* brand of "personality": the battle-hardened German frontline soldier. "And as soon as we have recognized this," according to Schauwecker, "it is irrelevant what actually happens in this skirmish, in that battle. For us, the battle and the war are already won, even if outwardly they are lost."[48] The frontline metaphysical experience has elevated a group of people—"our generation"[49]—beyond the realm of mere soldiers into a new breed of political fortune makers. In other words, although it is on its surface a book to commemorate and remember the First World War through the Soldier's "objective" eyes (here equated with the photographic lens), *So war der Krieg!* is far more concerned with a contemporary struggle about the war's enduring legacy: "After the peace agreement came time for the frontline soldier to reflect. He began to ponder. He looked for the meaning, the answer that he had not found out there in the scourge of war. And he found a new meaning and a new answer: nationalism."[50] Fate prevented Germany from defeating its many enemies, but the legacy of the war is still up for grabs. "Today we strive to understand the meaning of that dark, mysterious fate."[51] What Schauwecker's combination of text and image in *So war der Krieg!* contributed to the contested commemoration of the First World War was a heroic

45. Schauwecker, *So war der Krieg!*, 134.
46. Schauwecker, *So war der Krieg!*, 44.
47. Schauwecker, *So war der Krieg!*, 10.
48. Schauwecker, *So war der Krieg!*, 44.
49. Schauwecker, *So war der Krieg!*, 8.
50. Schauwecker, *So war der Krieg!*, 11.
51. Schauwecker, *So war der Krieg!*, 10.

vision that accepted the war's brutalities—wide-scale human casualties and material destruction—as a cleansing of "the rotten spirit of the past."[52] The overwhelming amount and variety of physical destruction pictured in the volume is framed, therefore, not as senseless violence, but as a necessary purging of the old: "This work shows destruction in almost every one of its images, namely the destruction of a past world."[53] The violence of the trenches represented both "the death spasms of a dying age and the birth spasms of a coming age, whose convulsions still continue today and whose final form is only now being prepared."[54] Although explosions, devastation, and death pervade the volume, *So war der Krieg!* attempts to crystallize a perspective on the war that finds spiritual triumph in tragedy, metaphysical transformation in physical destruction. In doing so, it instrumentalizes the heroic memory of war in service of a particular claim of authenticity for the "front generation" representation of war and a position of moral legitimacy for that group in the larger political and cultural debates of the late Weimar Republic.

The understanding of the war at the heart of *So war der Krieg!* stands in clear contrast to competing interpretations by pacifists, and its political agenda is framed in contrast to democrats and communists alike. Schauwecker criticizes all these groups explicitly. He espouses radical nationalist views, including a willingness to serve the nation at all costs, to submit to the will of fate, even if that entails death. Such a fate is beyond the grasp of pacifists, whom he decries as ignoring the metaphysical experience of the war's violence by concentrating on the technical qualities of cannons and machines. Fate does not reveal itself "in the insubstantial speculation of the smartest calculator,"[55] as pacifists are guilty of in stressing the number of men killed or the amount of money wasted in war. For Schauwecker, someone who counts the destroyed homes, or translates the manpower of troops at the front into the number of new homes that could have been built, or estimates the liters of blood lost, would just as likely measure the value of a statue by its weight, the effect of a painting by its size, and the truth of a claim by the number of its believers—"This is how German democracy came into being, this is how it thinks, and this is how it will perish."[56] Cold rationality is anathema to Schauwecker's insistence on an emotional transformation through

52. Schauwecker, *So war der Krieg!*, 8.
53. Schauwecker, *So war der Krieg!*, 8.
54. Schauwecker, *So war der Krieg!*, 20.
55. Schauwecker, *So war der Krieg!*, 7.
56. Schauwecker, *So war der Krieg!*, 8.

war, although he does not see the irony in the various instances throughout the book in which he interrupts his melodramatic prose with lists of facts and figures, including the number of casualties among combatant nations, shown so that they "become effective in history and guarantee the future."[57] His claim that "death for the country obliges the survivors; death begets action"[58] is not rhetorically much different from the pacifist cry for "Nie Wieder Krieg" (Never again war); it is simply a matter of seeing the same numbers from a contrasting vantage point. But, as he insists, "Anyone who sees only the 'senseless slaughter' of war proves that he himself saw nothing else in the war."[59]

Ad hominem attacks on pacifists as "irrelevant" and "cowardly and effeminate,"[60] with a "hole in their character,"[61] round out Schauwecker's diatribe, and he casts soldiers into a type of victim role made familiar by the phrase "geschlagen aber unbesiegt" (beaten but not defeated). Despite their extraordinary merit and sacrifice, soldiers could only stand by helplessly in November 1918 as they were betrayed by the likes of Spartacists Karl Liebknecht and Rosa Luxemburg, and then by Philipp Scheidemann, who proclaimed the German republic, and Matthias Erzberger, who as a minister in Scheidemann's government pressed for acceptance of the Treaty of Versailles: "Then the frontline soldier, bleeding from a hundred wounds, exhausted, with shaking knees, lowered his head and leaned on the burnt post of a destroyed house. That was Germany and that was the end. None of us were guilty. And yet reckoning came for Germany."[62]

Because of this supposed betrayal and the "intellectual-business interests" of democratic groups that ran counter to the war effort, there is only one movement that grasps the meaning of German fate: "It is only nationalism that is given the strength to do this in the future, and thus the German future; a tremendous responsibility given through fate."[63] These are the words that immediately precede the book's very first photograph, labeled "This is how the infantry marched to the front in 1918" (fig. 45). It shows a long column of German soldiers winding their way through an unspecified countryside. The photographer is positioned relatively high above the scene,

57. Schauwecker, *So war der Krieg!*, 124.
58. Schauwecker, *So war der Krieg!*, 124.
59. Schauwecker, *So war der Krieg!*, 7.
60. Schauwecker, *So war der Krieg!*, 7.
61. Schauwecker, *So war der Krieg!*, 8.
62. Schauwecker, *So war der Krieg!*, 11.
63. Schauwecker, *So war der Krieg!*, 12.

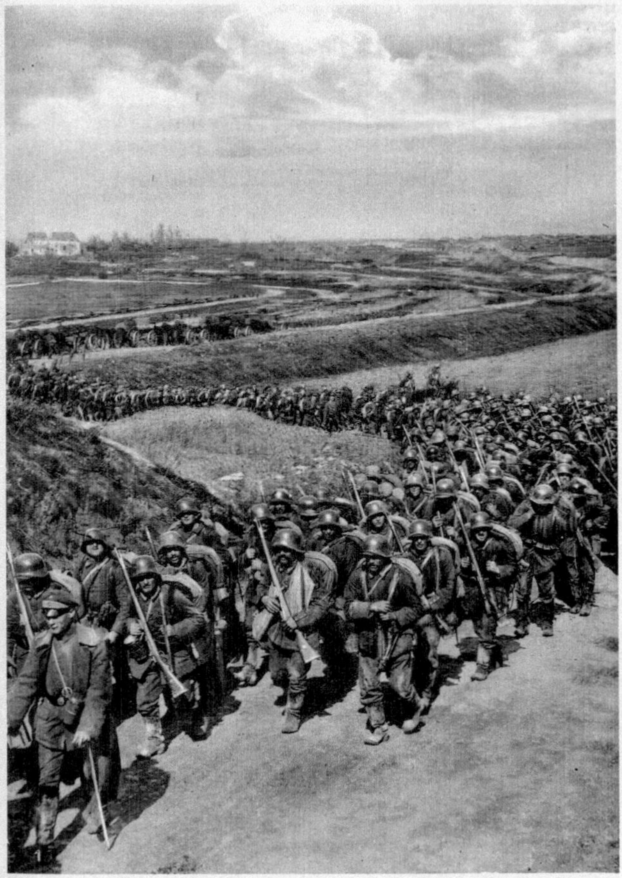

So marschierte die Infanterie 1918 zur Front.

Fig. 45. Franz Schauwecker, *So war der Krieg!* (Berlin: Frundsberg-Verlag, 1927), page 13.

perhaps standing on a cart or a nearby embankment, enabling him to capture the line of soldiers stretching into the distance. The photographer's position also means the soldiers who do pay the camera any attention must look up toward it. Their expressions are mostly blank, but their chins are held hopefully high, despite the photograph's origins in the war's later stages. The preceding text concerned with "the German future" casts this image, which is a tightly cropped version of a photograph that shows up in other picture books in different contexts,[64] as the embodiment of both a storied past and a sign of what is to come. Schauwecker's claim that nationalism is the only force suited to "give expression" to the "meaning of German fate" in the postwar era is made literal through the suggestion that the legacy of the soldiers pictured marching to the front in 1918 is taken up by nationalist factions, such as the paramilitaristic Stahlhelm, which jostled for political and symbolic power in the late 1920s.

Although it is rife with telling textual rhetoric, it is not enough to simply quote *So war der Krieg!*, as Schauwecker's book takes pride in its apparent success in (re)creating the war experience in both text *and* image. The title page sets the tone: "The book represents two books in one: the frontline soldier's diary of experiences [*Erlebnisbuch*] in words and pictures. Both parts merge into a coherent whole, something previously unknown."[65] *Erlebnis* (experience) is key to understanding the book, which—more than a "journal in pictures" for the frontline soldier,[66] as it claims elsewhere—is closer to a virtual immersion into the frontline experience (at least as Schauwecker fashions it) for those who missed out on the real thing. In transcribing the frontline experience into text and image, Schauwecker sought the induction of a type of affective prosthetic memory that would change subjectivities in the present and shape national politics. In this regard, the different qualities of text and image were strategically employed to have the greatest effect in immersing readers into his vision of war. As stated above, *So war der Krieg*'s thematic sections are all divided into two parts: in each, he provides several pages of text—often a curious mix of historical facts and figures with bombastic narrative prose and ideological ruminations—followed by several pages of photographs illustrative of the theme at hand. The photographs are given only short, descriptive captions—"Mine detonation" or "Tank guns take up position," for example—devoid of Schauwecker's characteristic pathos. Photographs are only sporadically attributed to a specific date or location, and no credit is given to individual photographers. This, combined with the fact that Schauwecker groups together photographs that have similar content matter and share formal qualities like perspective and framing, allows him to ignore the particularities of what is being pictured in favor of a more general yet specifically curated version of the war.

64. The same photograph appears in Ernst Jünger's *Das Antlitz des Weltkrieges* with the less charged title "Replacements" (page 21) and in *Der Weltkrieg im Bild* as "German columns on the march to the front" (see fig. 39 here).

65. Schauwecker, *So war der Krieg!*, title page.

66. Schauwecker, *So war der Krieg!*, 3.

For the less astute reader, historical exactitude and verifiable authenticity will not be an issue, and text and image *will* "merge into a coherent whole" as intended; simply put, it is not a stretch to imagine readers becoming engrossed by Schauwecker's oftentimes melodramatic prose accompanied by the photographs' visual excitement. On the surface, the thematic correlation between the texts he wrote and the photographs he selected and arranged is enough to tie these elements together. The lack of meta-reflection on the visual mediation of war serves this harmony, which goes hand-in-hand with a naturalistic presentation style that conceals the means of production for its illusion of reality. For example, Schauwecker's captions never directly infringe on the photographs' meaning in a satiric, ironic, or clearly falsifying way that would draw attention to the fraught relationship of connotation and denotation between text and image. Rather, he crafts the textual sections in a particular way so they could fit any of the corresponding photographs that follow. Conversely, photographs are constrained to function on the level of resemblances to cement this relationship to the text; the photographs' indexical moment is eclipsed by their iconic status, which is ensured by short, imprecise captions meant to impart an impression of what battle was like more so than to point to a specific historical moment. Pictures that share a likeness are grouped together to typify a theme and further trigger the photographs' iconic potential, as do those on pages 29–36, taken on many different dates and at many different locations but all showing explosions of some sort and together giving an impression of "Grenade explosions, artillery barrage, and gas" (see, for example, figs. 46 and 47). The symbolism is provided by the text: along with his typical metaphysics of the frontline experience, Schauwecker adds an account of poison-gas usage, which at first glance appears quite factual due to statistics cited from another publication, but ends up being entirely revisionist in its claim that the French were the first ones to use gas in the trenches.

That Schauwecker's writing style frequently shifts between hyperbolic, emotive descriptions of battles and rational, distanced presentation of statistics, although their exactitude can be called into question, is indicative of the relationship between fact and fiction at the book's core, and, as shown, plays out prominently in the constructed relationship between text and image. Lists of the number of casualties at sea among all belligerent nations or statistics about the explosive power of different grenades and artillery munitions,[67] to name two examples, add another layer to Schauwecker's

67. Schauwecker, *So war der Krieg!*, 92, 87.

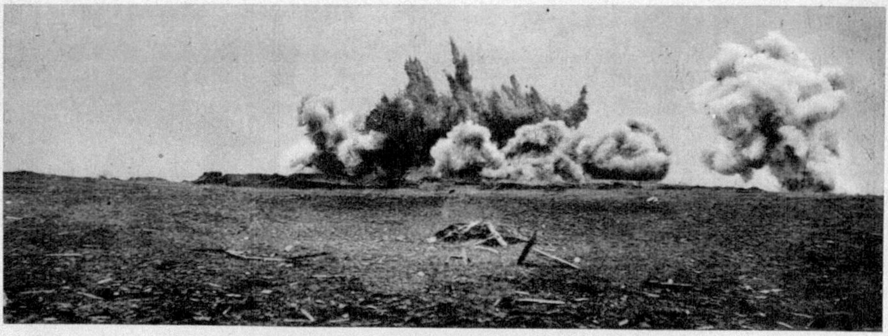

Fliegerangriff auf Etray. (Ende Oktober 1918.)

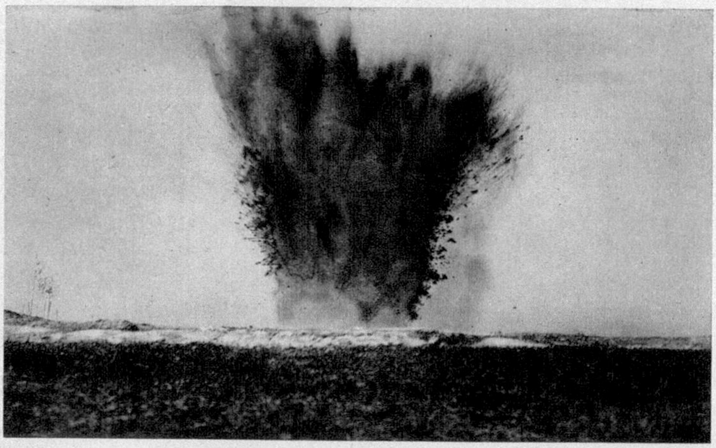

Minensprengung.

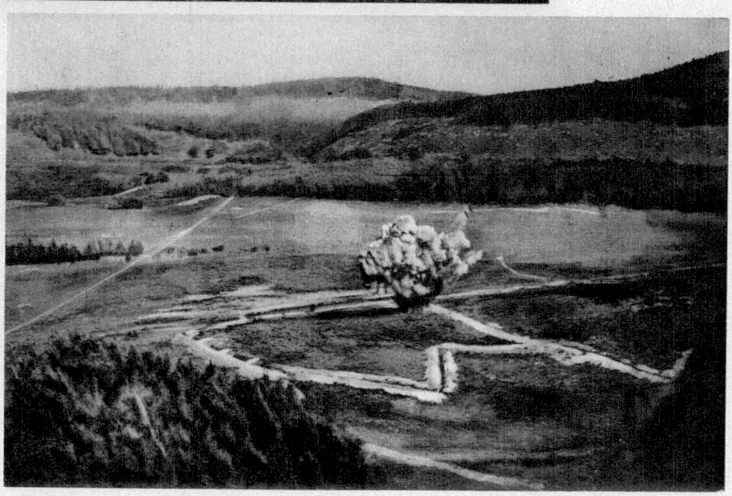

Erster Schuß auf neue Stellung. (Vogesen, Mudra-Riegel.)

Fig. 46. Franz Schauwecker, *So war der Krieg!* (Berlin: Frundsberg-Verlag, 1927), page 30.

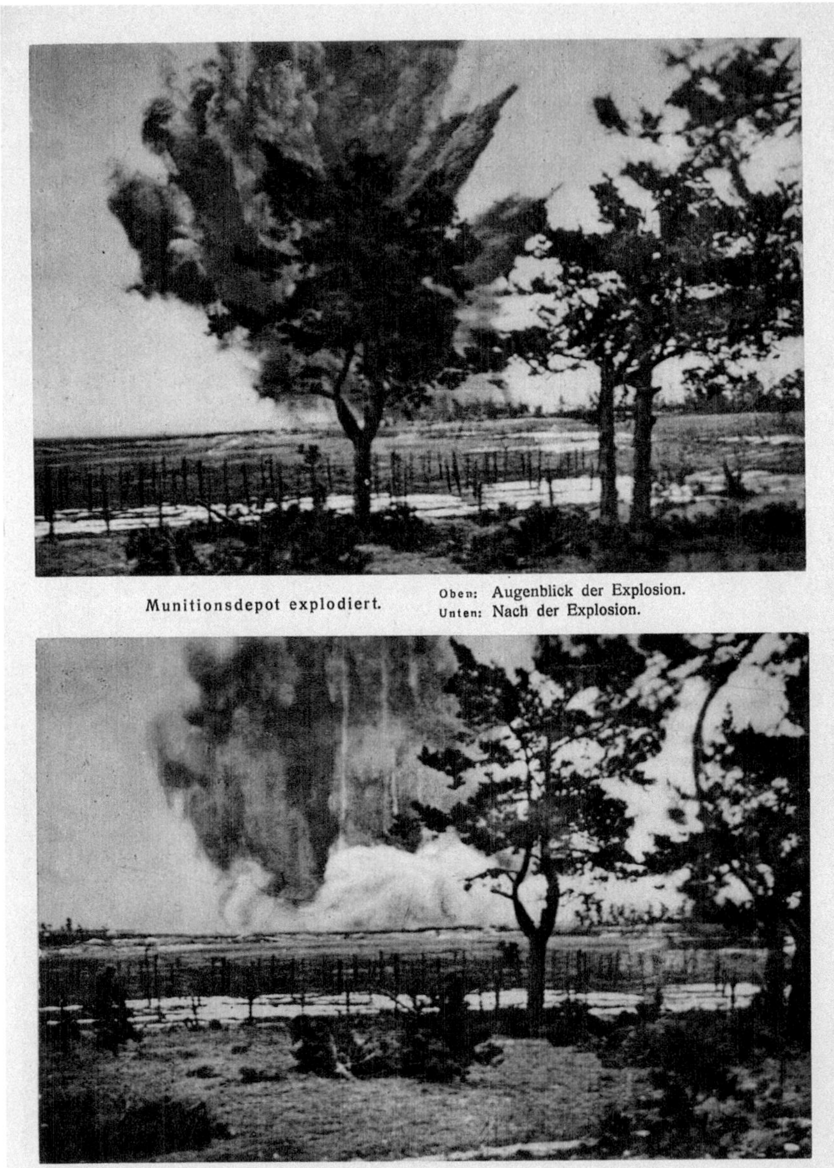

Fig. 47. Franz Schauwecker, *So war der Krieg!* (Berlin: Frundsberg-Verlag, 1927), page 31.

authoritative voice in *So war der Krieg!*, which strives to be a reliable source of factual knowledge about the war at the same time that it evokes an emotional testimony ultimately meant to shape political mentalities. If the first voice is concerned with the reproduction of "facts" and figures to impart an air of truth, the second voice is limited specifically to a more literary prose style, which mines that "truth" for its symbolic meaning.

Instead of reporting accounts of the front in a diary style à la Ernst Jünger's *In Stahlgewittern*, Schauwecker writes in a first-person narrative present that masquerades as his own actual experience while also standing in to represent a generic lived experience at the front. This can be seen as he effortlessly glides between an "I" perspective and a "we" perspective, grounding the narrative in his own lived experience while also allowing him to speak as the representative of an (imagined) "front generation." An obvious example of this is in the section titled "Shock troops, attack, and defense," which details the anxious motions of his autobiographical narrator as he awaits an attack: "I run through the trench, I press myself against the trench wall, I crouch on an ammunition box, I climb into a shelter, I turn around and climb up, I stare at the clock." But when the ordained moment comes to attack, the narrator switches to the first-person plural: "We climb out of the ditch and run," as if the very movement of attack had united the disparate individuals into one body.[68] Although he slips back into the first-person singular, by the end of the passage the "we" of his company has consolidated into one perceptive body that sees, thinks, and acts in unison, driven not by individual concerns but pulled by the fate of battle: "We move forward on a path of victory just a few meters wide, driven by an irresistible instinct, drawn by this vacuum that sucks us in with an irresistible attraction."[69]

More than a personal diary, *So war der Krieg!* functions as a repository of impressions in which the historical recounting of the particularities of certain battles is not as imperative as demonstrating the transformative impact of the war's visual, aural, and haptic stimuli on the sensorium of the frontline soldier. This is accomplished by an elision of most identifying information and a preference for highly stylized textual descriptions of generic battle scenes from the perspective of an entrenched frontline soldier. Throughout the book, Schauwecker's expository voice, which provides the distanced historical overview of the war and his political interpretation thereof, slips freely back and forth into an expressionistic prose style that seeks to convey

68. Schauwecker, *So war der Krieg!*, 39.
69. Schauwecker, *So war der Krieg!*, 42.

the frontline experience. Action and its effect on the body are emphasized in present tense as dramatic descriptors accumulate to impart a vision of hell, such as in this account of artillery fire: "a ceaseless banging and thundering, an endlessly monotonous ripping up and turning of the earth, a fury of rage and frenzy, in which one crash chases after another, one impact bursts into another, one smoke rolls into another."[70] Ellipses frequently interrupt the narrative to mark instances when he hears the voices of other soldiers speaking around him (see, for example, page 25), emphasizing a sense of shared experience. These rich textual descriptions are included in the picture book to give meaning to the soldier's emotions, which are largely closed off to the photographic lens. His lengthy passages of expressionistic prose reveal that he does not completely trust photography's power to convey the emotions he wishes to ascribe to the war experience; the realm of feeling is too important to his cause to leave it up to the surface appearance of photographs.

Take, for example, the section titled "Shock troops, attack, and defense," which begins *in medias res* as frontline soldiers wait for friendly artillery to flatten enemy defenses for a planned attack. There is no indication of where or when this particular skirmish is taking place, and that information is largely inessential, as Schauwecker admits himself, as the text does not intend to narrate a historical occurrence but rather relay an experience. By witnessing the artillery barrage and the resulting wall of fire and smoke, the frontline soldier forgets facts and slips into a transcendental realm:

> One hardly perceives the images of the kilometer-long front of smoke resulting from the impacts, which surpass all imagination, as reality any more. Instead, one stares into them, as if one's soul is being drawn out of one's flesh, and stands there with a body through which everything passes for minutes, like water through a pipe. Suddenly, everything becomes a vision, an apparition from another, higher realm, in which everything that happens has its unspeakable meaning shrouded by terrible sights.[71]

That the soldiers cannot process the surplus of stimuli during the artillery barrage—their bodies becoming mere channels through which impressions flow—typifies Schauwecker's metaphysics. The war escapes rational explanation and can only be understood as "apparitions from another, higher

70. Schauwecker, *So war der Krieg!*, 26.
71. Schauwecker, *So war der Krieg!*, 37–38.

realm." By the end of the narrative, the "champions for a new German man" are making their way into battle. Unconcerned with the outcome, they are "geschlagen, aber unbesiegt."[72] On the next pages, photographs show German troops caught up in the frontline's (meta)physical tumult: troops rush over craters into flattened wastelands where smoke and fire envelop them. Again, captions impart little emotive quality and serve only to clarify what is pictured, for example, "Assault troops advance in shrapnel fire."[73] However, the preceding text lingers in the reader's mind as he sees photographic—and therefore seemingly incontrovertible—evidence of the intense stimuli of battle, which, of course, were felt exclusively by the frontline soldier. Text and image thus stand in a subtle reciprocal relationship, in which the text activates the photograph's icon (What the Soldier pictured here has experienced is unimaginable!), while the photograph's index authenticates the text's political testimony (We are the Front Soldiers; to what ends have we suffered greatly?).

Another way of thinking through this mutual relationship is by paying attention to the way Schauwecker navigates around the limits of the two media forms. At stake in *So war der Krieg!* is the claim that the internal experience of the frontline soldier in war awakened a new political consciousness. Representations of this transformative spiritual encounter will necessarily be impeded by the cleft between surface appearances and the inner world of the mind and spirit. Unable to satisfactorily convey the new German *Mensch*'s internal qualities, photography, because it is limited to a surface representation of objects in a single moment, seems best accompanied by written description, a form better suited to unfurl the entire gamut of emotions, thoughts, and impressions that are waiting, latent in the imagination. As we see in *So war der Krieg!*, Schauwecker is quite at home in giving shape through writing to the more intense emotional and physical experiences of war that a photograph on its own is not certain to engender. Photography does offer, however, an indexical connection to reality that is stronger than words alone. The writing style of *So war der Krieg!* is often bombastic and in many instances skirts the bounds of believability through its melodramatic nature. This type of language works, however, much differently when combined with photography, which as a medium—especially in a popular sense—is tied closely to reality. Instead of reading like the hyperstylized fiction it is, the text (and its ideological undercurrent) gains an air of authen-

72. Schauwecker, *So war der Krieg!*, 44.
73. Schauwecker, *So war der Krieg!*, 50.

ticity in combination with photography. And conversely, the text activates the photographs' emotional potential, allowing Schauwecker to shape his own vision of the war experience and draw the intended meaning from it.

So war der Krieg! explicitly comments on photography as a medium in order to undergird Schauwecker's claim of representing the front experience authentically and authoritatively. Foremost is the insistence that the photographs in the book represent, in a sort of direct translation, the front experience. The title page asserts: "The 200 images contained in this work were selected from 25,000 photographs provided by frontline soldiers"; and the introduction states: "The structure and sequence of the images was determined by the experience of the frontline soldier."[74] Schauwecker employs an acritical approach to photography that elides questions of its capacity for presenting reality in the service of an apparently self-evident realism. Schauwecker bases the authenticity of his picture book on an exaggeration of the camera's technical properties: "The war . . . has soberly and wordlessly inscribed itself into the undeceivable light-sensitive layer of the photographic plate."[75]

Later in the book, a notable comparison between photography and memory also serves to authenticate the soldier's war account as unassailable. In the section "Shock troops, attack, and defense," in the middle of an attack, Schauwecker writes:

> And when we sometimes look to our sides, the retina of the eye unconsciously records the landscape there like a photographic plate and determines that soldiers are moving forward there too, at about the same level as us, but when we look away, that impression has disappeared, completely blurred. Only later, much later, do such insignificant things stand before our memory with the sharpest clarity, as if thrown onto a screen by a spotlight.[76]

This passage illuminates the threads tying photography, memory, and authenticity together in *So war der Krieg!*: it reiterates the technological perfection of photography made in the introduction; it exemplifies the primal yet ultimately transformative state soldiers experienced at the front, becoming mere receptors for overwhelming sensory information; and it asserts

74. Schauwecker, *So war der Krieg!*, 3.
75. Schauwecker, *So war der Krieg!*, 3.
76. Schauwecker, *So war der Krieg!*, 43.

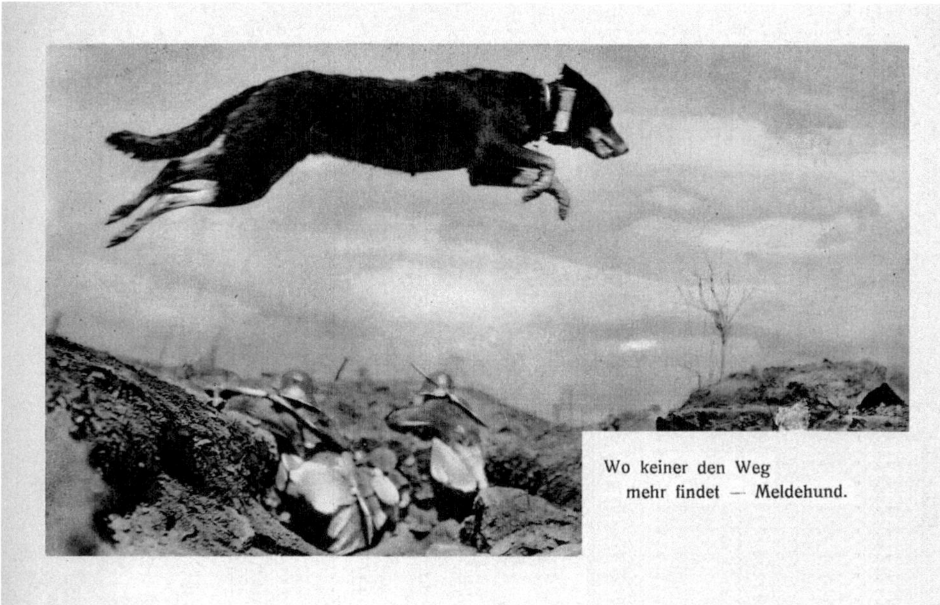

Fig. 48. Franz Schauwecker, *So war der Krieg!* (Berlin: Frundsberg-Verlag, 1927), page 105.

the authoritative memory of the front soldier, who remembers "with the sharpest clarity." This last point also speaks to a central concern of *So war the Krieg!*: the war's cultural meaning was still hotly contested even ten years after its end. The sociopolitical ramifications of the war's interpretation had too wide an impact for Schauwecker to just give his own account à la Jünger's *In Stahlgewittern*. Rather, he was compelled to stake the claim to be the *sole* inheritor of the war experience, the authenticator of the *Fronterlebnis* (frontline experience), which was, all things considered, specific to his highly constructed vision of the war that proceeded from an acritical utilization of photography.

Beyond the foundational question of the extent to which photography accurately represents reality or lived experience, let alone the experience of millions of soldiers idealized into one frontline soldier type, is the dubiousness of Schauwecker's claim that the photographs in his volume were supplied by amateur cameramen in the trenches. Bernd Hüppauf has found reason to suspect a fair portion of the photographs were actually taken by official war department correspondents for propaganda purposes, including a spectacular shot of a messenger dog leaping across the gap of a trench (fig.

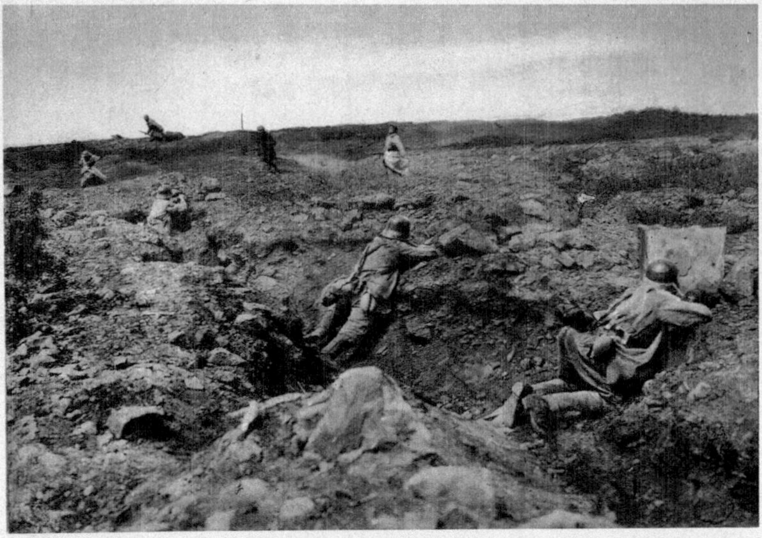

Der Franzose greift an.

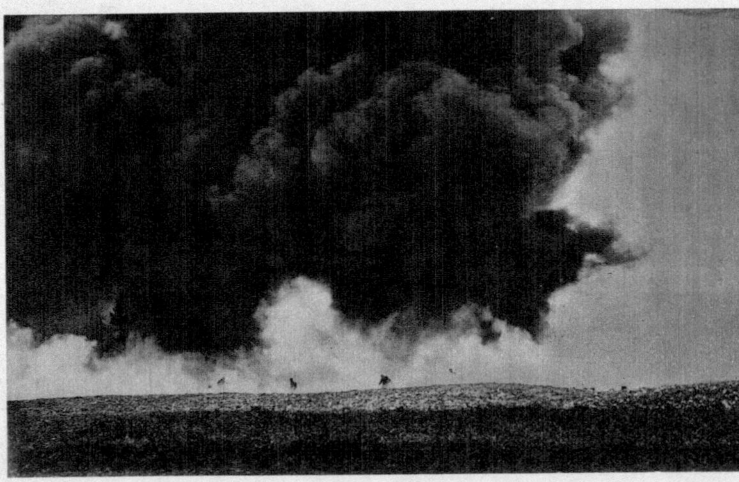

Deutscher Stoßtrupp geht unter dem Rauchschutz von Flammenwerfern vor.

Fig. 49. Franz Schauwecker, *So war der Krieg!* (Berlin: Frundsberg-Verlag, 1927), page 46.

48), a well-known photograph used to soften the image of war for a domestic audience in the effort to sell war bonds.[77] Bodo von Dewitz makes the general claim about the First World War that "genuine scenes of battle did not appear in photographs, though snapshots taken of individual explosions, often of one's own artillery fire, could convey an impression of the war."[78] While this might be overgeneralizing, it is clear that many photographs in *So war der Krieg!* fit this category. Take, for example, "The Frenchman attacks" (see fig. 49). It is hard to imagine a photographer exposing his position in such a vulnerable way in the middle of an enemy's attack for a photograph; it was more probably taken during a routine training exercise. Other photographs, especially aerial views of the destroyed landscape of battlefields, clearly suggest that Schauwecker is lying about the photographs' quotidian origins. To trace the provenance of every image in the volume would be an arduous undertaking, yet it suffices to state here that the reason the photographs and text "merge into a coherent whole" is because Schauwecker has obscured any details surrounding individual photographs. They are transplanted from a variety of sources and contexts—without attribution—to become illustrative pieces of his version of the war.

The connection asserted between the "undeceivable light-sensitive layer of the photographic plate"[79] and the veracity of *So war der Krieg!* is clear; whether it was enough to persuade its readers is another matter, although many reviewers from different backgrounds found Schauwecker's picture book to be highly convincing. Xaver Schaukroff, writing in the Catholic literary journal *Der Gral* (The grail), praises the entire enterprise as "exemplary,"[80] and a "Dr. L.," in the Pan-German nationalist journal *Deutschlands Erneuerung* (Germany's renewal), extols Schauwecker's ability "to exploit the educational content of the images."[81] The book is for him "an invaluable possession for anyone who has retained pride in his time as a soldier and is prepared to raise his children in the spirit of this frontline fighter."[82] At the same time that he criticizes the sometimes hyperbolic and long-winded prose of *So war der*

77. Hüppauf, "Zwischen Metaphysik und visuellem Esayismus," 234.

78. Dewitz, "German Snapshots," 157.

79. Schauwecker, *So war der Krieg!*, 3.

80. Schaukroff, review of *So war der Krieg*, 735. The journal's editor, Friedrich Muckermann, was a well-known German Jesuit priest and early Nazi opponent who fled the country in 1934.

81. L., review of *So war der Krieg*, 328. The author is likely the journal's editor, Julius Friedrich Lehmann, Beer Hall Putschist and NSDAP, or Nazi Party, member.

82. L., review of *So war der Krieg*, 328.

Krieg!, Oscar Illing admits in *Die neue Zeit* (The new times), a local weekly for politics, art, and literature from the German-American stronghold of New Ulm, Minnesota, that when one looks at the photographs in the book, "one immediately finds oneself with the frontline soldier in the tumult and fury of the World War."[83] According to Illing, photography "appears realistic and natural" and relays "the most vivid insight into a reality that has now become the past."[84]

These reviews duplicate Schauwecker's own stance on the power of photography and reflect attitudes of a popular reading audience who expected the immersive, authentic experience of a picture book. Indeed, the book must be taken seriously as a publication success; despite its price, which made it an unaffordable luxury item for many consumers, it sold well and had seventh and eighth editions published in 1928 and 1929. Schauwecker explains in the introduction to the seventh edition: "I welcome this new edition of a book that is difficult to sell due to its not insignificant price as a sign of growing nationalism. The World War, this stormy dividing line between two eras, already contains the present in its laboring womb and is more significant as a germinal point for the future than some may think."[85] Alterations made for the seventh edition of *So war der Krieg!* heighten many of the book's themes discussed up to this point, including its emphasis on soldiers as the "bearers of the ideas of an inevitably coming nationalist era."[86] Schauwecker decries attempts by liberal democracy in Germany "to attempt something in literary matters that, to the less instinctive, might almost look like nationalism."[87] What this veiled attack specifically refers to is less important than the fact that, even 10 years afterwards, the war's legacy was still contested with current political ramifications in mind.

For the seventh edition, *So war der Krieg!* was revised and 80 new photographs were added—some new, others replacing "less effective photographs"[88]—for an increased total of 230 (the original had 200). As stated earlier, the section on civilian populations in the first editions did not lend itself to Schauwecker's soldier-centered, nationalist interpretation of the war experience, and it was accordingly excised in the revised edition in favor of new sections on "Verdun" and "Material." The latter perpetuates a standard

83. Illing, "Buecher- und Schriftschau," 12.
84. Illing, "Buecher- und Schriftschau," 12.
85. Schauwecker, *So war der Krieg!*, 7th ed., 1.
86. Schauwecker, *So war der Krieg!*, 7th ed., 1.
87. Schauwecker, *So war der Krieg!*, 7th ed., 2.
88. Schauwecker, *So war der Krieg!*, 7th ed., 1.

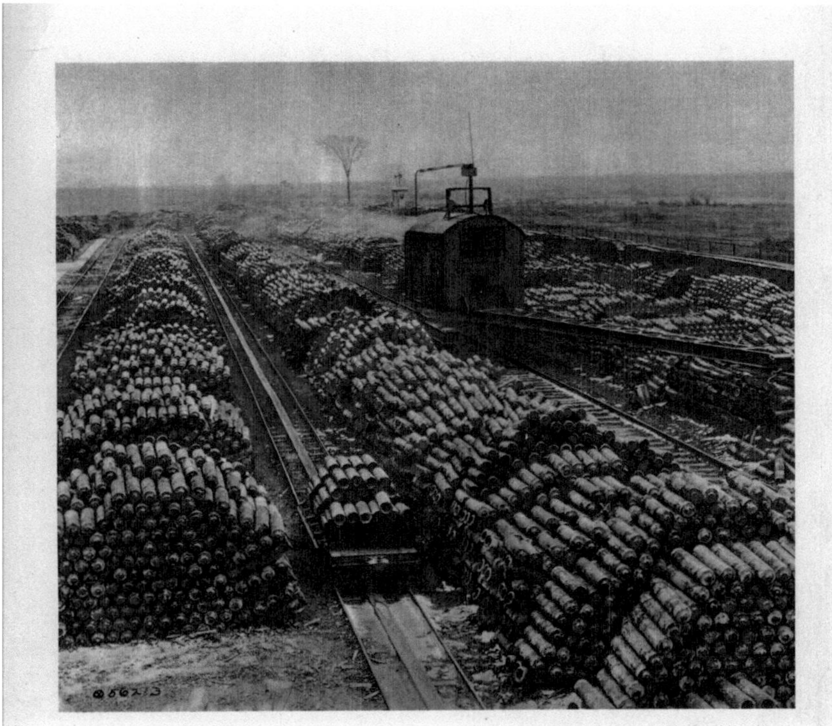

Fig. 50. Franz Schauwecker, *So war der Krieg!* (7th ed., Berlin: Frundsberg-Verlag, 1928), page 123.

line of argument among proponents of soldatischer Nationalismus: the front line was beaten mainly by its material disadvantage, yet the spirit of the front line (Schauwecker criticizes the home front and the *Etappe*) lives on. Seeming evidence of the Entente's material superiority is quite effectively illustrated in six photographs new to the seventh edition that show, for example, rows upon rows of Entente vehicles and stacks of English artillery that stretch from foreground to horizon (fig. 50). The new section on "Verdun" continues many of the same lines of thought from the original edition that support the legend of the frontline warrior. A short narrative of a company sent to the front lines quickly descends into the quintessential Schauweckerian experiences of battle: the mental and physical confusion occasioned by artillery barrages and other explosions, the whole-body perception of nature's forces (here, fire and rain), the fragile metaphysical balance between life and death, and the indubitable heroism of the front soldier in embracing fate: "Why did we stay? Why didn't we run away? . . . Only we know: fate wanted it, and we must want what fate wants."[89] Many of the pictures in the "Verdun" section are rearranged from other parts of the original edition, and added photographs simply expand the book's archive of visual destruction by showing the wasted landscapes of Verdun with short, identifying captions (see, for example, fig. 51).

Although *So war der Krieg!* is largely focused on the perspective of the frontline soldier who was transformed through the war experience and lived to claim the war's legacy, even those soldiers who did not escape death are included in Schauwecker's vision of nationalism. He elevates death on the battlefield to a symbolic sacrifice for the nation, as many other patriotic and nationalist thinkers do, but he does so also with a message for the present, for those who may have to follow suit in a "coming war," as he calls it elsewhere.[90] In "Grave," the last section of *So war der Krieg!*, Schauwecker uses the figure of the upturned war grave to show the physical nexus between life and death, thereby asserting a metaphorical connection between the living and the dead, united in the life of the nation:

> Often the war tore the graves back open, dragged the dead out, and tossed them around. The graves opened up. The dead rose, and among the dead fell the living, and new dead were thrown in. Life and death were intertwined, accompanied by the thunderous Nocturno of the battle, the dark dance of death. Here, the ultimate things were revealed.[91]

This apocalyptic vision of the living, dead, and soon-to-be-dead physically merging on the battlefield serves not only the broader idea that the frontline soldier's brush with death has steeled him for the present age but also suggests a future-oriented argument that death is not to be feared as it is a natural aspect of life; by extension, to die for the nation should not be feared, as it is a natural aspect of life as a member of the nation. This is the meaning of those who died during the war: "There are many words written on the miserable wooden crosses of the frontline graves. Their meaning is: 'To love life does not mean to fear death.'"[92] As will become clear in the next chap-

89. Schauwecker, *So war der Krieg!*, 7th ed., 56.
90. Schauwecker, *So war der Krieg!*, 67.
91. Schauwecker, *So war der Krieg!*, 133.
92. Schauwecker, *So war der Krieg!*, 134.

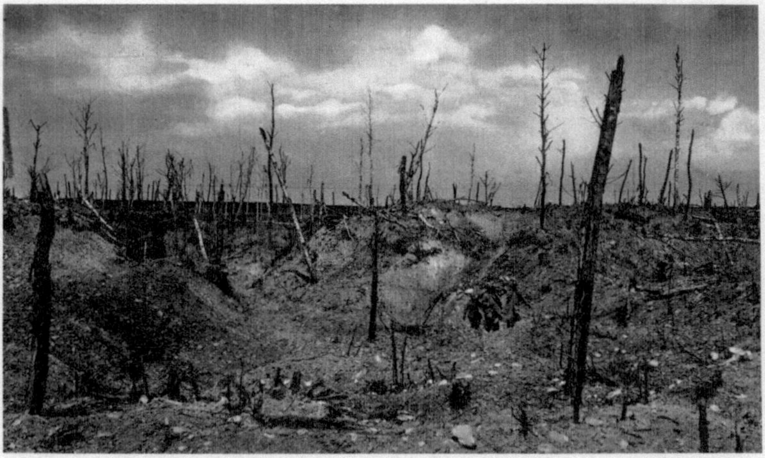

Caillette-Wald vor Verdun.

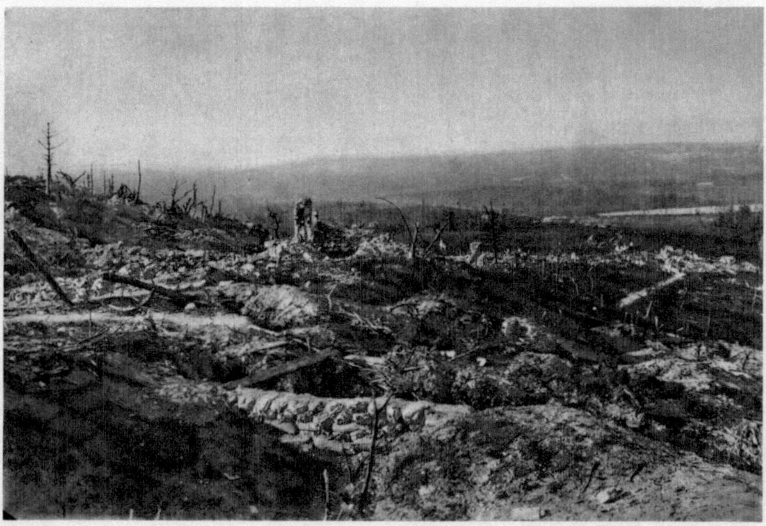

Französische Höhe bei Pargny.

Fig. 51. Franz Schauwecker, *So war der Krieg!* (7th ed., Berlin: Frundsberg-Verlag, 1928), page 64.

ter on Schauwecker's picture book *So ist der Friede*, the follow-up to *So war der Krieg!*, the nationalism born of the war experience is a powerful force that extends beyond 1918 to shape Germany and the world. In the unstable postwar world of *So ist der Friede*, in which political, social, and economic upheaval anticipates future conflict, the war dead remind the living that the nation relies on death for life. In Schauwecker's words: "For us, our connection with the nation as a whole inevitably and necessarily means living with it. But living with it could one day mean dying with it."[93]

93. Schauwecker, *So war der Krieg!*, 133.

CHAPTER SIX

Indicting the War's Political Legacy

Franz Schauwecker's *So ist der Friede* and a New German Nationalism

The follow-up to Franz Schauwecker's *So war der Krieg!* was published in 1928 by the Frundsberg-Verlag under the title *So ist der Friede: Die Revolution der Zeit in 300 Bildern* (This is what peace is like: The revolution of our times in 300 pictures). As the similarity between the two titles suggests, the "peace" described in *So ist der Friede* is highly interwoven with the war's legacy and Schauwecker's interpretation thereof. The picture book continues the text-and-image strategies of *So war der Krieg!*, which make its visual form almost identical to the first picture book. Many of the incriminating arguments directed against the Weimar "system" made in passing in the first book are developed fully in the follow-up, foremost among them the denunciation of liberalism, the championing of nationalism in an era of international uncertainty, and the need for Germany to remilitarize in the face of a global weapons race. In contrast to Walter Bloem and George Soldan, whose military-affirming accounts of the past reinforced only broad patriotic and nationalist mentalities in the present, Schauwecker's account of the war's legacy stakes out a far more explicitly political standpoint. He understands the First World War as "the first confrontation between liberalism and nationalism, which subsequently can only bring about the defeat of liberalism."[1] The political issues of the late 1920s are refracted through this interpretation of the war. Schauwecker decries the inability of liberalism—broadly construed as democracy, parliamentarianism, individualism, and internationalism—to both govern effectively and attend to the nation's inner soul that was awakened through sacrifices at the front. He understands all evidence presented in *So ist der Friede* to signal the impending rise of Ger-

1. Schauwecker, *So ist der Friede*, 7.

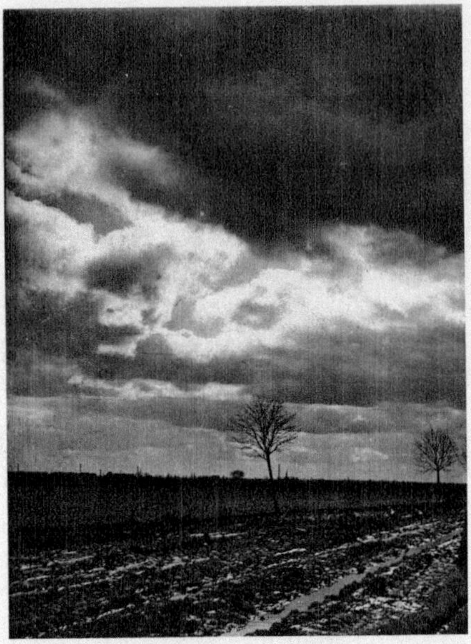

Diese Zeit

Franz Schauwecker

Über fernen Gräbern steht kein Zeichen.
Hügel schweigen kreuzlos. Erde fällt.
Trümmerfeld und Schädelstätte bleichen,
Über denen niemand Wache hält.

Keine Fahne flattert über'm Volke,
Weiten Scharen geht kein Schritt voran.
Massen murren, eine schwere Wolke,
Die nicht Blitz noch Regen werfen kann.

Schuld in lang und leicht vertanen Jahren,
Schuld an Erbe und an neuem Gut.
Wie Gesetze steh'n die Kriegerbahren.
Dunkel um die Wurzeln kreist das Blut.

Fig. 52. Franz Schauwecker, *So ist der Friede* (This is what peace is like) (Berlin: Frundsberg-Verlag, 1928), page 3.

man nationalism, which the political morass of the Weimar Republic has until now repressed but which will soon reassume political authority and the mantle of German-ness so valiantly fought for during the war. He asserts in the introduction: "Whoever puts his ear to the ground of events and facts can hear the steps of the future."[2] In this sense, the book offers an argument for looking back to the war for lessons and inspiration, all the while remaining

2. Schauwecker, *So ist der Friede*, 7.

future-oriented and offering veiled warnings to political enemies about the coming rise of nationalism (which is provisionally tied to National Socialism at the book's close). Beyond a post-1933 historical perspective that recognizes the trajectory of the Weimar Republic as it collapses into the Third Reich, *So ist der Friede* yields powerful evidence for how contemporaries established frames of meaning for understanding and making connections between the First World War, the Weimar era, and the anticipated future.

The book begins with an original poem by Schauwecker that signals the connection between the war's legacy and the failure of Germany's government to attend to the war's meaning, an argument used to bolster the supposed moral authority of nationalism that pervades the book (see fig. 52). "Diese Zeit" (These times) is comprised of three rhyming stanzas with four lines each. The first stanza speaks of distant graves left unmarked by crosses and over which no one keeps watch. The stanza relates most directly to the photograph placed above the text, which shows a flat, muddy field with a few young trees breaking the horizon. There are indiscernible shapes in the far background, perhaps the hint of other trees, or even the chimneys of a small village, but the field that fills the majority of the photograph's space is largely barren and unused. As the poem suggests about many former sites of combat during the war, there are no obvious visual signs that the pictured field necessarily was once a battlefield, as trenches or grave markers might indicate.

Despite the lack of such visual cues, the text bestows upon the unassuming pictured field an apparent sacred status. Amplifying the interpretation of the field as hallowed ground is the recognizable photographic manipulation of the cloud-filled sky that fills over two-thirds of the image. When the photograph was printed, the sky's upper portions were—in the parlance of darkroom photography—"burned in," meaning this section of the photographic paper was exposed to the light projected through the negative longer than other parts in order to enhance the contrast in the clouds and increase the image's visual dynamism. The result is a dramatic play of light and dark in the sky that draws the viewer's eyes upwards, calling to mind both a foreboding storm (or a passing one, as the muddy ground might attest to) and the presence of some higher power. Schauwecker's text uses the word *Schädelstätte* (site of skulls), which bears religious connotation with Golgotha, the site of Christ's crucifixion, but the darkened clouds echo primarily the supernatural forces of the frontline experience characterized by Schauwecker in *So war der Krieg!* That the field remains unconsecrated by any typical markers of commemoration, like cemetery crosses, reinforces the idea that Germans are neglecting the spiritual meaning of the fallen soldiers' sacrifice in the face of some higher purpose.

The photograph's darkened clouds are assigned a more specific metaphor in the second stanza of "Diese Zeit." The unattended war grave sites from the first stanza are connected with the supposed directionless politics of the present, in which the masses grumble in inactivity like a heavy cloud that produces neither rain nor lightning. This stormy, foreboding cloud, referenced in both text and image, does not only hang over the unmarked former battleground, but casts its impenetrable shadow over the present-day situation in Weimar Germany. The introduction that follows the poem makes some of the references from the second stanza clear. As in *So war der Krieg*, Schauwecker understands the war positively as an "awakening of idealism, action, nation, sacrifice, devotion, death, community, will" wasted by the political elite following the war.[3] Instead of nation-building based on the Volk, revolution, chaos, and greed reigned, the polarization of class identity was aggravated, and politics was made hostage to economics. The political corruption of parliamentarianism and the occupation of German lands by the war's victors are two of the most egregious postwar transgressions in his view.

Criticisms of the postwar situation alluded to in "Diese Zeit" and then explicated in the book's introduction are wide-ranging, and Schauwecker incriminates opposing ideologies like socialism and capitalism, often in the same sentence. Blurring the political lines of "right" and "left" that govern the thinking of "older" nationalist groups, he represents a new brand of nationalism that mixes freely from political ideologies, while striving foremost for the creation of a new order.[4] Armin Mohler has characterized a group of writers who share Schauwecker's new nationalist impulses as the *Nationalrevolutionäre* (national revolutionaries). Among its most prominent representatives are Ernst Jünger, Friedrich Georg Jünger, Ernst von Salomon, and Ernst Niekisch. Mohler's category also encompasses representatives of right-wing paramilitary *Wehrverbände* (combat leagues) and their publishing organs, such as the Stahlhelm and its newspaper *Standarte*, as well as other publications, such as *Arminius*, *Der Vormarsch*, and *Widerstand*.[5] Authors most representative of soldatischer Nationalismus, like Schauwecker or Werner Beumelburg, constitute a more specific subset within the broader national-revolutionary category. The larger grouping, however, encompasses authors who were born between 1890 and 1905 and

3. Schauwecker, *So ist der Friede*, 8.
4. Mohler, *Die konservative Revolution in Deutschland*, 145–46.
5. Mohler, *Die konservative Revolution in Deutschland*, 295.

had their most foundational coming-of-age experiences during their war service.[6] The group is set apart from older strands of nationalism that also were present after the war, such as the *völkisch* and *bündisch* movements or the *Jungkonservativen* around Arthur Moeller van den Brueck, as much through generational differences as through new revolutionary convictions. Based less on specific ideas—for example, the way *völkisch* ideology was centered around race theory and ethnic nationalism—the *Nationalrevolutionäre* envisioned a modern, dynamic, and radical movement toward grander yet oftentimes less clearly defined ideals, such as the rebirth of the "nation."[7]

Indeed, although he reveals his political viewpoint more freely than other authors addressed in this study (Ernst Friedrich excluded), Schauwecker is not concerned with exact political diagnosis of the postwar situation in *So ist der Friede*. An analysis of the book's introduction is best guided by lines in the second stanza of "Diese Zeit," in which the Volk, leaderless and directionless under no flag, stagnates as the "masses." What is most important in his understanding of the war's legacy is the very lack of a single motivating principle that could unite the German nation and address the war's economic, political, and, most important, spiritual impact: "The masses had cried out for leadership in a hundred revolts, but no voice had answered them. So the plundering revolt continued. The masses remained masses. It did not become a nation. It became a state with people. But no people found itself as a nation in this state form."[8] Furthermore, the task of unifying the masses into a true Volk would have to take its lead from a single charismatic leader. The introduction ends with the claim that soldiers, the ones most betrayed by the mishandling of the postwar situation, wait patiently for "the decisive leader [*Führer*]" to lead the movement of nationalism that arose among their ranks.

The final stanza of "Diese Zeit" reinforces the idea of a lost legacy from the front and laments the guilt assigned to Germany. For Schauwecker, the war never truly ended, and old wounds have not healed. Any mention of the war's victors in the book's introduction are surrounded by quotation marks—"*Sieger*"—used sardonically to alert the reader to the adage that Germany was "geschlagen aber unbesiegt" (beaten but not defeated), and the war was lost not because of some spiritual or motivational deficiency on the part of soldiers. Schauwecker not only rehashes the typical issues that were

6. Mohler, *Die konservative Revolution in Deutschland*, 142.
7. Mohler, *Die konservative Revolution in Deutschland*, 143–44.
8. Schauwecker, *So ist der Friede*, 8.

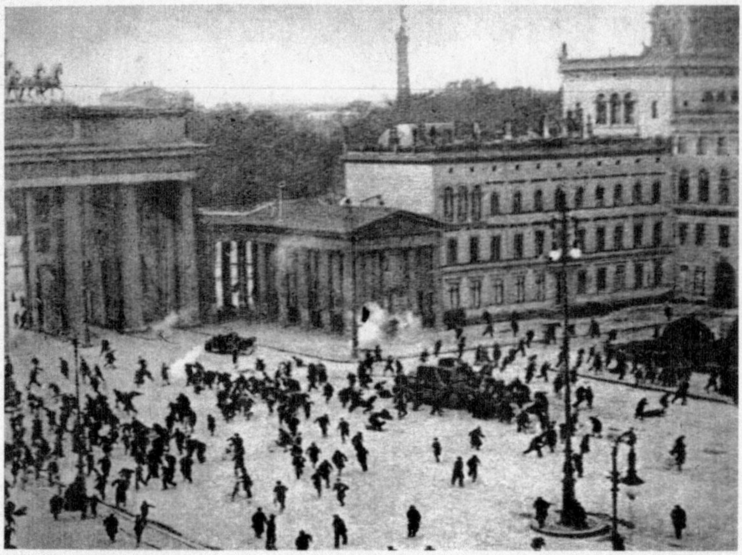

Panik am Pariser Platz U.

Fig. 53. Franz Schauwecker, *So ist der Friede* (Berlin: Frundsberg-Verlag, 1928), page 13.

especially onerous for patriotic Germans, including the bottomless anger over the occupation of German lands by foreign powers, but his entire frame of understanding the Weimar Republic's political and social conflicts is also the continuation of mindsets of war and myths about the war. He pines for the camaraderie among soldiers as much as he imagines the soldiers as comprising a unified political front, a group uniquely betrayed by the war's outcome but now occupying the moral high ground in a new conflict of "us" versus "them." While hostilities with old war enemies linger, an internal set of foes mentioned by name—liberalism, capitalism, communism, parliamentarianism, indeed whatever force was perceived as standing in the way of nationalism—represents the new antagonist. The Soldier must now fight the "tyranny of the irresponsible,"[9] which, like the enemies of the war, similarly seeks to impede the true German nation from flourishing. That this conflict should spill blood, as the poem attests, not only speaks to the fact of violent revolutions and putsches post-1918 but to a militarized mindset of seeing the world that remains a decade later.

Moving beyond the poem "Diese Zeit" and the book's introduction, the first set of photographs, titled "Revolution, Communism, and Occupation," testifies to the warlike nature of the Weimar Republic's early days. Over a little more than 20 pages, Schauwecker presents a photographic account of the postwar political situation that ties disparate matters, such as the Spartacist uprising, the proclamation of the German republic by the Social Democrat Philipp Scheidemann, the Ruhr occupation, the Hungarian Soviet Republic under Béla Kun, and the effects of Bolshevism in Soviet Russia, into one series of images incriminating the crisis of "these times." The captions that accompany the photographs succinctly identify the pictures but in no case do they elaborate any of the pictured contents' nuances or how the various issues might be related. The effect is at times disorienting. Take, for example, two pictures that are captioned "Panic at Pariser Platz" (fig. 53). Both show a crowd from the high perspective of a neighboring building. Whether the people were gathered there intentionally or were just passing through is unclear, but they are pictured running from the aftermath of some sort of explosion or gunfire, denoted by clouds of smoke near the Brandenburg Gate's north portico. The second picture, which is placed below the first and therefore must be read as a moment after, shows that some people are now lying on the ground. Perhaps they have tripped while running away or were shot. What the exact commotion was, who or what caused it, and who the affected people were all remain unknown.

---

9. Schauwecker, *So ist der Friede*, 9.

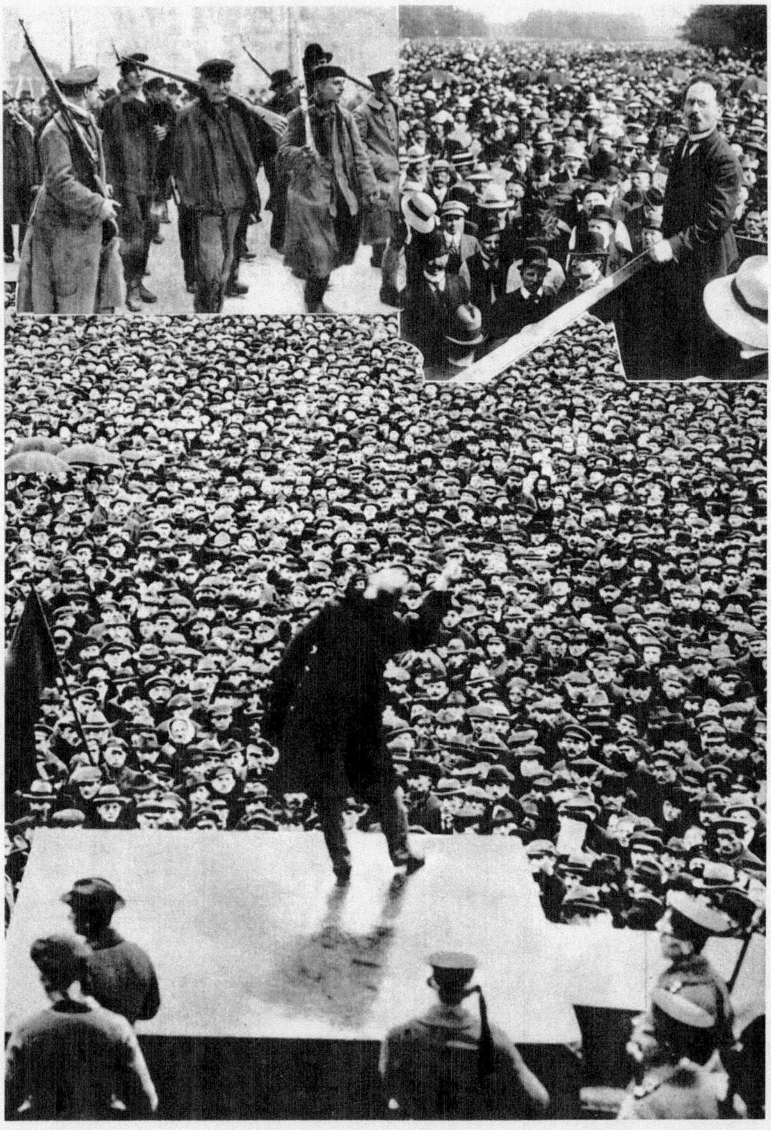

Ansprache eines sozialistischen Redners U.

Oben links:
Spartakustruppen Unter den Linden U.

Oben rechts:
Karl Liebknecht H.

Fig. 54. Franz Schauwecker, *So ist der Friede* (Berlin: Frundsberg-Verlag, 1928), page 12.

Such moments of crisis captured with photography reflect larger discourses at the time on the Weimar Republic as a time of struggle and impending catastrophe. Daniel Magilow traces how snapshot photography was newly employed in the late 1920s to exacerbate the rhetoric of "critical moments" that became increasingly present in Weimar cultural and political discourse. Photo essay forms mirrored the polemical essay culture at the time in contributing to the sense of "crisis" and the subsequent need for radical measures to respond to "decisive" historical moments.[10] Critically, as Magilow notes, and can be seen in the "Panic at Pariser Platz" spread, such public discourse was often uncritical and ahistorical. That the exact facts of the occurrence in Schauwecker's book could likely be traced in other archives is inconsequential here, as the photographs take on a different function from historical objectivity when embedded into the larger series of the book. Readers hoping to understand the enigmatic photographs would naturally look beyond the two images and their brief caption to the pictures that precede them on the opposite page (fig. 54). There one finds a collage of three images: a larger picture of an unidentified "socialist speaker" from behind who looks over a vast and dense crowd of tiny heads straining to hear him, above which two smaller pictures, one of a group of Spartacist troops on Unter den Linden, the second a candid image of Karl Liebknecht addressing a crowd, cut into the larger image's frame along an irregular, jagged line, itself suggesting instability through visual form. The collage works to make a plain connection between Spartacist violence, denoted by their pictured weapons, and the apparent broad support for (undifferentiated) leftist politics, denoted by the large crowds gathered to hear the speakers. With the book open to these two pages, that is, the collage of Spartacists and socialists and the "Panic at Pariser Platz," the pictured commotion is ascribed new connotations. The crowds of socialist supporters gathered on the left page are dispersed visually on the right. The political weight suggested by the gathered masses supporting the Spartacus League on the left page has clear violent potential, as the viewer sees it (or something like it) explode onto the Pariser Platz in the images on the adjacent page. Even if the pictures do not document the same series of events, it is easy to imagine the book's viewer drawing causal connections among the photographs' surface information, despite that connection being purely a construct of Schauwecker's design.

This sort of incrimination by visual proximity is characteristic of Schauwecker's proclivity to play loose with facts, and it typifies the first series of

10. Magilow, *The Photography of Crisis*, 121–23.

images in the book. The end effect of this jumble of photographs is an almost breathless damning of postwar Germany that brings together the many targets of his ire and entangles them in a combination that provides an undifferentiated view of the postwar situation. The series is in no way intended to historicize the events it depicts; rather its focus remains largely on perpetuating a sense of continued, acute crisis, in which political instability, street violence, and mass movements weaken Germany from within. Whereas the title of Schauwecker's first picture book, *So war der Krieg!*, refers literally to the war, the title of *So ist der Friede* takes on its first shade of ironic meaning in the initial series of photographs: the peace that followed the war was no peace after all.

For Schauwecker, the German "spirit" has been especially betrayed in the postwar realm of politics by a cold and calculating liberalism, combined with the rigid organization of parliamentarianism that has extinguished all potential life-giving energies of the German nation; politics has lost its connection to the "organic world" above and inside man.[11] In the second series of *So ist der Friede*, "Das Gesicht des Liberalismus: Der große Gegensatz" (The face of liberalism: The great contrast), he compares the political calculation of liberalism negatively with the metaphysical awakening of the German spirit so characteristic of *So war der Krieg!* Liberalism, for Schauwecker, represents an unnatural "apparatus" imposed by cold-minded technocrats and motivated purely by money; both capitalism and socialism, then, are "creatures of pure money."[12] In a six-page preface to the photographs in this section, he claims that liberalism reduces everything to calculation, tactics, and negotiation, so that it experiences no love or hate, but only infatuation and malice. Its embers are like those of an oven, hot and soulless. In contrast to liberalism, which Schauwecker labels a "worldview of materialism" that turns the Volk into the "masses," there exist natural forces proving that "there is still life beyond the mechanism."[13]

Schauwecker introduces the case of the Novarupta volcano in Alaska's Katmai National Park that erupted for the first time in 1912 and left a crater equal to the area of Berlin and Potsdam combined. The volcano's physical destruction is testament to the extraordinary forces of nature and reveals the sense of wonder masked by the apparatus of science, technology, and civilization that reaches its pinnacle in an age of liberalism. The moment of

11. Schauwecker, *So ist der Friede*, 35.
12. Schauwecker, *So ist der Friede*, 36.
13. Schauwecker, *So ist der Friede*, 38.

the volcano's eruption compels man to think beyond materiality—a moment sometimes felt, but which nevertheless quickly vanishes, as a sort of simmering of real life below the surface of daily existence governed by the automatons of business. The power of a volcano—its latent potential to destroy life in a flash of violence—serves as a visual reminder of primality, of man's precarious position between life and death; in contrast, the "magic of intellect" can only bring someone up the elevator of a radio tower.[14]

The cold-thinking, money-minded parliamentarians of Weimar Germany have, according to Schauwecker, destroyed a sense of the opposing forces—taken to its extreme, life and death—that give birth to ideas and action. The postwar government has become "organization instead of organism," the shell of a body "from which the sound of a gramophone record resounds, fooling people to believe that a living being is still speaking."[15] Whereas parliamentarianism and liberalism are false constructs that impose irrational limits on the human soul through a claimed rationality, the generation of frontline soldiers have learned better from the "glowing areas of life."[16] Like the eruption of a volcano, or the ephemeral feeling that life resembles an automobile speeding toward a cliff, driven by someone who refuses to turn or brake, there exist moments that unmask "life" from "construction."[17] No one knows this better than the "frontline warrior," who stood for years on the precipice between life and death. In the continued crisis of the postwar era, the frontline soldiers have special knowledge that enables them to see through the failings of the present with a future-oriented vision: "In this time of transition and preparation for the decisive things to come, mental attitude and independence drives us toward the essential and makes a conscious move to get to the core of things, processes, phenomena, and people. It was never any different at the front."[18]

The answer for the callous, economically driven calculations of parliamentarianism is for Schauwecker politics, which unleashes the creative and procreative forces inherent in tension and conflict.[19] He understands "politics" as something larger than "daily politics," and the term has clear ties to the brand of nationalism he advocates. The subordination of "politics" to "economics" in postwar German governance—the characterization is as

14. Schauwecker, *So ist der Friede*, 38.
15. Schauwecker, *So ist der Friede*, 35.
16. Schauwecker, *So ist der Friede*, 39.
17. Schauwecker, *So ist der Friede*, 38.
18. Schauwecker, *So ist der Friede*, 39.
19. Schauwecker, *So ist der Friede*, 35.

broad in the original as it is in this brief summary—has entailed the "subjugation of the nation to purely material interests."[20] Complicit in inhibiting the nation's potential to flourish are international trade, banking, and finance. To fight against the apparent banner of liberalism—"economics is fate"—is the greatest challenge facing the nation today, because where economics drives history and politics, "life stops, and the apparatus begins."[21] "This demand also applied at the front," Schauwecker concludes, again linking the war experience to the postwar situation.

What photographs, then, exhibit the "Face of Liberalism"? In the introductory text, Schauwecker posits that liberalism's "apparatus," "construct," or "mechanism" inhibits the sort of natural forces that comprise the "core of things," in the sense of both the physical power of nature over man and the soul's longing for the nation. This "face" of liberalism masks the nation's true spirit through the soulless economic decisions of parliamentarians, which were in many cases forced upon the Germans through the terms of surrender. The idea of a "face" takes on a more literal meaning in a series of honorific portraits featuring socially prominent individuals in the series. Here, Schauwecker taps into the contemporary revival of interest in and use of physiognomy, the analysis of external face and body features to uncover internal psychological and spiritual truths. Portrait photography played a prominent role in the hundreds of physiognomic publications from the interwar period, and the discipline, now discredited as misguided and bigoted but then widely regarded as an useful analytical tool, "offered thinkers and photographers a powerful means by which to probe the roots of the chaos lurking beneath Weimar Germany's fragile façade of stability."[22] For Schauwecker, the face of liberalism is represented by the cold, calculating politicians who squandered the vitalism of the front experience's legacy and who are visually depicted in staid and emotionless portraits.

Pictured in Schauwecker's liberalism series are former and current ministers of the Weimar Republic, Reichstag members, and international statesmen. The German politicians include predominantly members of the Sozialdemokratische Partei Deutschlands (German Social Democratic Party, or SPD), the Deutsche Demokratische Partei (DDP), the Catholic Deutsche Zentrumspartei (Zentrum), and the center-right Deutsche Volkspartei (DVP, successor to the Nationalliberale Partei), all political parties that were active

20. Schauwecker, *So ist der Friede*, 39.
21. Schauwecker, *So ist der Friede*, 40.
22. Magilow, *The Photography of Crisis*, 93.

in forming and sustaining the Weimar Republic and that in Schauwecker's eyes embodied the sort of soulless liberalism plaguing Germany. Foremost among those pictured are Matthias Erzberger, Gustav Stresemann, and Philipp Scheidemann, whose portraits prominently begin the series (fig. 55). All three men had important ties to both the war's legacy and the economic realities during the Weimar Republic. Schauwecker does not criticize these or any of the politicians in the series by name, nor do his captions include anything but simple identifications, but upon consideration of their roles in Germany's response to the war and its aftermath, it becomes clear why these politicians are so obviously tied to the preceding text's polemics.

Matthias Erzberger of the Catholic Zentrumspartei was the bogeyman of conservative and national liberal parties on the right and the target of inflammatory and violent right-wing propaganda, not least because he was a principal signer of the Armistice, advocated for the Treaty of Versailles, and pushed social reforms that disadvantaged the wealthy. He was assassinated in late August 1921 by two former navy officers, members of the ultranationalist Organisation Consul, which formed from the remnants of a Freikorps unit when that organization was officially disbanded following the failed Kapp Putsch in 1920. The Organisation Consul was responsible for the murder of more than 350 of their political opponents, including the foreign minister under Joseph Wirth of the Deutsche Volkspartei, Walter Rathenau. Rathenau was assassinated in 1922 after angering national extremists by supporting Germany's obligations under the Treaty of Versailles and for negotiating the Treaty of Rapallo (1922), which normalized relations with the Soviet Union and bilaterally renounced all territorial and financial claims made against the other from the war. Rathenau's portrait is included on a later page in the "Face of Liberalism" series.

Along with Erzberger, Gustav Stresemann and Philipp Scheidemann receive a primary position in the series of portraits of apparently undesirable liberal politicians. Despite the deep fractionalization of party politics during the Weimar Republic, the differences among the various parties are inconsequential to Schauwecker's larger argument against those who "sold out" the nation for peace.[23] Stresemann, chancellor for a few short months in the fall of 1923 and then Germany's foreign minister from 1923 to 1929, was

23. This accords with the general characterization by historian Dirk Schumann of political violence in the Weimar era: "In den Konfrontationen zwischen gegnerischen politischen Gruppen bzw. zwischen ihnen und den staatlichen Ordnungskräften [ging es] im Prinzip immer um die Grundlagen des politischen Systems . . . und nicht bloß um Detailforderungen" (Schumann, *Politische Gewalt in der Weimarer Republik*, 17).

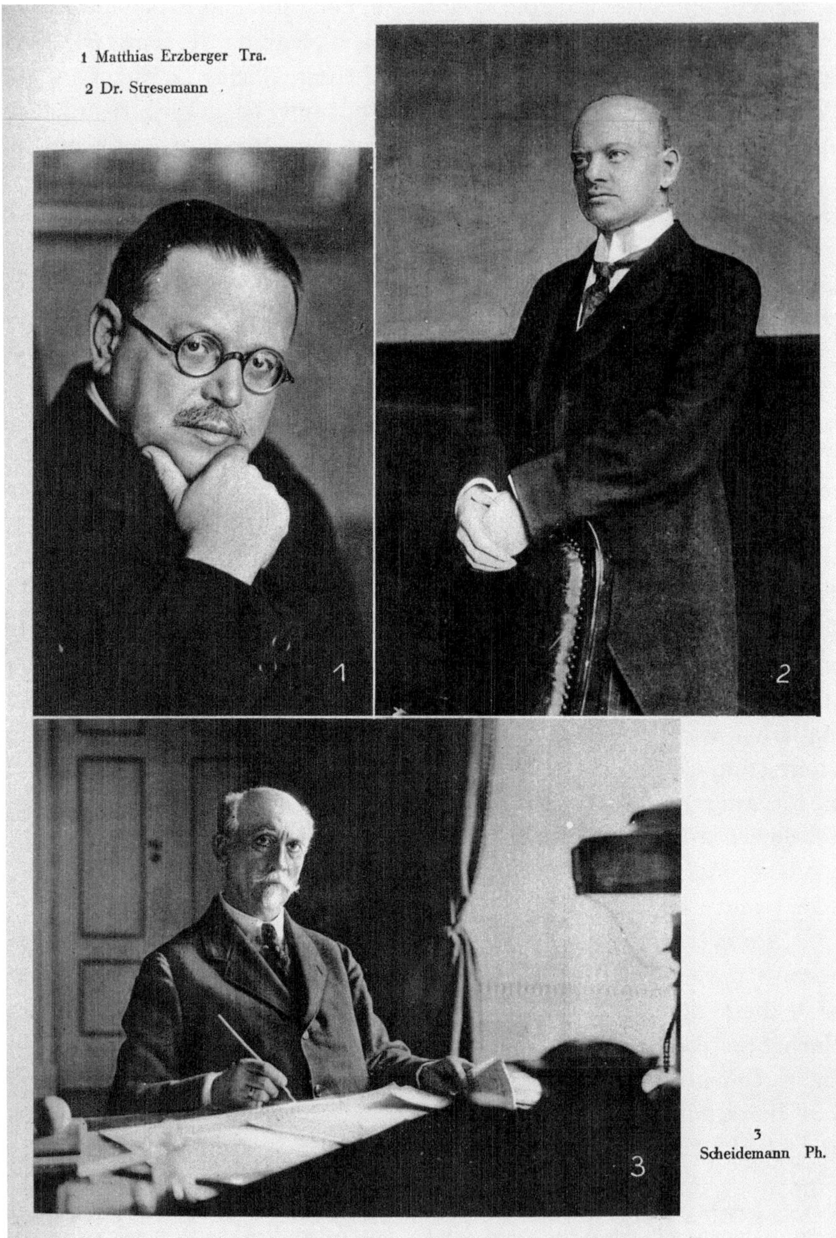

Fig. 55. Franz Schauwecker, *So ist der Friede* (Berlin: Frundsberg-Verlag, 1928), page 41.

criticized from the right as a *Vernunftrepublikaner*, someone who remained a monarchist at heart but who was obliged to openly accept the reality of a democratic republic for the sake of reasonableness. He drew conservative ire for his actions on the international stage that were perceived as too willing to cooperate with Germany's former—and bitter—rivals and too unconcerned with the nation's own interests by taking a pragmatic, internationalist economic stance.

Stresemann's co-laureate for the 1926 Nobel Peace Prize, the French prime minister Aristide Briand, is pictured near the end of the series of portraits, where two pages are dedicated to non-German statesmen who affected postwar Germany's economic situation or represented a new breed of cooperative European diplomats who were understood by Schauwecker and his ilk to be undermining German nationalism. Among portraits of Richard von Coudenhove-Kalergi (the central figure in the Paneuropean Union), Alfonso Costa (League of Nations chairman in 1926), and various French prime ministers and diplomats, the British statesman Austen Chamberlain is pictured. Chamberlain worked with Stresemann and Briand to negotiate the Locarno Treaties, which guaranteed postwar peace in Western Europe by settling lingering border disputes, normalizing Germany's relationships with its neighbors, and affirming that Germany would never again declare war on any of the treaty's signatories. Stresemann, Briand, and Chamberlain are indicative of the type of internationalists incompatible with Schauwecker's brand of fervent nationalism, which relied on a continuation of war attitudes and antagonisms for its moral legitimacy.

The final politician pictured on the first page of "The Face of Liberalism" is Philipp Scheidemann (SPD), who became for many on the far right the face of the hated democratic Weimar Republic. On November 9, 1918, hearing that the Spartacist leader Karl Liebknecht planned to declare a German Soviet Republic out of the administrative confusion and violence of the November Revolution, Scheidemann declared the German republic from a balcony in the Reichstag. The action was largely spontaneous and went against the wishes of Chancellor Friedrich Ebert, Scheidemann's SPD colleague, who wanted to preserve the imperial system if possible. Even though Scheidemann served for less than half a year and surrendered the chancellorship over his cabinet's indecision regarding the Treaty of Versailles, his "betrayal" of Germany through the proclamation of the republic was not forgotten by right-wing forces.

Erzberger's, Stresemann's, and Scheidemann's roles in the ending of the war, the Weimar Republic's foundation, and the postwar economic situation make them representative of the "face" of liberalism that, from Schauwecker's perspective, had killed the German national spirit. Despite the lack of any specific textual support differentiating the various pictured politicians, a moderately informed contemporary reader could have reconstructed the motivation for the portraits' inclusion by considering the text of his broad polemic. Among many other biographies that illuminate the actual specifics of Schauwecker's complaints are a slew of German chancellors: Gustav Bauer (SPD), Hermann Müller (SPD), Constantin Fehrenbach (Zentrum), Joseph Wirth (Zentrum), and Wilhelm Marx (Zentrum). In one of the only extended captions in the series, he notes that Müller (as secretary of state) and Johannes Bell (Zentrum; a Reichstag vice president from 1920 to 1926), who are pictured with Ebert and Marx on the second page of the series (fig. 56), were "the two signatories of the Versailles Peace Treaty."[24] In a caption for Ebert, he quotes the Reichspräsident on June 18, 1919, saying, "We will never accept this peace, come what may; we reject it."[25] The effect is sarcastic, as the Treaty of Versailles was signed eleven days later following Scheidemann's resignation on June 21 and Ebert's insistence that Bauer form a new government and accept the treaty's terms.

The photograph of Ebert's speech quoted above is one of the exceptions in the series that is not an official-looking posed portrait, although such a photograph of Ebert is also included on the same page. The visual stasis of the staged portraits positioned around it on all four sides make the photograph of Ebert's speech initially seem out of place. A dense crowd gathered below Ebert, who speaks from a window balcony (recalling Scheidemann's proclamation of the republic), connotes a level of movement or commotion before and after the photograph's particular moment. However, any sense of political dynamism suggested by the photograph is undercut by the irony of the quotation in the caption; Ebert's words were an empty promise, and the government accepted the Treaty of Versailles in the end.

The photograph of Ebert's speech stands out in "The Face of Liberalism" series precisely because it offers a sense of action or movement beyond the photographic moment that the other portraits cannot. One can imagine Ebert's hand gestures and facial expressions as he speaks as well as the crowd's movement as it raises and lowers signs, calls back to the speaker, and shuffles in place. Although they are in the end also normal photographs capturing just one instant in time, the posed portraits, often cropped or framed

24. Schauwecker, *So ist der Friede*, 42.
25. Schauwecker, *So ist der Friede*, 42.

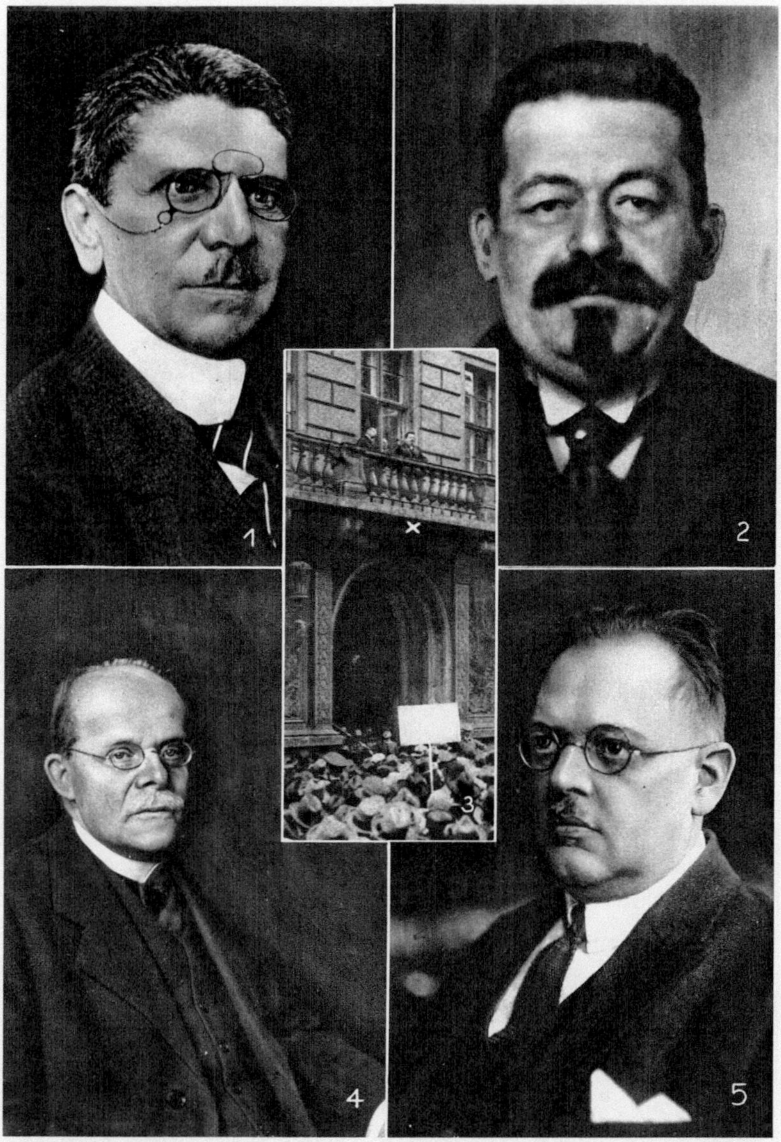

1 Dr. Bell, Vizepräsident des Reichstages Ph. 5 Abgeordneter Müller, Reichskanzler a. D., Sozialdemokrat Ph. (die beiden Unterzeichner des Versailler Friedensvertrages)

2 Reichspräsident Ebert S. 3 Präsident Ebert am 18. Juni 1919: „Wir werden diesen Frieden nie und nimmer annehmen, mag kommen was da will; wir lehnen ihn ab". D.V. 4 Reichskanzler Dr. Marx At.

Fig. 56. Franz Schauwecker, *So ist der Friede* (Berlin: Frundsberg-Verlag, 1928), page 42.

to show just the subject's face or bust, have a strong sense of frozen time. This visual stasis is useful to support the claims Schauwecker makes in the introductory text that the "apparatus" of liberalism and parliamentarianism has extinguished all the living forces of healthy tension and polarity.[26] The subject's faces are also predominantly expressionless, reflecting the criticism of the "soulless" calculations of the ruling political class.

Schauwecker's textual argument about liberalism being an "apparatus" or "mechanism" imposed from above is visualized in the contrast between the public realm's pictured dynamism in the first section, in which the masses gather and violence is enacted, and the static, constrained interior realm of the political elite typified by their portraits in the second section. Armin Mohler, editor of the handbook on *Die Konservative Revolution in Deutschland*, identifies "motion" or "being in motion" as key terms for the national-revolutionary authors,[27] and the idea of motion figures powerfully in *So ist der Friede* in the visual contrast between political action in the first section and political stultification in the second. (It will also reappear in the section on "Disarmament," in which the rest of the world moves forward rapidly with technological advances and rearmament while Germany falls behind.)

Take, for instance, the contrast between two photographs of Scheidemann, one found in each of the sections. In the first series, he is seen addressing a large crowd from a window of the Reich Chancellery (see fig. 57), visually mirroring his proclamation of the republic from the Reichstag. He is standing on the windowsill, is being held by his coattails from falling, and has both arms stretched wide as he speaks.[28] Schauwecker does not provide any more context than this, but it is clear from the tightly packed crowd, some holding placards, and Scheidemann's dramatic gesturing that he associates this picture with the titular "revolution," a time of "uncertainty, inability, insignificance," in which one singular voice did not rise to guide the national will.[29] Taken together with the other photographs in the series of competing political forces during the time, Scheidemann embodies the chaos of postwar politics, which, at least on the surface, appears dynamic and vital but in Schauwecker's estimation did not meet the needs of the nation. He writes in the first section of the immediate postwar situation's squandered potential:

26. Schauwecker, *So ist der Friede*, 35.
27. Mohler, *Die konservative Revolution in Deutschland*, 144–45.
28. Schauwecker, *So ist der Friede*, 16.
29. Schauwecker, *So ist der Friede*, 8.

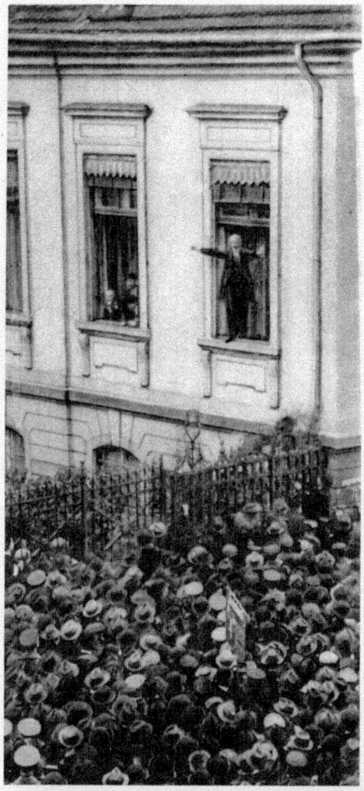

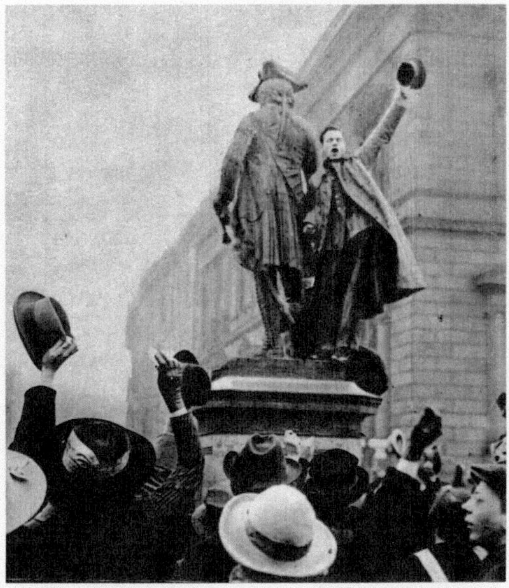

Sozialdemokratischer Redner auf dem Wilhelmplatz U.

Oben links:
Scheidemann, am Rockschoß gehalten, spricht aus dem Fenster des Reichskanzlerhauses in der Wilhelmstraße U.

Unten:
Regierungstruppen auf dem Brandenburger Tor U.

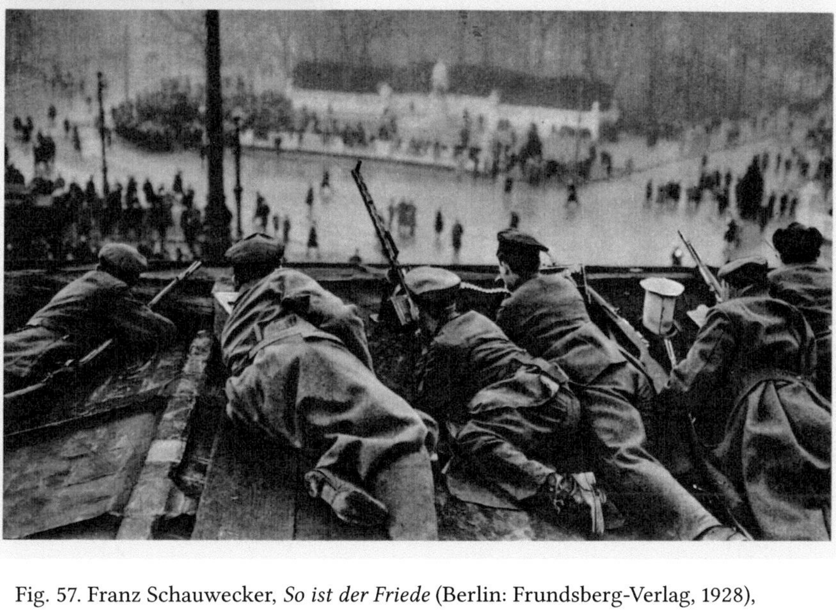

Fig. 57. Franz Schauwecker, *So ist der Friede* (Berlin: Frundsberg-Verlag, 1928), page 16.

> The last of the Nation's strength was wasted in vain on strikes, demonstrations, meetings, speeches, revolts, and putsches. . . . Meanwhile, the clever ones went about their business without much fanfare. The state was hastily reorganized and rewritten. When the passionate ones awoke from their dreams, they found the state completely reorganized. . . . In the first chaos, the Nation could have been recreated within the state, but now, in the new order, it was even more impossible.[30]

The portrait of Scheidemann in the second section (see fig. 55), "The Face of Liberalism," echoes this textual argument from the first section. In this photograph he is sitting at his work desk, holding a pen in his right hand and a few papers in his left. His face is expressionless; if not tired, he is calm. Whereas the gesticulating orator Scheidemann was part and parcel of the postwar political chaos in the first section, the bureaucrat Scheidemann typifies the "clever ones"[31] who stymie any alternative political rearrangement in the present. In two contrasting photographs, Scheidemann thereby typifies for Schauwecker the sort of rationalistic politician who "successfully" harnessed the chaos of revolution for his own political goals, not those of the nation. Schauwecker does not address the apparent contradiction that Scheidemann comes to embody both the "clever ones" and "passionate ones" described in his text, but it could speak further to his estimation of such liberal politicians as maliciously calculating. Nevertheless, that two photographs of outwardly contrasting appearances point to an array of possible inner qualities—Is Scheidemann clever? Passionate? Both? Did he change from one to the other? Does he use one to mask the other?—problematizes the whole physiognomic approach of "The Face of Liberalism." In the end, though, coherent analysis and historicizing do not lie at the heart of *So ist der Friede.*

Beyond a contrast between the first and second series, there is evidence in individual photographs for the type of political detachment from the heartblood of the Volk that Schauwecker denounces. In the second photograph of Scheidemann (his posed portrait in "The Face of Liberalism"), we see visual representation of his separation from the outside world's pulse. His desk is situated next to a window, through which sunlight illuminates his face and the papers spread out before him. It suggests initially that his decisions are informed by the outside world, but his relationship to it is severed

30. Schauwecker, *So ist der Friede*, 8.
31. Schauwecker, *So ist der Friede*, 8.

by the photograph's visual composition. By nature of the camera's optical limitations the photograph was exposed for what was likely a dark interior, meaning the photograph's right third including the window is overexposed. Anything that the photographer would have seen outside the window is rendered as white space for his viewer. The interior realm of Scheidemann's office is visually cut off from the realities of the outside world, and is perhaps merely a blank canvas on which Scheidemann crafts his policies as he pleases. His firm grip on the pen and paper reinforce the emotionless rationality that is so antithetical to Schauwecker's fiery worldview. The portraits of Erzberger and Stresemann, to return to the two other examples offered above, perpetuate the same sense of isolated political calculation as the Scheidemann portrait. A closely framed portrait of a bespectacled Erzberger with his chin resting in the grip of his right hand suggests a self-absorbed political thinker, and a portrait of Stresemann standing with his hands folded over the back of a chair, staring off into the distance, gives the impression of an out-of-touch daydreamer. The photograph of Ebert's speech, then, although it is subverted by its ironic caption, is a clear exception to the politician's stodgy interior world represented among the classic studio or studio-like portraits in the "Face of Liberalism" series.

Portraits of leaders of international diplomatic organizations, such as the Paneuropean Union and the League of Nations, found on the last page of "The Face of Liberalism," segues into the next section on "Disarmament," which encompasses the book's lengthiest series of photographs. Like the other sections it begins with several pages of text. In it Schauwecker decries the League of Nations as "the stronghold of liberalism," which "does not practice pacifism, but only precautionary war prevention."[32] In contrast to what is being preached at the League of Nations, rearmament across the world is obvious to Schauwecker, who sees "the next imperial war" being prepared with all possible force.[33] And despite the League's intention of ensuring the self-determination of all nations, Schauwecker offers examples that ran counter to that ideal: the quick negotiation of hostilities during the Polish-Lithuanian War (1920) to neither side's preference, the "rape" of Morocco by France, of the Middle East by England, and of China by the Entente powers combined.[34] Germany, a cofounder of but not a participant in the League of Nations, likewise was deceived by the Entente's demands, foremost that

32. Schauwecker, *So ist der Friede*, 49.
33. Schauwecker, *So ist der Friede*, 50–51.
34. Schauwecker, *So ist der Friede*, 50.

Germany have a democratic republic, while "America is completely autocratic, and England is a monarchy."[35] The title of *So ist der Friede* takes on further ironic meaning in "Disarmament" to show how Germany—long after the signing of the Treaty of Versailles in 1919—continues to be duped by its acceptance of surrender while the world seemingly prepares for another war. As Schauwecker asserts, "It is the method of the liberal victors of the World War."[36]

Schauwecker lists a range of facts and figures showing Germany's material disadvantage in a rapidly rearming world. He lists the numerical strength of militaries (both their personnel and equipment) from nations across the globe, gives the technical details of innovative American and French tanks, describes the more powerful artillery classes of new British destroyers, and sheds light on advances in chemical warfare. In contrast, Germany (and Austria, Bulgaria, and Hungary) are disadvantaged by "peace." Germany is limited to just 100,000 men, possesses no heavy artillery, and is not permitted to have tanks or airplanes—all terms of the Treaty of Versailles. Visual evidence to support Schauwecker's argument about spurious disarmament includes around 40 pages of photographs attesting to global rearmament: the newest tanks, artillery, warships, airplanes, and military recruits of the world powers. In face of the international effort to preserve peace through the League of Nations and accords like the Kellogg–Briand Pact (1928), which denounced war as an instrument of settling international disputes, the photographs are meant to show the reality of the situation. Compared to the "cloak of dishonesty" of international conferences, speeches, and agreements,[37] the photographs reveal concrete evidence that the military establishment endures and regenerates itself during peacetime. Although some individual photographs are dynamically composed and give a sense of the pictured weapon's distinctive power, the 40 pages of images are best understood together as one body of evidence. Schauwecker notes ironically: "In the following images we gain a conviction, namely the conviction of general disarmament, which is radically making its way throughout the world. You see: Never again war!"[38] Captions differentiate among the various pictured militaries, but the photographs work together to create an undifferentiated and unignorable impression of the postwar situation. That

35. Schauwecker, *So ist der Friede*, 50.
36. Schauwecker, *So ist der Friede*, 54.
37. Schauwecker, *So ist der Friede*, 51.
38. Schauwecker, *So ist der Friede*, 51.

the series brings together photographs of English tanks and American airplanes with Swedish submarines and columns of marching Greek infantry means the images add up to a general visual impression of the claim that "a world armed to the teeth stands across from us,"[39] perpetuating the common sentiment that it was Germany against the world (as seen also prominently in Walter Bloem's *Deutschland* picture book).

America, however, occupies a principal role in the photographs, just as its apparent war-motivated economic interests and its booming trade in gas warfare technology are especially called out in the introductory text.[40] Whereas the vast majority of captions in the series are neutral identifications of the pictured content, the most sarcastic captions are directed against American militarism, if in a subtle manner. For example, US Secretary of War Dwight F. Davis is caught by the camera as he "smiles from inside a giant new American tank,"[41] and the caption "the inauguration of President Coolidge" accompanies a photograph showing American infantry marching in the inauguration parade.[42] Both are subtle suggestions of America's thriving and joyous militarism. "The only real picture of disarmament," as Schauwecker claims, is a photograph of a row of American ships set to be dismantled. It is compared sarcastically to Germany: "The combat value of these old iron ships is probably almost equal to that of the republican German navy."[43] American military entanglement across the world is also evident in the photographs: American tanks are unloaded in China for use during the Chinese civil war;[44] American troops are recognized by a French general for aiding the colonial forces in fighting Berber tribes during the Rif War (1920–26);[45] and the American navy flexes the might of its warships from San Diego to Cuba.[46]

The only collage of photographs in the "Disarmament" series (fig. 58) reinforces the threat of an undifferentiated remilitarizing world. Seven images of artillery, tanks, airplanes, submarines, and military parades overlap each other in an almost haphazard way. A photograph of a submarine cuts across the middle of the page at a 45-degree angle, and the corners of

39. Schauwecker, *So ist der Friede*, 60.
40. Schauwecker, *So ist der Friede*, 55.
41. Schauwecker, *So ist der Friede*, 68.
42. Schauwecker, *So ist der Friede*, 87.
43. Schauwecker, *So ist der Friede*, 82.
44. Schauwecker, *So ist der Friede*, 67.
45. Schauwecker, *So ist der Friede*, 88.
46. Schauwecker, *So ist der Friede*, 81.

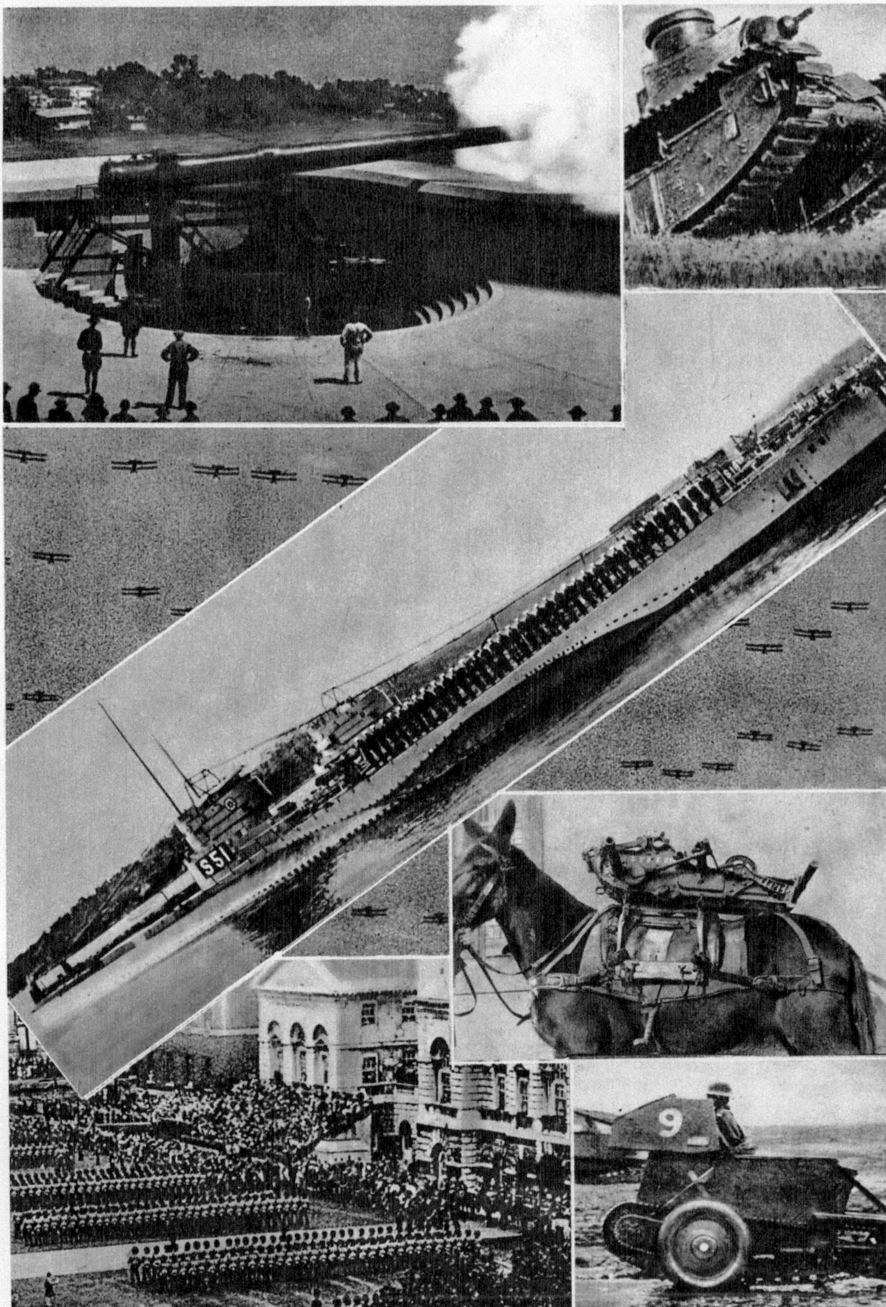

Fig. 58. Franz Schauwecker, *So ist der Friede* (Berlin: Frundsberg-Verlag, 1928), page 98.

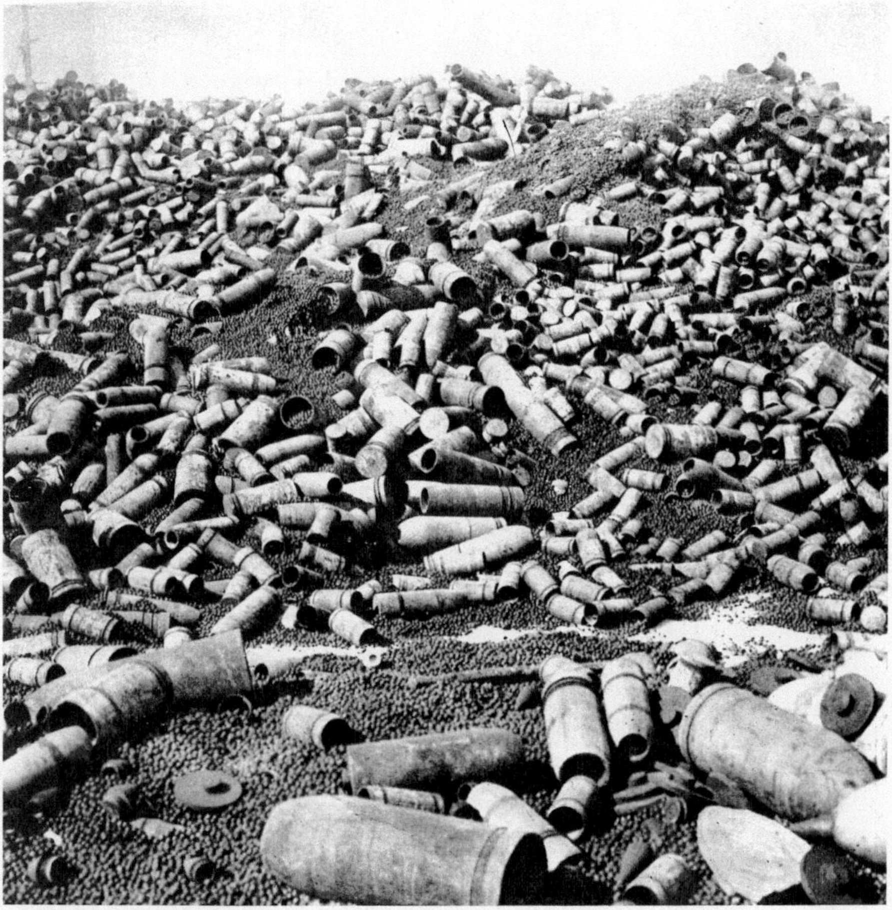

Deutschland allein rüstet wirklich ab:
Deutsche Munition, zum Einschmelzen bestimmt U.

Zertrümmern eines großen Geschützes in den Spandauer Heeres-Werkstätten U

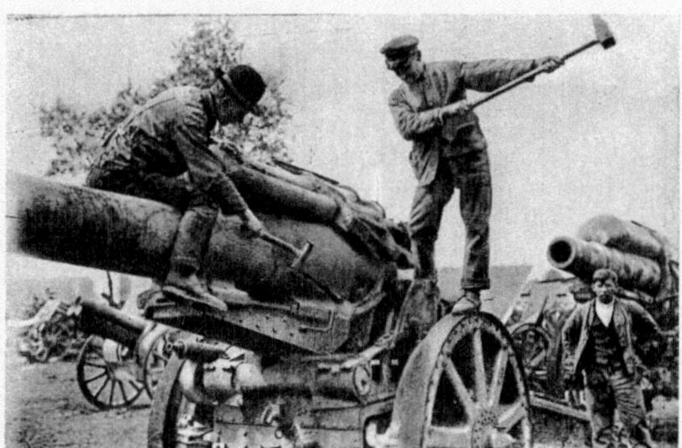

Fig. 59. Franz Schauwecker, *So ist der Friede* (Berlin: Frundsberg-Verlag, 1928), page 99.

some pictures jut into their neighbor's frame. The technique mirrors the page from "The Face of Liberalism" that included the group shot with police commissioners Bernhard Weiß, Albert Grzesinski, and Karl Zörgiebel, and the submarine image's visual skew reflects much of the same sense of unsettlement as that group shot. A photograph of airplanes flying high under a darkened sky serves as the bottom or background layer of this collage, reflecting a threat from the air with which Germany would not be able to contend, as Schauwecker also warns in the text. In contrast to all the other images in the series, none of the photographs in this collage have captions. Only a true expert would be capable of discerning the national identity of the pictured equipment or armies, but that is not the point. The collage functions to give a final overall impression of the disarmament that the pictures should prove has played out much more akin to rearmament.

After the collage, the final two pages turn the series' attention to the German situation. Contradicting his own claim that the photograph of the soon-to-be dismantled American warships was the only image of actual disarmament, Schauwecker includes two photographs of Germany's efforts to disarm that should reveal the pathetic reality of its postwar military. A large photograph captioned "Germany alone is truly disarming: German ammunition, destined to be melted down" (fig. 59) shows large piles of useless munitions set to be destroyed (a visual echo to the rows upon rows of English artillery pictured in *So war der Krieg!*). Below it, a smaller photograph of "Destroying a large gun in the Spandau Army Workshops" shows two men hammering away at an artillery cannon. In contrast to the newest, most elite technology pictured on the opposite page, these two photographs show Germany's wasted potential and military backwardness. The pile of munitions appears as a sort of abstract landscape, a sad wasteland of Germany's former military might now neutered by the terms of surrender. The two men at work dismantling the artillery gun appear hapless; from the photograph it seems they have only managed to open a crack in the cannon's bore by sheer dint of their rudimentary tools. Furthermore, their plain laborer clothes seem provincial and dingy in contrast to the sharply dressed military men who parade across the preceding pages, and a third man who stands by aimlessly gaping at the two workers adds to the photograph's sense of incompetence. If the cracked cannon and the broken munitions capsules are read as phallic symbols, they evince Germany's castration, and the long, sleek submarine titled at a 45-degree angle in the collage on the opposite page takes on a different sexual connotation.

The final page of the series cements the argument about German mili-

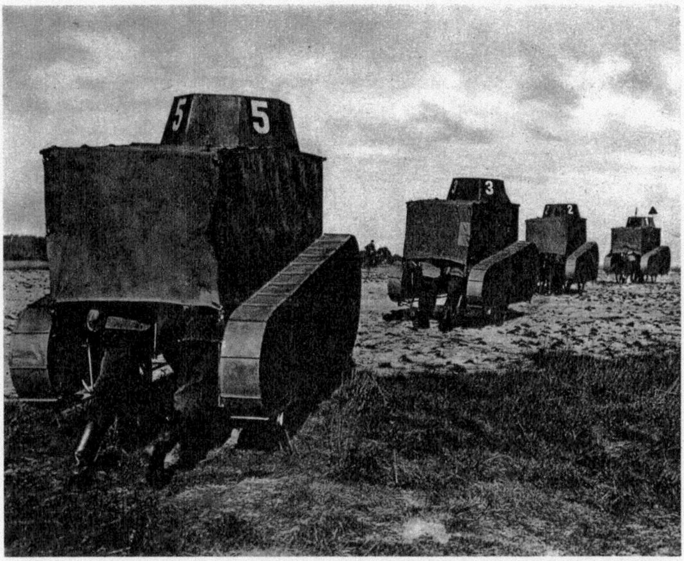

Deutsche „Tanks" im Gefecht auf dem Vormarsch Ph.-U.

Fig. 60. Franz Schauwecker, *So ist der Friede* (Berlin: Frundsberg-Verlag, 1928), page 100.

tary inferiority in the face of world remilitarization. On that page is a single photograph (fig. 60), captioned "German 'tanks' on the advance in battle."[47] The quotation marks are meant ironically as the pictured "tanks" are fakes. Their obviously shoddy construction points to the subpar materials used to create them—certainly not steel—and the two pairs of feet poking out from their undercarriages reveal their true source of power. These are the "cardboard tanks on soldier legs" mentioned in the section's introductory text. They are one more pathetic consequence of the "dictated reduction of army strength to the point of defenselessness" and one final damning piece of visual evidence in the series of "modern Germany as a liberal republic, as an empire under the sign of Versailles and as a country under the worldview of liberalism," as Schauwecker has it in the section's introductory text.[48]

47. Schauwecker, *So ist der Friede*, 100.
48. Schauwecker, *So ist der Friede*, 57–58.

The dynamism present in the book's first section recurs in "Disarmament" after the marked static nature of "The Face of Liberalism." Troops march, battleships fire, and tanks roll across the landscape. But Germany has been forced into a disadvantaged position, betrayed by the liberals who accepted the terms of surrender and forged the republic. The sense of "being in motion" that is central to the works of national-revolutionary authors is evident in the "Disarmament" series but, to the chagrin of Schauwecker, not in Germany, where the unfavorable postwar situation has constrained the nation's vitalism. German guns have been physically dismantled, leaving the nation metaphorically neutered, and German technology has been confined to the realm of playthings. The contrast between the very first image in the series, showing the "Armed tank practice at Fort Wadworth [*sic*], United States,"[49] and the very last image of Germany's cardboard tanks pushed by manpower, visually clarifies Schauwecker's accusations. It is conceivable that the "Disarmament" series would incite the intended feelings of indignity, even in a reader who was not already sympathetic to Schauwecker's nationalist rhetoric. After almost 40 pages of photographs showing the military might, innovation, and dynamism of former war rivals, the final two pages showing the present situation of Germany's military would be a massive source of shame.

The final section of *So ist der Friede* continues one of the book's central arguments: the open warfare may have ended, but war mentalities continue in an ideological struggle between liberalism and nationalism. Titled "Der Nationalismus aller Länder" (The nationalism of all lands), the section presents a broad history of postwar nationalism as evidenced in various countries around the globe. Whereas the World War was incited by liberalism, imperialism, and capitalism and brought Europe to its knees, countries outside of Europe are experiencing the dawning of a new age; Schauwecker explains that liberalism brought about its own end in the war, and the world now belongs to nationalism.[50] Nationalism is a new "world feeling" finding expression in different forms across the globe, from China to Egypt, in Germany as in India. Its manifestations are united by a simple driving impulse: "People, united in history, language, culture, landscape, and feeling, long with passion for an independent community and self-determination, which liberalism has cleverly and calculatingly spoken of in its mendacious peace

49. Schauwecker, *So ist der Friede*, 61.
50. Schauwecker, *So ist der Friede*, 101.

agreements."[51] For Schauwecker, nationalism will bring a true end to imperialistic wars, like that of the World War, as nations will respect each other as nations made legitimate by the will of their peoples. He imagines a future "International of nationalism" that will restore the lost dignity of nations and ensure that any future wars will only be those necessary to realize the people's will. Because it replaces the international bonds of class and clears away the systems of global capitalism, effectively reorganizing the world based on ties of existing communities, nationalism both reveals communism to be the "manure on the field of nations" while freeing the people from the "international slavery of money."[52]

Schauwecker's characterization of nationalism, which lets out "the true cry of the oppressed nations to the world,"[53] is still firmly rooted in the war experience, as he established in *So war der Krieg!*: "[Nationalism] arises from the soil to which we owe all our strength, from the earth that has drunk blood and is fertilized by it."[54] He assigns a sense of inevitability to the rise of nationalism, saying it was born with the "irresistible power of organic growth" and promising that there is no use in trying to impede its growth.[55] After the section on "Disarmament," which is more carefully reasoned (at least by his standards), here Schauwecker slips back into a characteristic style of argumentation: emotionally charged, metaphor-laden, and stubbornly narrow-minded in its assertion of the war's enduring legacy. Schauwecker's picture books are certainly not meant as treatises on political science, and, from his own account, intellect is anathema to the spiritual feelings of nationalism. Not only does nationalism create a "connection of character, spirit, feeling" that places "the nation over the party, conviction over intellect, spirit over reason," but the wellspring of nationalism also could have never been pure reason, "because intellect denies the earth and derives life from constructs."[56]

The sketches following the short introduction present the story of nationalism's rise in countries around the globe. Schauwecker characterizes the successes and failures of nationalism in Italy, Turkey, Poland, Spain, Hungary, Ireland, Morocco, China, India, Saudi Arabia, Macedonia, the United States, and Germany. He also considers Zionism, outlining a positive plan

51. Schauwecker, *So ist der Friede*, 101–2.
52. Schauwecker, *So ist der Friede*, 102–3.
53. Schauwecker, *So ist der Friede*, 102.
54. Schauwecker, *So ist der Friede*, 104.
55. Schauwecker, *So ist der Friede*, 103.
56. Schauwecker, *So ist der Friede*, 104.

for Jews' survival as a nation, while regurgitating antisemitic clichés. Each subsection comprises a few pages of introductory text and then short photographic series. Without summarizing the particularities of each subsection, there are several patterns that Schauwecker brings forth across the larger series and that should be addressed here as they bear significance on his assessment of the German situation, which is, after all, the core issue of his picture book and this study.

"The Nationalism of All Lands" begins with Italy and Benito Mussolini. One of the most defining characteristics of Schauwecker's brand of nationalism, soldatischer Nationalismus, is embodied in the story of Mussolini's rise to power: "the wonder of personality."[57] Amid the economic and political chaos in Italy following the war, Mussolini broke through as the charismatic leader of a people's revolution that conquered the communists, marched against the state, and inspired the Italian people: "His personality radiates and rules unconditionally. The masses act according to his will, soft material that he shapes."[58] Schauwecker's praise for Mussolini is boundless. He is a "dazzling diplomat," a "naturally born genius," and an "unswervingly confident statesman."[59] Even the brutality engendered by Mussolini's movement is normalized as necessary action against forces that threaten the Italian nation, especially communism.

Mussolini is the epitome of the Schauweckerian "personality." Part of this is pure charisma: "A magic emanates from him and, like a converging lens, unites every gaze onto him."[60] But not only is his image a "symbol of the new"[61] for the people, Mussolini has the essential characteristics of "a burning heart" and "a cold-thinking brain," a rare combination of character types uniting the energy and sheer willpower to force change and the know-how to guide it to fruition.[62] Schauwecker admires Mussolini for his political intelligence, but is careful to avoid attributing this characterization to "intellect" or "reason." He understands the essence of Mussolini's "personality" more as a future-oriented vision: "Mussolini always sees what is, but he also sees at the same time what can be and must be, and he decides that it should be."[63] His leadership of the Fascist takeover in 1922 is the prime example of his ability to combine the nation's emotional impulse with the political know-how

57. Schauwecker, *So ist der Friede*, 105.
58. Schauwecker, *So ist der Friede*, 109.
59. Schauwecker, *So ist der Friede*, 110–12.
60. Schauwecker, *So ist der Friede*, 109.
61. Schauwecker, *So ist der Friede*, 106.
62. Schauwecker, *So ist der Friede*, 106.
63. Schauwecker, *So ist der Friede*, 106.

ITALIEN

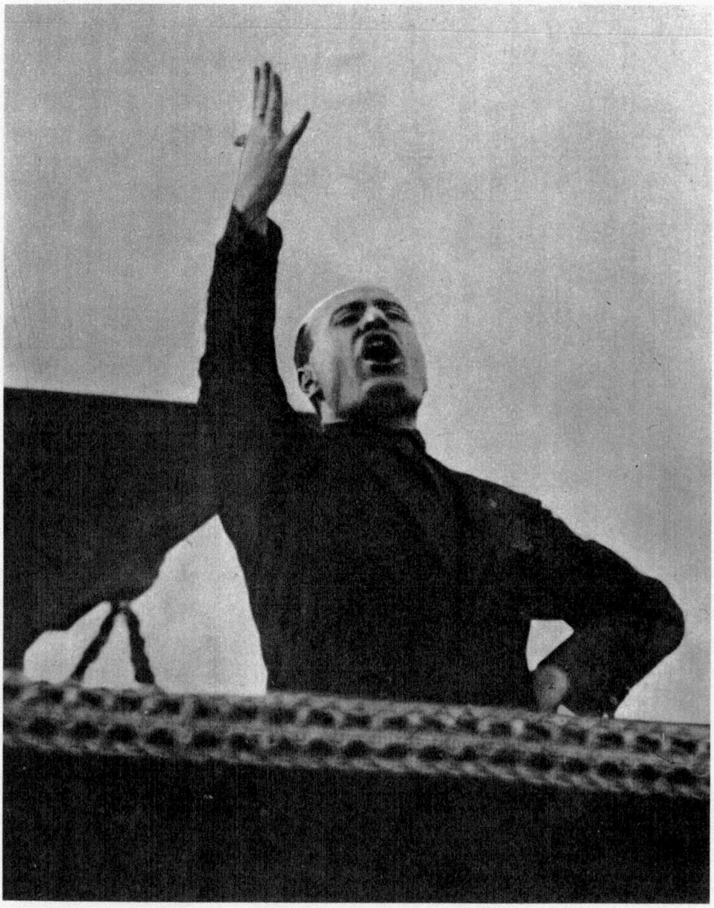

Mussolini spricht L. U. C. E.

Fig. 61. Franz Schauwecker, *So ist der Friede* (Berlin: Frundsberg-Verlag, 1928), page 113.

necessary to organize and govern. Mussolini's achievements are tied directly to his character and role as "engine and driver in a double-built body."[64] He is "a man of destiny, and his work is the same."[65]

The photographs following the text visualize Mussolini's burning "personality." The first image, "Mussolini speaks" (fig. 61), is a dynamic snapshot of Mussolini delivering a speech, and it clearly serves as the illustration of a passage of text that came about five pages earlier. In it, Schauwecker dips into the expressionistic writing style that is so characteristic of his first picture book:

> Mussolini! There he stands. Above the crowd. He speaks. He is on fire. He breaks through the tension with a downward strike of his arm. Drumming. He hurls incitement. In the middle of a sentence he falls silent. A second. The crowd trembles with anger. And then he cuts through the wound-up passion like a taut rope. And into the silence his voice rises, ringing, metallic, a flickering flame: "What use are words! Come with me!"[66]

The photograph catches Mussolini with mouth open and his right arm outstretched in front of him, suggesting the passion he is lending to his speech. His left arm, however, is relaxed at his side, the top of his hand perched naturally on his hip. The physicality of these gestures evinces Schauwecker's idea of Mussolini's dual impulses: the fiery dramatics of his speech and his raw charisma are made reasonable by a sense of natural composure and confidence. Mussolini's position described in the text is also mirrored in the photograph's visual perspective. The camera, positioned below Mussolini, pictures him as "above the crowds." Whom he is addressing is not apparent from the photograph, though, as the shot is framed quite closely, yet the viewer is interpolated into the crowd through the perspective. Besides a few shapes suggesting the outline of a speaking platform, Mussolini looms large against a blank sky. The photograph is also printed large to cover most of the page. The visual effect of these qualities is meant to inspire awe and reverence; the viewing position of looking up *at* Mussolini becomes a metaphorical looking up *to* him.

The photograph of Mussolini is clearly far more visually dynamic than the formal, almost somber portraits in "The Face of Liberalism." Even when

64. Schauwecker, *So ist der Friede*, 111.
65. Schauwecker, *So ist der Friede*, 112.
66. Schauwecker, *So ist der Friede*, 108–9.

compared to two other photographs of speeches that came earlier in the book and were discussed earlier, this image captures the vigor and feeling of the individual to a far greater extent. Both the photograph of Scheidemann speaking from a window of the Reich Chancellery and the other of Ebert addressing a crowd from an unidentified balcony are framed from a distance, bringing both speaker and crowd into the frame. Scheidemann and Ebert appear therefore the same size as the people in the crowd, special only because of their raised position, echoing a critique from the text that their rank over the Volk is a construct, a nasty symptom of liberalism's apparatus. Both men are visually positioned above the masses, suggesting their leadership, but the text asserts that they lack the sort of vital connection to the people to truly shape the masses, something Mussolini in contrast achieves naturally. In the first photograph, Scheidemann spreads both his arms wide as he speaks and he must be held by the coattails of his jacket so he does not fall from his perch. In contrast to Mussolini, who unites passion and reasoned thought, Scheidemann's speech appears precarious and desperate. The caption of the Ebert photograph explains that the politician is decrying the terms of the Treaty of Versailles, when common knowledge tells the viewer that he accepted the terms just ten days later. The caption reveals the disconnect between the man's promises to the crowd below him and his actual actions. Although these two photographs seem initially to show the actions of charismatic leaders, the text subverts the visual content as artifice. Mussolini, by contrast, is pictured from a close distance and from a perspective in which he towers over the crowd. The viewer takes on the crowd's perspective through the camera and is drawn into the cult of personality characteristic of Italian fascism and lauded by Schauwecker. The remaining five pages of photographs that follow the dynamic portrait of Mussolini in the series on Italy continue the idea of Mussolini's personality being central to the Fascist movement. In all but a few of the pictures, he is the central figure, and even if he is not pictured, as in some of the photographs showing the famous March on Rome in 1922, his presence is still felt.

The other subsections in the "Nationalism of All Lands" series continue the pattern of tracing a nation's success or failures through the personalities of its leaders. Mustafa Kemal Atatürk (Turkey), Miguel Primo de Rivera (Spain), and Miklós Horthy (Hungary), although they are men of different natures and circumstances and are in Schauwecker's estimation certainly not of the high caliber of a Mussolini, are praised as decisive leaders who ended periods of unrest and restored the dignity of their respective nations. Correspondingly, they are all represented with photographs that are intended to inspire confidence in their leadership model. Horthy, for example, is dramatically pictured saluting his men atop a white horse after his forces have reclaimed Budapest from the Hungarian Soviet Republic under Belá Kun.[67] Even the otherwise static studio portraits of Atatürk and Horthy found in the series are meant to exude an air of unflappable and honorable leadership. Initially they appear to share the same static interiority of the portraits in "The Face of Liberalism," but Schauwecker seems to be aware of any perceived inconsistencies in representation. His laudatory text and the careful selection of accompanying images ensures that the interpretation of the portraits will be received as intended. Horthy's portrait is followed by two photographs of him dramatically retaking Budapest, and Atatürk's portrait is positioned above a photograph of a celebratory parade of his troops after the taking of Constantinople.[68] The positive reading of the portraits, and by extension the two leaders' "personality," is bolstered by their heroic actions, which are tied visually to the men's very faces. The context created by the text and accompanying images is also the reason why the portraits in "The Face of Liberalism" are not seen by the viewer as they otherwise would be; instead of the typical reverent portraits of important members of society, they become in this context the face of ineffective, corrupt, and uncaring politicians. Schauwecker betrays an understanding that from a physiognomic point of view, photography is a second-order form of signification, and signifying power is not inherent in the face but vested in the rhetoric of photographic representation.[69] In this sense, J. J. Long's assertion about the discourse of physiognomy being a "flexible discourse" in the Weimar era rings clear: "[physiognomy] cannot be thought of without reference to its performative dimension."[70]

As a counterexample to the positive nationalism centered on a strong leader, the situation in Poland is lambasted in the text and mocked through the selected photograph of Józef Piłsudski, the "First Marshal of Poland" (fig. 62). According to Schauwecker, Poland owes its existence to the failures of its enemies and the "egotistical" interests of France in upholding it as a counterweight to Germany, facts that do not bode well for the future of "this impossible state structure."[71] Placed next to a photograph of Spain's Primo de Rivera looking magisterial with the sun hitting his profile as he

67. Schauwecker, *So ist der Friede*, 128.

68. Schauwecker, *So ist der Friede*, 125.

69. See Long, "Faces," 201.

70. Long, "Faces," 213.

71. Schauwecker, *So ist der Friede*, 122.

POLEN

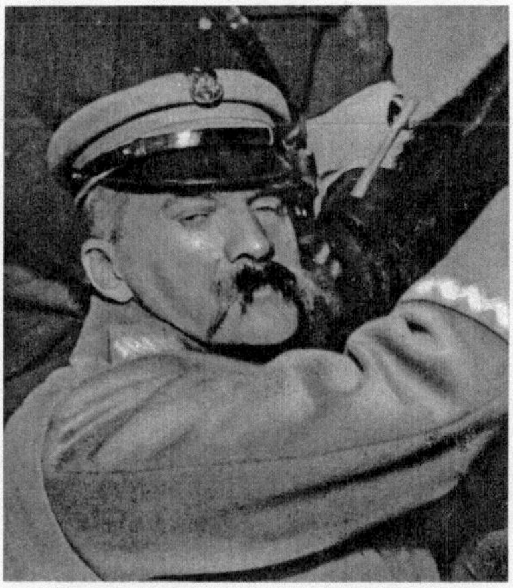

Der polnische Marschall Pilsudski U.

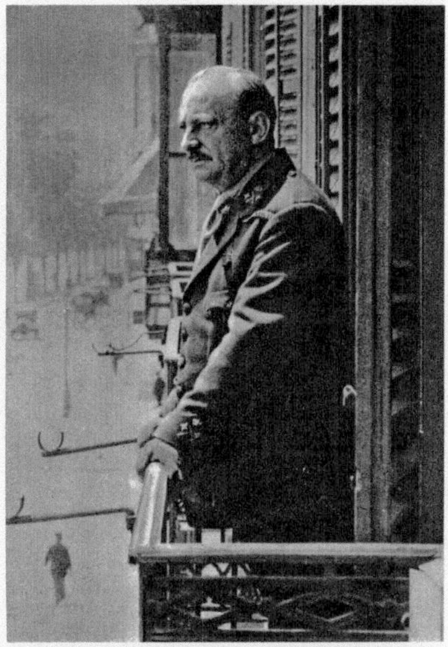

Mitte:
General Primo de Rivera U.

Unten:
Primo de Rivera dekoriert den Leichnam des in Marokko gefallenen Coronel Francis mit der Militär-Medaille

SPANIEN

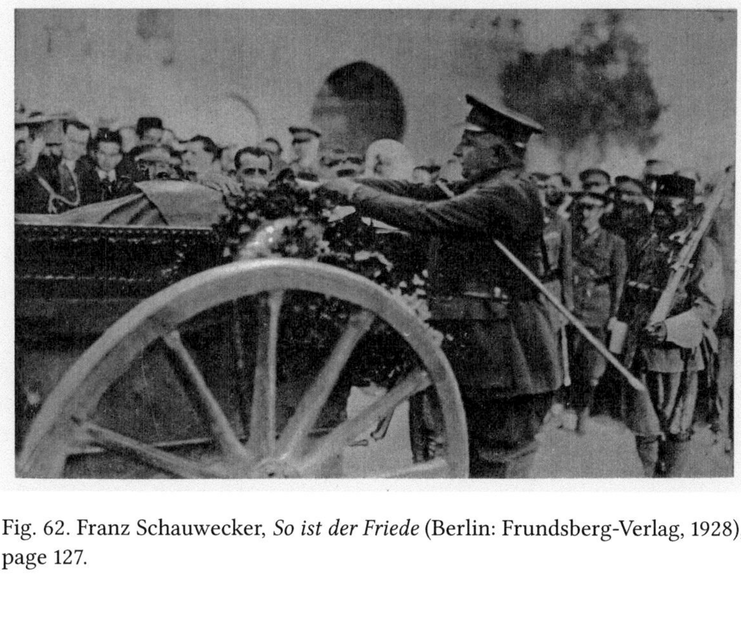

Fig. 62. Franz Schauwecker, *So ist der Friede* (Berlin: Frundsberg-Verlag, 1928), page 127.

looks out from atop a balcony, the photograph of Piłsudski—the only one in this subsection representing Poland—is highly unflattering. He is pictured in a contorted posture, with his right arm bent upwards in front of him as he turns his face toward the camera. It is not obvious what the picture is actually showing, as the image has evidently been cropped to focus on his upper body and face, although the photograph seems to have been a candid shot. This fact is clear in Piłsudski's unbecoming facial expression, with eyes half open to the camera, making him appear drunk or feeble-minded. Such an unflattering and manipulated snapshot should serve as proof for Piłsudski's absence of Schauweckerian "personality," but the image reveals practically nothing on its own, and such a reading is possible only through the negative characterization of the Polish postwar situation in the preceding text. It betrays again the contradictory beliefs that Schauwecker ascribes—consciously or unconsciously—to photographs: their evidentiary force is indisputable, but their meaning is only activated through textual explanation and juxtaposition.

The stories of Ireland and Morocco introduce another pattern to the section on the "Nationalism of All Lands" that is significant for understanding how Schauwecker sees attitudes toward war simmering into the postwar era. Both comprise evidence for his critique of the Allies' continued violent exploitation of other nations. The national movements of Sinn Fein in Ireland and of the Berber-speaking Rif tribes in Morocco under the leadership of Mulai Ahmed er Raisuli and Abd el-Krim represent the oppression of ethnic populations by English and by Spanish and French imperialists, respectively. The pictures of Ireland show English military forces occupying Dublin, and those of Morocco include French airplanes bombing Ajdir (then capital of the Republic of the Rif, 1922–26) as well as images of other native tribes loyal to France outfitted with French weaponry. The intervention of world powers to stop uprisings of local peoples who seek independent status clashes with the stated principles of the postwar peace, including the self-determination of countries and the disarmament of the world outlined by President Woodrow Wilson in his Fourteen Points. Schauwecker explains of the Rif: "The same immense superiority that had been on the side of the Entente in the World War crushed here too—with its immense, formless mass—the enemy fighting for his life, the nation fighting for its existence."[72]

The final subsection in "The Nationalism of All Lands" and the final seven pages in *So ist der Friede* concerns Germany. After around 80 pages

72. Schauwecker, *So ist der Friede*, 135.

of considering other nations around the globe, Schauwecker returns to the heart of the matter: Germany's position in a post-Versailles world. The series' introductory text decries the cozy relationship between Reichstag members and big business ("The democrat Dr. Hermann Fischer held 20 supervisory board positions alone"), the costs of a liberal government ("All the ministers accepted the pension, even though the people were starving"), and the inefficacy of parliament ("The National Assembly wrote a book of 5,733 pages, the first Reichstag a work of 12,830 pages, the third, the shortest, a tome of 11,050 pages").[73] In Schauwecker's eyes, German nationalism was born in the life-and-death experience of war, but the postwar disappointments strengthened and emboldened nationalism.[74] He provides a brief overview of the various groups that arose in the national movement, including the National Socialist Party (Nazis) and many paramilitary veterans' organizations, such as the Wehrwolf, the Jungdeutsche Orden, the Reichsflagge, and the Wikking, many of which were formed from members of disbanded Freikorps divisions. Although he is likely biased by writing for the Frundsberg-Verlag, the author assigns the Stahlhelm, Bund der Frontsoldaten (the Steel Helmet, League of Frontline Soldiers), a primary role among these combat leagues, characterizing it as the largest and the most politically active of them all. Many of the smaller organizations, then, as well as the public at large, look to the Stahlhelm for "the realization of the 'internal and external liberation of Germany.'"[75]

The photographs in the "Deutschland" series support Schauwecker's claim to political legitimacy for the "front generation" and avow typical nationalist indignations, such as anger over the execution of Albert Leo Schlageter, which is shown in the first photograph in the series. Schlageter was sentenced to death for sabotage actions against the French occupation of the Ruhr. The photograph is ascribed special sacral meaning as the "only image" of the event and it is given a whole page to itself, setting it apart from the series.[76] Beyond the Schlageter photograph, the overwhelming majority of images in the series are intended to show the nationalist movement's strength in Germany, embodied foremost by the Stahlhelm, and to a lesser extent by the Nazi Party. The second page, showing three photographs of "former frontline fighters in the Kapp-Putsch (March 1920),"[77] announces

73. Schauwecker, *So ist der Friede*, 179.
74. Schauwecker, *So ist der Friede*, 179.
75. Schauwecker, *So ist der Friede*, 180.
76. Schauwecker, *So ist der Friede*, 181.
77. Schauwecker, *So ist der Friede*, 182.

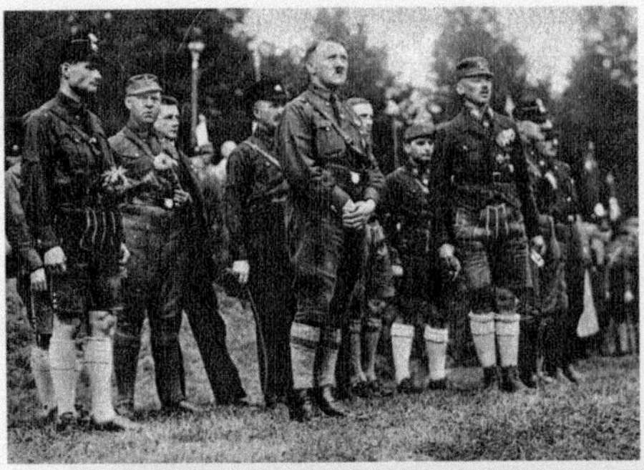

Der Führer der Nationalsozialisten
Adolf Hitler Ro.

Mitte:
Nationalsozialisten an der Ruhr
Ro.

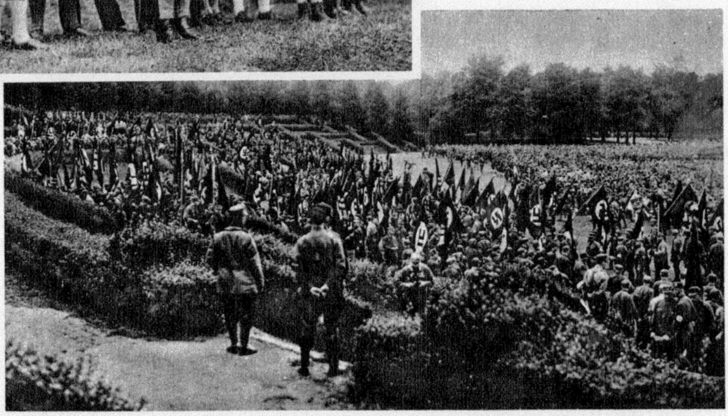

Frontkämpfer des Stahlhelm-Bundes im Lustgarten, Berlin (Mai 1927) Tra.

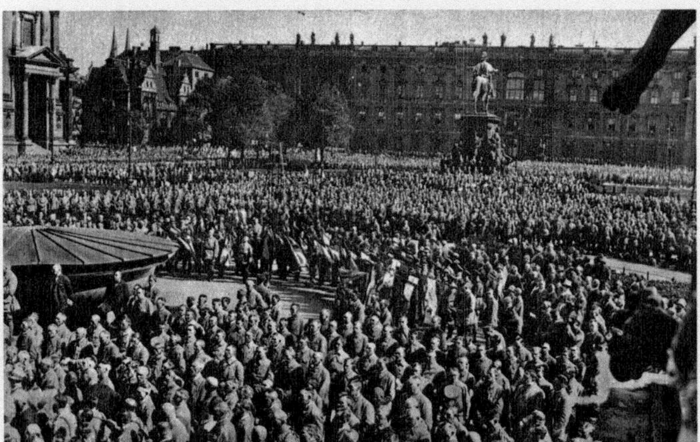

Fig. 63. Franz Schauwecker, *So ist der Friede* (Berlin: Frundsberg-Verlag, 1928), page 183.

the militaristic nature of the nationalist groups' strength, and the message is carried through the end of the series. Frontline soldiers of the Stahlhelm, dressed in military uniform, are shown across four pages gathering for massive "Front Soldiers Day" rallies in early May 1927 on Unter den Linden, by the Berliner Dom, and in the Berlin Stadium.

Two photographs of demonstrations by the National Socialists mirror the Stahlhelm march and visually link the groups under one movement (fig. 63).[78] The first photograph shows Adolf Hitler in uniform, standing stately among other higher-ups and looking out of frame to the right. The picture is positioned so that it cuts into the top left corner of a photograph below it, which shows a Nazi rally in the Ruhr. The perspectives of the two photographs do not merge, but the positioning suggests that Hitler is looking out over the rally in the second picture. The visual effect is a clear assertion of Hitler's role as *Führer* of the Nazi movement. A third picture below the first two, showing a gathering of "frontline fighters" of the Stahlhelm, visually suggests the melding of the two movements with Hitler at the head of both. The same connotation is continued on the next page, where Franz Seldte, "Führer of the Stahlhelm," is shown in military uniform inspecting participants of the Front Soldiers Day demonstrations.[79] The groups' strong leaders, their militaristic nature, and, perhaps most important, their masses of supporters are united visually in the photographs following the text's assertion that the two groups are the standard-bearers of German nationalism. The only obvious visual cue of the groups' difference is the swastika flags seen in the crowd of the Nazi rally and the German Imperial flags carried by Stahlhelm supporters.[80]

So ist der Friede ends with a picture of "The gray army of former German frontline fighters in the German Republic of German parliamentarianism" (fig. 64). The crowd, photographed from a distance, fills the image's entire frame, giving a strong final impression of the movement's support. Under the photograph, written in large capital letters, is the slogan "Nicht Masse, sondern Volk; nicht Klasse, sondern Nation" (Not the masses, but the people; not class, but nation).[81] The phrase sets an exclamation point on many of the politicized arguments made by Schauwecker throughout the book and

78. Schauwecker, *So ist der Friede*, 183.

79. Schauwecker, *So ist der Friede*, 184.

80. For a consideration of how photographs from the First World War were employed as part of National Socialist propaganda from 1926 to 1939, see Protte, "Das 'Erbe' des Krieges."

81. Schauwecker, *So ist der Friede*, 186.

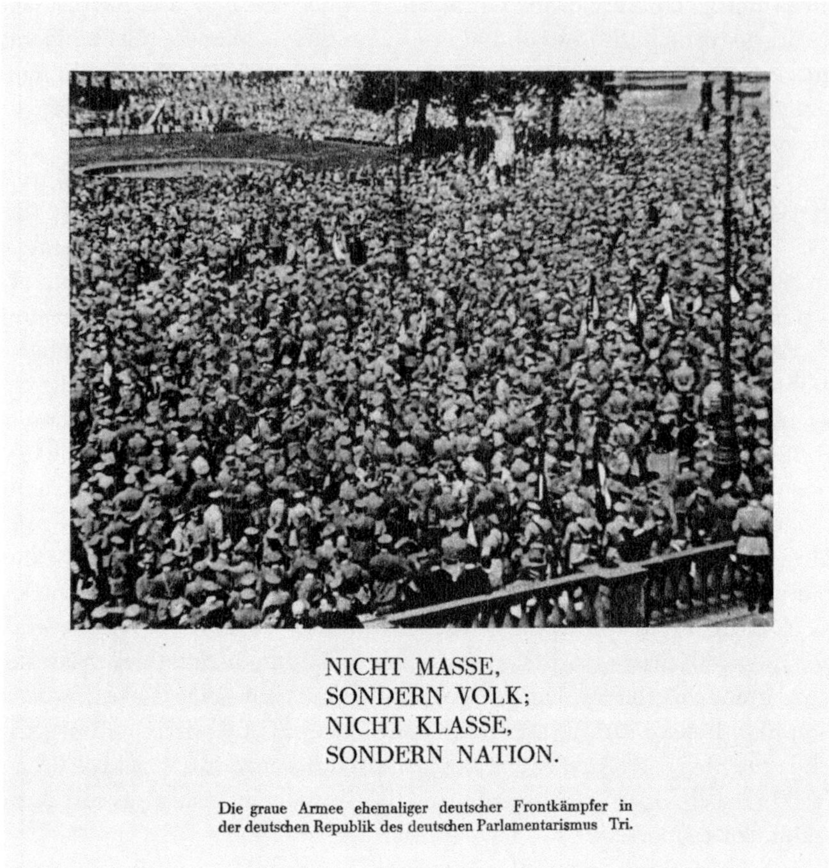

Fig. 64. Franz Schauwecker, *So ist der Friede* (Berlin: Frundsberg-Verlag, 1928), page 186.

correlates directly to the poem that began the book, "Diese Zeit." There, the Volk are left leaderless after the war, consigned to grumble as "masses" under "a heavy cloud."[82] The squandered legacy of the war introduced in "Diese Zeit" (which is typified by the unmarked graves of erstwhile battlefields) is "proven" in the apparent failures of liberalism and parliamentarianism. The war's fallen soldiers have been betrayed by the Weimar situation but receive their deserved redemption in the nationalist movement spearheaded by former frontline soldiers (and, to a lesser degree here, by the Nazi Party).

82. Schauwecker, *So ist der Friede*, 3.

These groups represent a positive wave of nationalism and as such they alone provide the answers to the crises plaguing Weimar Germany that are laid out from the start of the picture book. For the Stahlhelm, their asserted legitimacy to reshape the country in a nationalist image is firmly anchored in the war experience. That Schauwecker freely applies aspects of the war experience to a postwar vision of Germany, including the need for decisive and inspirational authoritarian leaders and the continued agitation of international rivalries, is a natural extension of the mentalities of war that persisted for a decade after 1918 and contributed to the unstable Weimar political landscape.

Such mentalities are voiced in the widespread positive reception *So ist der Friede* received in the conservative press. The editorial board of the *Allgemeine schweizerische Militärzeitung* (General Swiss military newspaper) praised the picture book as a "very timely book that tears the mask off the hypocritical face of modern pacifism in all its mendacity." With its "naked, unvarnished truth" and "unbeatable imagery," *So ist der Friede* offers a clear lesson for the present: "To be prepared is everything."[83] A reviewer under the abbreviation "G. Sch." maintains in *Der Ring* that the book proves "how the photograph can be used as an effective weapon in the national struggle."[84] Xaver Schaukroff, writing in *Der Gral*, similarly praises the book's factual nature and the "correctness" of its anti-Marxist, antiliberal message for the present. He goes a step further and recognizes the book's community-building potential: "The honesty of the book and the pictures are more than worth reading; their objectivity will easily create enthusiastic followers for the new movement."[85] Richard Neumann claims in *Deutsche Blätter für erziehenden Unterricht* (German papers for educational instruction) that Schauwecker's "idea of the nation will one day help form the new national substance, which has its nucleus in the most deceived: the soldiers of the Great War who are silent."[86] And a review in the national-revolutionary *Der Vormarsch* recommends it to "every nationalist," claiming "he will return with a new view of the world."[87] In short, at the same time that the political ideas espoused in *So ist der Friede* found positive resonance with a wide conservative audience, Schauwecker's arguments about photography were uncritically accepted by his reading public. His reviewers shared with him

83. Review of *So ist der Friede* in *Allgemeine schweizerische Militärzeitung*, 358.
84. Sch., review of *So ist der Friede*, 220.
85. Schaukroff, review of *So ist der Friede*, 956.
86. Neumann, review of *So ist der Friede*, 156.
87. Review of *So ist der Friede* in *Vormarsch*, 253.

the belief that photography naturally held an immense power to change people's subjectivities and politics for the future.

Schauwecker's picture book *So ist der Friede* is strong evidence of the way nationalists assessed the war's meaning in the postwar era and envisioned a radically different state than the Weimar Republic. The work is unique for the strong relationship it shares with its precursor, *So war der Krieg!* Together, the books assert a highly specific version of the war experience that is meant to have political purchase after the war. They achieve this through the careful selection, editing, and arrangement of photographs, which at times must be guided by textual explanation and at other times develop meaning beyond the text through specific sequencing, juxtaposition, and patterns. In this way Schauwecker's works share aspects of the genre common to other picture books discussed in this study, but the way in which the war experience is tied so explicitly to an indictment of the Weimar Republic is unique to him. Both *So war der Krieg!* and *So ist der Friede* are representative of soldatischer Nationalismus specific to a subset of the national revolutionaries that drew on myths of the "frontline warrior" and the "front generation" to reckon with the war's aftermath. The picture books are highly revealing not only for how mentalities of the age were shaped by the war but for how they also sought to shape the postwar era through visual representations.

Conclusion

Werner Beumelburg asks in the opening lines to the picture book *Eine ganze Welt gegen uns* (A whole world against us; 1934): "A new book with pictures from the Great War? Why?"[1] As is clear from the rest of his introduction, the rhetorical question is meant to address the war's enduring legacy, but it seems the book's editor, Wilhelm Reetz, is worried that it might be taken as an invitation to challenge the book's release in an already satiated market of war picture books. In a separate preface he offers a practical answer to Beumelburg's question that appeals to the reader who might have had enough of the genre and war pictures in general: he claims that most of the photographs in the book have not been seen in Germany or even previously published elsewhere, and he assures the reader that he personally looked through over 60,000 images to find the strongest ones possible.[2] Despite his marketing-minded outlook, Reetz nevertheless shares with Beumelburg the intention to draw from the war experience lessons that can be applied in a postwar era.

Beumelburg evinces strands of soldatischer Nationalismus that define Franz Schauwecker's earlier picture books—foremost the lauding of the frontline soldier's virtues as exemplary for the nation—when he writes that the intention is not to erect a monument to the frontline soldier, nor to simply express gratitude, but to remind the Volk again where "the deep roots lie from which their life force arises." The frontline soldier—modest, gray, rich in both wounds and virtues—stands on the border of two epochs and is, according to Beumelburg, the surest guarantor of a better and more just future. Reetz takes the future-oriented vision one step further in his preface,

1. Reetz, *Eine ganze Welt gegen uns*, 5.
2. Reetz, *Eine ganze Welt gegen uns*, 11.

writing that the book should encourage later generations, if needed, to freely accept becoming frontline soldiers themselves.

Eine ganze Welt gegen uns was published in 1934, after the end of the Weimar Republic and the National Socialist rise to power. As such, it does not engage in the sort of political posturing in the hotly disputed field of war memory that one contemporary characterized in 1929 as a political contest of "-isms" between antipodal "literatures of justification and accusation."[3] Because of its post-1933 publication date, Reetz's book stands clearly apart from the war picture books of the 1920s, which were, as seen throughout this study, concerned as much with shaping the memory of the war as with shaping the uncertain future of postwar Germany. For Reetz and Beumelburg, the war memory contests, including an increase of politicized war novels in the post-1929 crisis years,[4] had largely been settled. Their book is as far removed from the uncertain political horizon of Ernst Friedrich's *Krieg dem Kriege!* as it is from the military-affirming patriotism of Walter Bloem in *Deutschland: Ein Buch der Größe und der Hoffnung in Bildern, 1914–1924* or the self-legitimization of Reichsarchiv publications, all concerned with explaining war for immediate application in a turbulent postwar era. And although the book still intervenes in assessing the war's legacy and asserting the frontline soldier's centrality as an example for the nation, it is not in the terms of radical societal or governmental change, as it is in the works of soldatischer Nationalismus authors such as Franz Schauwecker, George Soldan, or even an earlier Beumelburg.

Furthermore, although photography from the First World War had a role in the self-fashioning of the NSDAP (Nazi Party), it was significantly less important than it was to soldatischer Nationalismus thinkers. As Katja Protte explains, "An illustrated book that would have become the epitome of a National Socialist 'war experience'—like Hans Zöberlein's frontline novel *Der Glaube an Deutschland* (Faith in Germany [1931]) in literature—cannot be found."[5] The handful of war picture books published after 1933, including Otto Danz's *Der Weltkrieg: Ein Bildwerk aus dem großen Kriege, zusammengestaltet aus dem Bildmaterial des Reichsarchivs Potsdam* (The World War: An illustrated work from the Great War, composed of visual material from the Reichsarchiv Potsdam; 1934), Hermann Ziese-Beringer's *Das Antlitz von Verdun* (The face of Verdun; 1936), and Erich Otto Volkmann's series

3. Weniger, "Das Bild des Krieges," 7.
4. See Gollbach, *Die Wiederkehr des Weltkrieges.*
5. Protte, "Das 'Erbe' des Krieges," 19.

Die unsterbliche Landschaft: Die Fronten des Weltkriegs, Ein Bilderwerk (The immortal landscape: The fronts of the World War, a pictorial work; 1934–35), do not wear their political views as transparently as those picture books of the 1920s. Whereas the latter group must be understood in the dynamically changing field of memory and politics that they reflected and helped to construct, post-1933 war picture books had no such concerns. But in making their politics relatively invisible, they normalized then dominant right-wing and National Socialist interpretations of the war.

Yet even if many of the photographs included in *Eine ganze Welt gegen uns* were previously unpublished—if Reetz's claim is true—they are not unlike what appears in earlier nationalist picture books (and some are, in fact, obvious repeats). The images show the war in its many facets, focusing like Schauwecker on a sense of action that hides the harshest aspects of (German) death on the front. Reetz's claim that he picked only the "strongest" images is evident in the book's preponderance of dynamically composed photographs. A variety of formatting techniques unseen in earlier works, such as the stretching of photographs to occupy entire pages and a more robust variety of image size and shape, increase the visual appeal but do not contribute to additional meaning-making. Brief, identifying captions are set in an attractive modern typeface but are free of ideological commentary—with the exception of an expected critical stance toward the Treaty of Versailles. These aesthetic details are evidence of certain technical advances in the war-picture-book genre in the half decade following Schauwecker's *So ist der Friede*, but the differences from those earlier books, even in a radically different political context, are slight.

Like the picture books before it, *Eine ganze Welt gegen uns* can provide only a general interpretation of the war experience. It distills from a massive collection of war photographs a message that, although notably less political, seeks to encapsulate "The War" into something easily and universally understood. By drawing freely from a general archive, all picture-book authors and editors covered in this book erased the photographs' respective creators, perspectives, and contexts from consideration to craft specific interpretations of the war that were then presented as paradigmatic. Unlike personal albums of photographs taken by German soldiers, which, despite their own gaps in representation, offer a richer impression of actual lived experience, picture books can only offer the typical as such. The process is shared between such radically opposed contemporaries as Ernst Friedrich and Franz Schauwecker, who both saw something emblematic in the war experience: for one, horror, and for the other, heroism. Although both have their respective nuanced presentation style (Friedrich's sarcastic juxtapositions, for example), the basic method of drawing specific visions of war from general archives highlights how the flexibility of the war's visual record can be instrumentalized for a variety of purposes, even ones on opposite sides of such entrenched political divides. The same holds true for less blatantly political practitioners, such as the Reichsarchiv's historiographers, who crafted the war's visual history in terms that reaffirmed the social order of the military as it came under threat at the end of monarchical rule. That war would engender such diverse reactions is not surprising, but the fact that the war's photographic archive was so malleable—in large part due to its myriad contributors and sheer amount of created images—offers a warning to any viewer trying to understand history through the camera's lens. This book has made the case against photography as mere illustration and has modeled how careful consideration of photography's use often reveals more about the mentalities and ideologies ascribed to images than their inherent ability to produce knowledge. The matter is of concern for historians of any decade, but the case of First World War memory in the Weimar era is an especially fraught example of how visions of the past competed for authoritative status in an ideological contest.

The pitfalls of such selective memory have been made clear throughout this book and include processes of distortion, censorship, and erasure. Although other media are certainly prone to similar abuse in shaping collective memory, photography was positioned by picture-book authors as unique in representing reality with perfect technical reproduction. Reetz, for one, carries the popular belief into the post-Weimar era when he calls photographs "serious, truthful documents" in the preface to *Eine ganze Welt gegen uns.* Other accounts, like the memoirs of military higher-ups popular in the immediate postwar years, made similar claims to represent the war authoritatively, but their effect was countered by alternative narratives, including Remarque's later *Im Westen nichts Neues,* that presented the war in a similarly convincing way. Among the authors and editors discussed here, there is rarely nuanced thinking about photography's representational limits, and little to nothing was included in the realm of popular picture books to question or counter the supposition of photography's authority. Ernst Friedrich believes in the shock power of photography to change hearts in the same way that Walter Bloem sees definitive proof of Germany's greatness in pictures of its ships and zeppelins. Yet all authors betray to a certain extent their uncertainty about the ability of photography to "speak for itself"; captions or lengthy passages of text are found in all picture books to frame or guide intended interpretations. The authors, however, do not reflect upon the contradiction. They remain either unaware of it or fear that naming it would undermine their purpose.

Although theoretical discussions about photography were occurring in other forums during the Weimar era, popular war picture books and their reviews indicate that general audiences were to a certain degree unaffected by the critical efforts of avant-garde photography practitioners like Albert Renger-Patzsch to "train" viewers to be more discerning in their consumption of images. The work of some German visual artists in the postwar era, such as the abstract photograms of Christian Schad or the photomontages of John Heartfield, was a direct response to the prevailing uncritical understanding of photography at the time. Their work sought to assert "individual creativity in the face of a dominant mechanical medium and the ostensibly absolute authenticity of its imagery."[6] In a longer trajectory of artists responding to the challenge photography posed to the traditions of painting and drawing, other visual artists occupied with the war, such as Otto Dix, championed the expressive power of classical media. Dix maintained that "photography can only record a moment, and that only superficially, but it cannot delineate specific, individual form, something that depends on the imaginative power and intuition of the painter."[7]

The enduring appeal of antiwar work by Weimar visual artists, among them Heartfield, Dix, Käthe Kollwitz, and George Grosz, is certainly due in part to the evocative nature of their visual representations. Analysis of what effect they had on the Weimar public's perception of the First World War is outside the scope of this book, but their example offers a significant counterpoint to the military-affirming, patriotic, or nationalist visions of war that prevailed in the realm of picture books. (Friedrich, for one, moved in the same circles as Kollwitz and shared with Dix and Grosz both a pacifist worldview and a fixation on the grotesque.) It would be difficult to assess definitively which genre, picture books or the fine arts, had a larger impact on the public's impression of the war, but due to the success and widespread availability of generally right-wing or patriotic war picture books, it is quite possible that the positive spin provided by picture books reached a broader audience. Even Friedrich's book was more of a curious, albeit sensational exception to the otherwise dominant right-wing affiliated interpretations. Contemporary perception of the First World War is far more influenced by

6. Eberle, *World War I and the Weimar Artists*, 14.
7. Quoted in Eberle, *World War I and the Weimar Artists*, 46.

the work of avant-garde artists, not only because of their artistic inventiveness but also because their political message is far more tenable in a post–Second World War era. It is the same reason Friedrich's *Krieg dem Kriege!* was rediscovered during the peace movements of the 1980s and is reprinted even today. Both the Anti-War Museum in Berlin, run by Friedrich's grandson, and the Spokesman Press, the publishing imprint of the Bertrand Russell Peace Foundation, have released editions of the book in the last decade. The pacifist view of war, stressing the excess of physical carnage, coincides also with modern myths about the First World War as a senseless fight about nothing,[8] while the Second World War has clearer narratives of good versus evil.

Why picture books or the photographs within them have failed to influence contemporary perceptions about the First World War in a way that Weimar-era fine artists continue to do could also be explained by photography's unrealized potential at the time. Working from an English context, Jorge Lewinski cynically observes that no photographer in the First World War captured both the "grandeur and the depths of the calamity"[9] of the war experience, and no photograph seems to capture the harsh realities of life in the trenches:

> They have a descriptive clarity, but very few show passion or commitment on the part of the photographers. . . . The photographers do not attempt to make a point, as if they did not expect that their pictures would be looked at. The power of the photograph to communicate a deeply felt emotion had not yet been realized.[10]

It is true that no photograph from the First World War has reached the same iconic status as later war photographs. No single image encapsulated the conflict in the way that Margaret Bourke-White's photographs of the liberated concentration camps summarized the Second World War and the Holocaust or Nick Ut's infamous photograph of Phan Thi Kim Phuc, the "Napalm Girl," came to represent the horrors of the Vietnam War. The fact is due in no small part both to the far more limited and censored nature of war reportage during the First World War[11] and the photographer's dug-in

8. See Todman, *The Great War.*
9. Lewinski, *The Camera at War*, 68–69.
10. Lewinski, *The Camera at War*, 70.
11. See Koszyk, *Deutsche Pressepolitik.*

vantage point in the trenches of the Western Front, which Bodo von Dewitz credits with a surplus of images that show spectacularly wasted landscapes from ultimately unspectacular perspectives.[12] The horrible images of mutilated faces in Friedrich's *Krieg dem Kriege!* are among the photographs that have come the closest to becoming icons of the First World War, but even those are known only to a narrow audience.

While photographs from the period can at times seem mundane to the modern viewer, there is no discounting the visual excitement they elicited among early twentieth-century audiences, especially during the "photoboom" of the 1920s. The channeling of the public's interest in photography, coupled with their engagement in contentious public debates surrounding the war's enduring legacy, explains the publication success of war picture books. Photographs and their textual frames were powerful tools for shaping the collective memory of the war, and the variety of approaches to doing so reflects as much the divisiveness of the debate as the openness of photography to being co-opted for ideological signification. Picture books from the Weimar Republic are therefore significant testimony both to the ways that the First World War was remembered visually and how those frames of interpretation sought to shape a turbulent postwar era.

---

12. Dewitz, *So wird bei uns der Krieg geführt,* 263.

Works Cited

Archival Materials

"Album mit Fotos aus dem 1. Weltkrieg vom Kriegsschauplatz an der Ostfront." Deutsches Historisches Museum in Berlin, Do2 98/236.

"Album mit Fotos, Postkarten und Theaterprogrammen deutscher Gefangener in englischen Lagern." Deutsches Historisches Museum in Berlin, Do2 89/148.

"Album mit Fotos und Kunstexponaten aus der Kriegsgefangenschaft in Sibirien im Ersten Weltkrieg." Deutsches Historisches Museum in Berlin, Do2 89/237.

"Album mit Postkarten, Fotos und Dokumenten zum Leben deutscher Kriegsgefangener in russischen Lagern." Deutsches Historisches Museum in Berlin, Do2 89/149.

"Fotoalbum aus dem Ersten Weltkrieg mit zahlreichen Aufnahmen von Kriegszerstörungen in Frankreich, Belgien und Polen." Deutsches Historisches Museum in Berlin, Do2 2013/186.

"Jako Sitzmann, Photo Album, 1914–1918." Department of Special Collections, Memorial Library, University of Wisconsin–Madison, MS 411 no. 10.

Soldan, George. "Die deutsche Geschichtsschreibung des Weltkrieges: Eine nationale Aufgabe." Bundesarchiv, R 1506, 41, fos. 49–90.

Books and Book Chapters

Berhmann, Franz. *Die Osterschlacht bei Arras 1917, I. Teil: Zwischen Lens und Scarpe (=Bd. 28, Schlachten des Weltkrieges).* Oldenburg/Berlin: Stalling, 1929.

Beumelburg, Werner. *Douaumont (=Bd. 1, Schlachten des Weltkrieges).* Oldenburg/Berlin: Stalling, 1925.

Beumelburg, Werner. *Loretto (= Bd. 17, Schlachten des Weltkrieges).* Oldenburg: Stalling, 1927.

Beumelburg, Werner. "Vorwort." In *Der Weltkrieg im Bild, Bd. 2: Frontaufnahmen aus den Archiven der Entente,* 5–7. Berlin: National-Archiv, ca. 1928.

Bloem, Walter. "Zehn Jahre Geschichte!" In *Deutschland: Ein Buch der Grösse und der Hoffnung in Bildern, 1914–1924, herausgegeben in Verbindung mit dem Reichsarchiv,* 5–7. Berlin: Otto Stollberg, ca. 1924–25.

Bose, Thilo von. *Das Marnedrama 1914, Teil III: Die Kämpfe des Gardekorps und des rechten Flügels der 3. Armee vom 5. bis 8. (=Bd. 24, Schlachten des Weltkrieges).* Oldenburg/Berlin: Stalling, 1928.

Bose, Thilo von. *Deutsche Siege 1918 (=Bd. 32, Schlachten des Weltkrieges).* Oldenburg/Berlin: Stalling, 1929.

Bose, Thilo von. *Wachsende Schwierigkeiten 1918 (=Bd. 33, Schlachten des Weltkrieges).* Oldenburg/Berlin: Stalling, 1930.

Claasen, Oswald. *Franz Schauwecker: Ein Leben für die Nation.* Berlin: Frundsberg, 1933.

Danz, Otto. *Der Weltkrieg: Ein Bildwerk aus dem großen Kriege, zusammengestaltet aus dem Bildmaterial des Reichsarchivs Potsdam.* Mettmann: Immalin-Werke, 1934.

Das 41. Reserve-Korps von der Somme zum Pripjat: Mit 438 Bildern. Munich: Piper, 1917.

Dellmensingen, Konrad Krafft von. *Der Durchbruch am Isonzo, Teil I: Die Schlacht von Tolmein und Flitsch (= Bd. 12a, Schlachten des Weltkrieges).* Oldenburg/Berlin: Stalling, 1926.

Der Krieg 1914 in Wort und Bild, Heft 1. Berlin: Deutsches Verlagshaus Bong, 1914.

Deutschland: Ein Buch der Grösse und der Hoffnung in Bildern, 1914–1924, herausgegeben in Verbindung mit dem Reichsarchiv. Berlin: Otto Stollberg, ca. 1924–25.

Friedeburg, Friedrich von. *Karpathen- und Dnester-Schlacht 1915 (= Bd. 2, Schlachten des Weltkrieges).* Oldenburg/Berlin: Stalling, 1925.

Friedrich, Ernst. *Krieg dem Kriege!* Berlin: Freie Jugend, 1924; reprint, Berlin: Christoph Links, 2015.

Habbig, Ernst, ed. *Eine deutsche Division zwei Jahre im Weltkrieg: Erinnerungsblätter aus West und Ost.* Bremen: Franz Teuwer, 1917.

Heydemann, Kurt. *Die Schlacht bei St. Quentin 1914, I. Teil: Der rechte Flügel der 2. deutschen Armee am 29. und 30. August (=Bd. 7a, Schlachten des Weltkrieges).* Oldenburg/Berlin: Stalling, 1925.

Jünger, Ernst. *Das Antlitz des Weltkrieges: Fronterlebnisse Deutscher Soldaten.* Berlin: Neufeld & Henius, 1930.

Jünger, Ernst. *In Stahlgewittern.* 1924; reprint, Stuttgart: Klett-Cotta, 2014.

Kalm, Oskar Tile von. *Gorlice (= Bd. 30, Schlachten des Weltkrieges).* Oldenburg/Berlin: Stalling, 1930.

Kleinau, Wilhelm. *Stahlhelm und Staat: Eine Erläuterung der Stahlhelm-Botschaften.* Berlin: Stahlhelm-Verlag, 1929.

Konsbrück, Hermann. *Großer Bilderatlas des Weltkrieges, Band 1.* Munich: F. Bruckmann, 1915.

Konsbrück, Hermann. *Großer Bilderatlas des Weltkrieges, Band 3.* Munich: F. Bruckmann, 1919.

Mertz von Quirnheim, Hermann. "Vorwort des Reichsarchivs zur 2. Auflage." In *Douaumont (=Bd. 1, Schlachten des Weltkrieges),* edited by Werner Beumelburg, 5–6. Oldenburg: Stalling, 1925.

Mühlmann, Carl. *Der Kampf um die Dardanellen 1915 (= Bd. 16, Schlachten des Weltkrieges).* Oldenburg/Berlin: Stalling, 1927.

Reetz, Wilhelm. *Eine ganze Welt gegen uns.* Berlin: Ullstein, 1934.

Reinhard, Wilhelm. *Das 4. Garde-Regiment zu Fuß (=Bd. 100, Erinnerungsblätter deutscher Regimenter).* Oldenburg: Stalling, 1924.

Rieben, Heinrich von. *Kaiser Franz-Garde-Grenadier-Regiment Nr. 2 (=Bd. 279, Erinnerungsblätter deutscher Regimenter).* Oldenburg; Berlin: Stalling, 1929.

Schauwecker, Franz. *So ist der Friede: Die Revolution der Zeit in 300 Bildern.* Berlin: Frundsberg, 1928.

Schauwecker, Franz. *So war der Krieg! 200 Kampfaufnahmen aus der Front.* Berlin: Frundsberg, 1927.

Schauwecker, Franz. *So war der Krieg! 230 Kampfaufnahmen aus der Front.* 7th ed. Berlin: Frundsberg, 1928.

Schmidt, Ernst. *Argonnen (= Bd. 18, Schlachten des Weltkrieges).* Oldenburg/Berlin: Stalling, 1927.

Schramm, Wilhelm von. "Schöpferische Kritik des Krieges. Ein Versuch." In *Krieg und Krieger*, edited by Ernst Jünger, 33–49. Berlin: Junker und Dünnhaupt, 1930.

Schulenburg-Wolfsburg, Carl Hans Gebhard von der. *Geschichte des Garde-Füsilier-Regiments nach den amtlichen Kriegstagebüchern und persönlichen Aufzeichnungen bearbeitet (=Bd. 157, Erinnerungsblätter deutscher Regimenter).* Oldenburg: Stalling, 1926.

Schwenke, Alexander. *Die Tragödie von Verdun 1916, Teil II, Das Ringen um Fort Vaux (= Bd. 14, Schlachten des Weltkrieges).* Oldenburg/Berlin: Stalling, 1928.

Soldan, George. *Zeitgeschichte in Wort und Bild.* Berlin: National-Archiv, 1931.

Soldan, George. "Zum Geleit." In *Der Weltkrieg im Bild, Bd. 1: Originalaufnahmen des Kriegs-Bild-und-Filmamtes aus der modernen Materialschlacht.* Berlin: National-Archiv, 1926.

Steuber, Werner. *Jildirim: Deutsche Streiter auf heiligem Boden (= Bd. 4, Schlachten des Weltkrieges).* Oldenburg/Berlin: Stalling, 1925.

Tucholsky, Kurt. *Deutschland, Deutschland über alles.* Berlin: Neuer Deutscher Verlag, 1929.

Volkmann, Erich Otto. *Die unsterbliche Landschaft: Die Fronten des Weltkriegs, Ein Bilderwerk.* Leipzig: Bibliographisches Verlag, 1934–35.

Ziese-Beringer, Hermann. *Das Antlitz von Verdun.* Berlin: Frundsberg-Verlag, 1936.

Zwei Jahre an der Westfront: 323 Bilder aus Artois, Pikardie und französisch Lothringen. Munich: Piper, 1917.

Zwischen Arras und Peronne: Mit 311 Bildern herausgegeben von einem deutschen Reservekorps. Korpsverlagsbuchhandlung Bapaume and Munich: Piper, 1916.

Newspaper Articles, Book Reviews, and Essays

"Aufhebung der Photographie-Verbote." *Die Photographische Industrie*, December 11, 1918.

Benjamin, Walter. "The Author as Producer." In *Walter Benjamin: Selected Writings, Volume 2, 1931–1934*, edited by Michael W. Jennings, Howard Eiland, and Gary Smith, 768–82. Translated by Rodney Livingstone and others. Cambridge, MA: Belknap Press of Harvard University Press, 1999.

Benjamin, Walter. "Little History of Photography." In *Walter Benjamin: Selected Writings, Volume 2, 1931–1934*, edited by Michael W. Jennings, Howard Eiland, and Gary Smith, 507–30. Translated by Rodney Livingstone and others. Cambridge, MA: Belknap Press of Harvard University Press, 1999.

Benjamin, Walter. "The Work of Art in the Age of Its Technological Reproducibility: Second Version." In *Walter Benjamin: Selected Writings, Volume 3, 1935–1938*, edited by Howard Eiland and Michael W. Jennings, 101–133. Translated by Edmund Jephcott, Howard Eiland, and others. Cambridge, MA: Belknap Press of Harvard University Press, 2002.

Brecht, Bertolt. "The *Threepenny* Lawsuit." In *Brecht on Film and Radio*, translated and edited by Marc Silberman, 147–99. London: Methuen, 2000.

"Der Krieg und der Amateurphotograph." *Photographische Rundschau und Mitteilungen* 51 (1914): 241–42.

"Der Verkauf kleiner Apparate an unsere 'Feldgrauen.'" *Die Photographische Industrie*, October 14, 1914.

"Die Filmnot." *Die Photographische Industrie*, February 10, 1915.

"Die Photographie als Hilfsmittel im Krieg." *Photographische Kunst* 15 (1916/17): 70.

"Die photographische Industrie im dritten Kriegsjahr." *Die Photographische Industrie*, January 3, 1917.

E., H. "Kriegstagebücher." *Photographie für Alle* 15/16 (1918): 131–34.

Eyermann, A. "Die Lichtbildkunst und Krieg," *Photographische Rundschau und Mitteilungen* 52 (1915): 190–91.

"Grabphotographien." *Das Bild: Monatsschrift für photographische Bildkunst* 14, no. 4 (July 1918): 49.

Iblher, Franz. "Photographie und Wirklichkeit. Anläßlich zweier Bücher vom Weltkriege." *Der Ring* 4, no. 37 (1931): 695–96.

Illing, Oskar. "Buecher- und Schriftschau," *Die neue Zeit* 9, no. 27 (1927): 12–13.

Jünger, Ernst. "Der unsichtbare Kern." *Vormarsch* 2 (1928/29): 329.

"Kleine Mitteilungen: Zentralstelle für die Zensur von Photographien." *Die Photographische Chronik* 74–75 (1915): 303–4.

Kracauer, Siegfried. "Die Photographie." *Frankfurter Zeitung*, October 28, 1927. Reprinted in *Das Ornament der Masse*, 21–39. Frankfurt: Suhrkamp, 1963.

L. Review of *So war der Krieg!*, by Franz Schauwecker. *Deutschlands Erneuerung* 2, no. 7 (1927): 328.

Lask, Berta. "Das wahre Gesicht des Krieges." *Die Rote Fahne*, September 21, 1924.

"Literatur." *Das größere Deutschland: Wochenschrift für deutsche Welt- und Kolonialpolitik* (1916): 1127.

"Neue Bücher." *Die Umschau: Wochenschrift über die Fortschritte in Wissenschaft und Technik* 20 (1916): 236.

"Neue Eingänge bei der Schriftleitung." *Blätter für Volksbibliotheken und Lesehallen* (1916): 138.

"Neue Eingänge bei der Schriftleitung." *Blätter für Volksbibliotheken und Lesehallen* (1917): 221.

Neumann, Richard. Review of *So ist der Friede*, by Franz Schauwecker. *Deutsche Blätter für erziehenden Unterricht* 56, no. 20 (1929): 156.

"Photographische Behelfe im Felde." *Photographische Rundschau und Mitteilungen* 52 (1915): 202–203.

Review of *Großer Bilderatlas des Weltkrieges. Band I*, by Hermann Konsbrück. *Kunstgewerbeblatt* 27 (1916): 200.

Review of *So ist der Friede*, by Franz Schauwecker. *Allgemeine schweizerische Militärzeitung* 75, no. 7 (1929): 358.
Review of *So ist der Friede*, by Franz Schauwecker. *Vormarsch* 22, no. 2 (1928): 253.
Sch., G. Review of *So ist der Friede*, by Franz Schauwecker. *Der Ring* 8, no. 11 (1930): 220.
Schaukroff, Xaver. Review of *So ist der Friede*, by Franz Schauwecker. *Der Gral: Monatschrift für Dichtung und Leben* 24 (1929–30): 956.
Schaukroff, Xaver. Review of *So war der Krieg!*, by Franz Schauwecker. *Der Gral: Monatschrift für Dichtung und Leben* 21 (1927): 735.
Schauwecker, Franz. "Südland." *Vormarsch* 1 (1927/28): 8.
Schiel, Max. "Photographische Arbeiten im Feld." *Photographische Rundschau und Mitteilungen* 53 (1916): 219–20.
Seger, Gerhart. Review of *Der Weltkrieg im Bild. Die Friedens-Warte* 27, no. 7 (July 1927): 221–22.
Steiger, Edgar. "Aus unserer Bücherei." *Die neue Zeit: Wochenschrift der deutschen Sozialdemokratie* 36, no. 1 (1916): 474–76.
Tucholsky, Kurt. "Auf dem Nachtisch." 1930. In *Gesammelte Werke, Band 8*, edited by Mary Gerold-Tucholsky and Fritz J. Raddatz, 136–43. Reinbeck bei Hamburg: Rowohlt, 1975.
Tucholsky, Kurt. "Die Tendenzfotografie." In *Gesammelte Werke, Band 4*, edited by Mary Gerold-Tucholsky and Fritz J. Raddatz, 104–5. Reinbeck bei Hamburg: Rowohlt, 1975.
Tucholsky, Kurt. "Waffe gegen den Krieg." *Die Weltbühne*, February 23, 1926.
Weißermel, W. "Die Feldkamera." *Photographische Rundschau und Mitteilungen* 52 (1915): 180–82.
Weißermel, W. "Entwickeln des Amateurs im Felde." *Photographische Rundschau und Mitteilungen* 53 (1916): 161–62.
Weniger, Erich. "Das Bild des Krieges: Erlebnis, Erinnerung, Überlieferung." *Die Erziehung: Monatsschrift für den Zusammenhang von Kultur und Erziehung in Wissenschaft und Leben* 5, no. 1 (1929): 1–21.

Secondary Literature

Alexander, Jeffrey C. *Trauma: A Social Theory*. Cambridge: Polity, 2012.
Anderson, Benedict. *Imagined Communities: Reflections on the Origin and Spread of Nationalism*. London: Verso, 2006.
Apel, Dora. "Cultural Battlegrounds: Weimar Photographic Narratives of War." *New German Critique* 76 (1999): 49–84.
Arendes, Cord. "Wirklichkeitsbilder? Fotografie und die Ernnerungen an den Ersten Weltkrieg." In *Der Erste Weltkrieg und die Folgen*, edited by Óscar Loureda Lamas, 25–46. Heidelberg: Winter, 2016.
Assmann, Aleida. *Der lange Schatten der Vergangenheit: Erinnerungskultur und Geschichtspolitik*. Munich: Beck, 2006.
Atkin, Alber. "Peirce's Theory of Signs." *The Stanford Encyclopedia of Philosophy*, spring 2023 ed., edited by Edward N. Zalta and Uri Nodelman. https://plato.stanford.edu/archives/spr2023/entries/peirce-semiotics/

Barthes, Roland. "The Photographic Message." In *Image, Music, Text*, translated by Stephen Heath, 15–31. New York: Hill and Wang, 1977.

Batchen, Geoffrey. *Forget Me Not: Photography and Remembrance*. New York: Princeton Architectural Press, 2004.

Bengsch, Nadja. "Franz Schauwecker—der 'Dichter des heldischen Lebens.'" In *Dichter für das "Dritte Reich," Band 2: Biographische Studien zum Verhältnis von Literatur und Ideologie*, edited by Rolf Düsterberg, 175–205. Bielefeld: Aisthesis, 2011.

Brandt, Susanne. "Bilder von der Zerstörung an der Westfront und die doppelte Verdrängung der Niederlage." In *Kriegserfahrungen: Studien zur Sozial- und Mentalitätsgeschichte des Ersten Weltkriegs*, edited by Gerhard Hirschfeld et al., 439–55. Essen: Klartext, 1997.

Brohm, Holger. "From Erlebnis to Erinnerung: Rereading Soldiers' Letters and Photographs from the First World War." In *German Life Writing in the Twentieth Century*, edited by Birgit Dahlke, 39–53. Columbia, SC: Camden House, 2010.

Burke, Peter. *Eyewitnessing: The Uses of Images as Historical Evidence*. Ithaca: Cornell University Press, 2001.

Canning, Kathleen. "The Politics of Symbols, Semantics, and Sentiments in the Weimar Republic." *Central European History* 43 (2010): 567–80.

Confino, Alon. *Germany as a Culture of Remembrance*. Chapel Hill: University of North Carolina Press, 2006.

Crew, David F. "Alltagsgeschichte: A New Social History 'from Below'?" *Central European History* 22, nos. 3–4 (1989): 394–407.

Deist, Wilhelm. "Censorship and Propaganda in Germany during the First World War." In *Les Sociétés européennes et la Guerre de 1914–1918*, edited by Stéphane Audoin-Rouzeau and Jean-Jacques Becker, 199–211. Nanterre: Université de Nanterre, 1990.

Dewitz, Bodo von. "German Snapshots from World War I: Personal Pictures, Political Implications." In *WAR /PHOTOGRAPHY: Images of Armed Conflict and Its Aftermath*, edited by Anne Tucker, Will Michels, and Natalie Zelt, 152–61. Houston: Museum of Fine Arts, 2012.

Dewitz, Bodo von. "Schießen oder fotografieren? Über fotografierende Soldaten im Ersten Weltkrieg." *Fotogeschichte* 12, no. 43 (1992): 49–60.

Dewitz, Bodo von. *So wird bei uns der Krieg geführt: Amateurfotografie im Ersten Weltkrieg*. München: Tuduv-Verlagsgesellschaft, 1989.

Dewitz, Bodo von, and Detlef Hoffmann. "Christus in aktualisierter Gestalt: Über ein Motiv in der Kriegsfotografie von 1914 bis 1954." *Fotogeschichte* 1, no. 2 (1981): 45–58.

Eberle, Matthias. *World War I and the Weimar Artists: Dix, Grosz, Beckmann, Schlemmer*. New Haven: Yale University Press, 1985.

Encke, Julia. *Augenblicke der Gefahr: Der Krieg und die Sinne*. Munich: Wilhelm Fink, 2006.

Erll, Astrid. *Kollektives Gedächtnis und Erinnerungskulturen: Eine Einführung*. Stuttgart: Metzler, 2011.

Evans, Jennifer. "Introduction: Photography as an Ethics of Seeing." In *Ethics of Seeing: Photography and Twentieth-Century German History*, edited by Jennifer Evans, Paul Betts, and Stefan-Ludwig Hoffmann, 1–22. New York: Berghahn, 2018.

Flusser, Vilém. *Towards a Philosophy of Photography*. Translated by Anthony Mathews. London: Reaktion Books, 2000.

Fox, Paul. *The Image of the Soldier in German Culture, 1871–1933*. London: Bloomsbury Academic, 2018.

Fritzsche, Peter. "Did Weimar Fail?" *Journal of Modern History* 68, no. 3 (1996): 629–56.

German Federal Archives. "Der Krieg im Bewegtbild—das Bild- und Filmamt." *Google Arts and Culture*. https://artsandculture.google.com/story/ggWRgGgAvxYA8A

Gerstner, Jan. *Das andere Gedächtnis: Fotografie in der Literatur des 20. Jahrhunderts*. Bielefeld: transcript, 2013.

Gollbach, Michael. *Die Wiederkehr des Weltkrieges in der Literatur: Zu den Frontromanen der späten Zwanziger Jahre*. Kronberg Taunus: Scriptor Verlag, 1978.

Grütter, Heinrich Theodor, et al., eds. *200 Jahre Krupp: Ein Mythos wird besichtigt. Katalog zur Ausstellung im Ruhr Museum vom 31. März bis 4. November 2012*. Essen: Klartext, 2012.

Haas, Claude. "Im Schatten der 'Unbekannten Soldaten': Trauer, Heldengedenken und Totenkult in der deutschen Literatur des Ersten Weltkriegs." *Weimarer Beiträge* 61, no. 2 (2015): 202–28.

Halbwachs, Maurice. *Das Gedächtnis und seine sozialen Bedingungen*. Translated by Lutz Geldsetzer. Berlin: Luchterhand, 1966. (Original: *Les Cadres sociaux de la mémoire*; Paris, 1925.)

Heiting, Manfred. "Autopsie: Anschauung, Information und Analyse. Über die Sammlung zur Wissenschaft." In *Autopsie: Deutschsprachige Fotobücher 1918 bis 1945*, vol. 1, edited by Manfred Heiting and Roland Jaeger, 6–10. Göttingen: Steidl, 2012.

Hermand, Jost. *Politische Denkbilder von Caspar David Friedrich bis Neo Rauch*. Cologne: Böhlau, 2011.

Hirsch, Marianne. *Family Frames: Photography, Narrative, and Postmemory*. Cambridge, MA: Harvard University Press, 1997.

Hirschfeld, Gerhard. "Das historische Erbe des Ersten Weltkriegs im 20. Jahrhundert." In *Der Erste Weltkrieg und die Folgen*, edited by Óscar Loureda Lamas, 139–64. Heidelberg: Winter, 2016.

Hollmann, Michael. "Die Gründung des Reichsarchivs im Jahre 1919." In *Erinnern an den Ersten Weltkrieg: Archivische Überlieferungsbildung und Sammlungsaktivitäten in der Weimarer Republik*, edited by Rainer Hering, Robert Kretzschmar, and Wolfgang Zimmermann, 29–61. Stuttgart: W. Kohlhammer, 2015.

Holzer, Anton. *Das Lächeln der Henker: Der unbekannte Krieg gegen die Zivilbevölkerung 1914–1918*. Darmstadt: Wissenschaftliche Buchgesellschaft, 2008.

Horstkotte, Silke. "Inkongruente Bilder: Ernst Jüngers Pferde." *Monatshefte* 109, no. 2 (Summer 2017): 215–28.

Hüppauf, Bernd. "Kriegsfotografie." In *Der Erste Weltkrieg: Wirkung, Wahrnehmung, Analyse*, edited by Wolfgang Michalka, 875–909. Munich: Piper, 1997.

Hüppauf, Bernd. "Schlachtenmythen und die Konstruktion des 'Neuen Menschens.'" In *Keiner fühlt sich mehr als Mensch . . . Erlebnis und Wirkung des Ersten Weltkrieges*, edited by Gerhard Hirschfeld and Gerd Krumeich, 43–84. Essen: Klartext, 1993.

Hüppauf, Bernd. "Zwischen Metaphysik und visuellem Essayismus. Franz Schauwecker: So war der Krieg (1928)." In *Von Richthofen bis Remarque*, edited by Thomas F. Schneider, 233–48. Amsterdam: Rodopi, 2003.

Hynes, Samuel. *The Soldiers' Tale: Bearing Witness to Modern War*. New York: Viking, 1997.

Imbrigotta, Kristopher. "Framing Brecht: Photography and Experiment in the Modellbücher, Arbeitsjournale, and Kriegsfibel." PhD diss., University of Wisconsin-Madison, 2013. ProQuest (3592653).

Jaeger, Roland. "Die Fülle der neuen Bilderbücher: Eine begriffsgeschichtliche Skizze zum 'Fotobuch.'" In *Autopsie: Deutschsprachige Fotobücher 1918 bis 1945*, vol. 1, edited by Manfred Heiting and Roland Jaeger, 24–29. Göttingen: Steidl, 2012.

Jäger, Helmut. *Erkundung mit der Kamera: Die Entwicklung der Photographie zur Waffe und ihr Einsatz im 1. Weltkrieg*. Munich: Venorion VKA, 2007.

Kansteiner, Wulf. "Finding Meaning in Memory: A Methodological Critique of Collective Memory Studies." *History and Theory* 41, no. 2 (2002): 179–97.

Keller, Ulrich. "Der Weltkrieg der Bilder: Organisation, Zensur und Ästhetik der Bildreportage 1914–1918." *Fotogeschichte* 33, no. 130 (2013): 5–50.

Koshar, Rudy. "What Should Haunt Us about World War I?" *Guernica*, February 6, 2014. https://www.guernicamag.com/daily/rudy-koshar-what-should-haunt-us-about-world-war-i/

Koszyk, Kurt. *Deutsche Pressepolitik im Ersten Weltkrieg*. Düsseldorf: Droste, 1968.

Kramer, Alan. "The First World War and Germany Memory." In *Untold War: New Perspectives in First World War Studies*, edited by Heather Jones, Jennifer O'Brien, and Christoph Schmidt-Supprian, 385–415. Leiden: Brill, 2008.

Krase, Andreas. "'Aber die armen Kerle, die in diesem Feuer sind!' Tagebuch und Bildchronik des Otto H. aus dem Ersten Weltkrieg." *Fotogeschichte* 11, no. 41 (1991): 15–30.

Krassnitzer, Patrick. "Die Geburt des Nationalsozialismus im Schützengraben: Formen der Brutalisierung in den Autobiographien von nationalsozialistischen Frontsoldaten." In *Der verlorene Frieden: Politik und Kriegskultur nach 1918*, edited by Jost Dülffer and Gerd Krumeich, 119–48. Essen: Klartext, 2002.

Krumeich, Gerd. "Die Präsenz des Krieges im Frieden." In *Der verlorene Frieden: Politik und Kriegskultur nach 1918*, edited by Jost Dülffer and Gerd Krumeich, 7–18. Essen: Klartext, 2002.

Krumeich, Gerd. "Ein einzigartiges Werk: Einführung zur Neuausgabe von 'Krieg dem Kriege.'" In *Krieg dem Kriege*, edited by Anti-Kriegs-Museum Berlin, vii–xxxvii. Berlin: Christoph Links, 2015.

Kuhn, Tom. "'Was besagt eine Fotografie?' Early Brechtian Perspectives on Photography." In *Young Mr. Brecht Becomes a Writer / Der junge Herr Brecht wird Schriftsteller (Brecht Yearbook 31)*, edited by Jürgen Hillesheim, 261–84. Madison: International Brecht Society / University of Wisconsin Press, 2006.

Landsberg, Alison. *Prosthetic Memory: The Transformation of American Remembrance in the Age of Mass Culture*. New York: Columbia University Press, 2004.

Langford, Martha. *Suspended Conversations: The Afterlife of Memory in Photographic Albums*. Montreal: McGill-Queen's University Press, 2001.

Lewinski, Jorge. *The Camera at War: War Photography from 1848 to the Present Day*. Secaucus, NJ: Chartwell Books, 1986.

Linder, Ann P. *Princes of the Trenches: Narrating the German Experience of the First World War.* Columbia, SC: Camden House, 1996.

Lipp, Anne. *Meinungslenkung im Krieg: Kriegserfahrungen deutscher Soldaten und ihre Deutung 1914–1918.* Göttingen: Vandenhoeck & Ruprecht, 2003.

Long, J. J. "Faces: Antlitz and Gesicht in the Weimar Republic Photobook." *Monatshefte* 190, no. 2 (Summer 2017): 201–14.

Long, J. J. "From *Das Antlitz des Weltkrieges* to *Der gefährliche Augenblick*: Ernst Jünger, Photography, Autobiography, and Modernity." In *German Life Writing in the Twentieth Century*, edited by Roger Woods, Birgit Dahlke, and Dennis Tate, 54–70. Rochester, NY: Camden House, 2010.

Lugon, Olivier. "'Photo-Inflation': Image Profusion in German Photography, 1925–1945." *History of Photography* 32, no. 3 (Autumn 2008): 219–34.

Magilow, Daniel. *The Photography of Crisis: The Photo Essays of Weimar Germany.* University Park: Pennsylvania State University Press, 2012.

Mayer, Dieter. "Aktiver Pessimismus: Kurt Tucholskys Deutschland, Deutschland über alles (1929)." In *Kurt Tucholsky: Das literarische und publizistische Werk*, edited by Sabina Becker and Ute Maack, 67–113. Darmstadt: Wissenschaftliche Buchgesellschaft, 2002.

McBride, Patrizia. *The Chatter of the Visible: Montage and Narrative in Weimar Germany.* Ann Arbor: University of Michigan Press, 2016.

Mitchell, W. J. T. *What Do Pictures Want? The Lives and Loves of Images.* Chicago: University of Chicago Press, 2010.

Mohler, Armin. *Die konservative Revolution in Deutschland, 1918–1932, ein Handbuch.* Darmstadt: Wissenschaftliche Buchgesellschaft, 1989.

Moriarty, Catherine. "'Though in a Picture Only': Portrait Photography and the Commemoration of the First World War." In *Evidence, History, and the Great War: Historians and the Impact of 1914–18*, edited by Gail Braybon, 30–47. New York: Berghahn, 2003.

Mosse, George. *Fallen Soldiers: Reshaping the Memory of the World Wars.* Oxford: Oxford University Press, 1990.

Müller, Hans-Harald. *Der Krieg und der Schriftsteller: Der Kriegsroman der Weimarer Republik.* Stuttgart: Metzler, 1986.

Nelson, Robert L. *German Soldier Newspapers of the First World War.* Cambridge: Cambridge University Press, 2011.

"NH 59638 German Vice Admiral von Spee's Cruiser Squadron." Naval History and Heritage Command. https://www.history.navy.mil/our-collections/photography/numerical-list-of-images/nhhc-series/nh-series/NH-59000/NH-59638.html

Pflug, G. "Lebensphilosophie." In *Historisches Wörterbuch der Philosophie*, vol. 5, edited by Joachim Ritter und Karlfried Gründer, 135–40. Darmstadt: Wissenschaftliche Buchgesellschaft, 1980.

Pöhlmann, Markus. "'Daß sich ein Sargdeckel über mir schlösse': Typen und Funktionen von Weltkriegserinnerungen militärischer Entscheidungsträger." In *Der verlorene Frieden: Politik und Kriegskultur nach 1918*, edited by Jost Dülffler and Gerd Krumeich, 149–70. Essen: Klartext, 2002.

Pöhlmann, Markus. *Kriegsgeschichte und Geschichtspolitik: Der Erste Weltkrieg. Die amtliche deutsche Militärgeschichtsschreibung 1914–1956*. Paderborn: Ferdinand Schöningh, 2002.

Protte, Katja. "Das 'Erbe' des Krieges: Fotografien aus dem Ersten Weltkrieg als Mittel nationalsozialistischer Propaganda im Illustrierten Beobachter von 1926–1939." *Fotogeschichte* 60 (1996): 19–41.

Prümm, Karl. *Die Literatur des Soldatischen Nationalismus der 20er Jahre (1918–1933): Gruppenideologie und Epochenproblematik*. Kronberg Taunus: Scriptor Verlag, 1974.

Rachamimov, Alon. *POWs and the Great War: Captivity on the Eastern Front*. Oxford: Berg, 2002.

Ramsbrock, Annelie. "The 'Face of War' in Weimar Visual Culture." In *Ethics of Seeing: Photography and Twentieth-Century German History*, edited by Jennifer Evans, Paul Betts, and Stefan-Ludwig Hoffmann, 57–78. New York: Berghahn, 2018.

Riesz, János. "Afrikanische Kriegsgefangene in der deutschen Propaganda." In *Gefangene Bilder: Wissenschaft und Propaganda im Ersten Weltkrieg*, edited by Benedikt Burkard, 58–71. Petersberg: Imhof, 2014.

Riha, Karl. "Den Krieg photographieren." In *Kriegserlebnis: Der Erste Weltkrieg in der literarischen Gestaltung und symbolischen Deutung der Nationen*, edited by Klaus Vondung, 146–61. Göttingen: Vandenhoeck & Ruprecht, 1980.

Rose, Gillian. *Doing Family Photography: The Domestic, the Public and the Politics of Sentiment*. Farnham, UK: Ashgate, 2010.

Rusinek, Bernd-A. "Die Kultur der Jugend und des Krieges: Militärischer Stil als Phänomen der Jugendkultur in der Weimarer Zeit." In *Der verlorene Frieden: Politik und Kriegskultur nach 1918*, edited by Jost Dülffer and Gerd Krumeich, 171–98. Essen: Klartext, 2002.

"Sacrario Militare di Pian di Salesei." Ministero della Difesa. Accessed June 1, 2018. https://www.difesa.it/il-ministro/ufficio-per-la-tutela-della-cultura-e-della-memoria-della-difesa/veneto/sacrario-militare-di-pian-di-salesei/49675.html

Schneider, Thomas F. "Narrating the War in Pictures: German Photo Books on World War I and the Construction of Pictorial War Narrations." *Journal of War and Culture Studies* 4, no. 1 (2011): 31–49.

Schumann, Dirk. *Politische Gewalt in der Weimarer Republik 1918–1933: Kampf um die Straße und Furcht vor dem Bürgerkrieg*. Essen: Klartext, 2001.

Schweizer, Stefan. *"Unserer Weltanschauung sichtbaren Ausdruck geben": Nationalsozialistische Geschichtsbilder in historischen Festzügen*. Göttingen: Wallstein, 2007.

Sekula, Allan. "Dismantling Modernism, Reinventing Documentary (Notes on the Politics of Representation)." In *Photography against the Grain: Essays and Photo Works, 1973–1983*, 53–75. Halifax: Press of the Nova Scotia College of Art and Design, 1984.

Sherman, Daniel. *Construction of Memory in Interwar France*. Chicago: University of Chicago Press, 1999.

Siebrecht, Claudia. "Seeing the 'Savage' and the Suspension of Time: Photography, War, and Concentration Camps in German South West Africa, 1904–1908." In *Ethics of Seeing: Photography and Twentieth-Century German History*, edited by

Jennifer Evans, Paul Betts, and Stefan-Ludwig Hoffmann, 37–56. New York: Berghahn, 2018.
Solomon-Godeau, Abigail. *Photography at the Dock.* Minneapolis: University of Minnesota Press, 1991.
Solomon-Godeau, Abigail. "Who Is Speaking Thus? Some Questions about Documentary Photography." In *Photography at the Dock*, 169–83. Minneapolis: University of Minnesota Press, 1991.
Sondhaus, Lawrence. *The Great War at Sea: A Naval History of the First World War.* Cambridge: Cambridge University Press, 2014.
Sontag, Susan. *On Photography.* London: Penguin, 2008.
Sontheimer, Kurt. *Antidemokratisches Denken in der Weimarer Republik: Die politischen Ideen des deutschen Nationalismus zwischen 1918 und 1933.* Munich: Nymphenburger Verlagshandlung, 1962.
Spree, Tommy. *Ich kenne keine "Feinde": Der Pazifist Ernst Friedrich, Ein Lebensbild.* Berlin: Anti-Kriegs-Museum, 2013.
Stauffer, Peter. *Walter Bloem: Biographie eines Verfechters, Geschichte eines Gekränkten.* Hilden: WJK Verlag, 2009.
Stetler, Pepper. *Stop Reading! Look! Modern Vision and the Weimar Photographic Book.* Ann Arbor: University of Michigan Press, 2015.
Stiftung Deutsches Historisches Museum. *Der Erste Weltkrieg in 100 Objekten.* Darmstadt: Theiss-Verlag, 2014.
Tagg, John. *The Burden of Representation: Essays on Photographies and Histories.* London: Macmillan Education, 1988.
Taylor, David. *Memory, Narrative and the Great War: Rifleman Patrick MacGill and the Construction of Wartime Experience.* Liverpool: Liverpool University Press, 2013.
Todman, Dan. *The Great War: Myth and Memory.* London: Hambledon and London, 2005.
Türk, Klaus. *Bilder der Arbeit: Eine ikonographische Anthologie.* Wiesbaden: VS Verlag für Sozialwissenschaft, 2012.
Ulrich, Bernd, and Benjamin Ziemann, eds. *Krieg im Frieden: Die Umkämpfte Erinnerung an den Ersten Weltkrieg. Quellen und Dokumente.* Frankfurt am Main: Fischer, 1997.
Wette, Wolfram. "Militärgeschichte von unten: Die Perspektive des 'kleinen Mannes.'" In *Der Krieg des kleinen Mannes: Eine Militärgeschichte von unten*, edited by Wolfram Wette, 9–47. Munich: Piper, 1992.
Wette, Wolfram. "Von Kellogg bis Hitler (1928–1933): Die öffentliche Meinung zwischen Kriegsächtung und Kriegsverherrlichung." In *Pazifismus in der Weimarer Republik*, edited by Karl Holl and Wolfram Wette, 149–72. Paderborn: Ferdinand Schöningh, 1981.
Winter, Jay. *Remembering War: The Great War between Memory and History in the Twentieth Century.* New Haven: Yale University Press, 2006.
Ziemann, Benjamin. *Contested Commemorations: Republican War Veterans and Weimar Political Culture.* Cambridge: Cambridge University Press, 2013.

Index

Note: Page numbers in *italics* refer to illustrations.